The Politics of
The Hunger Games

ALSO BY JAMEY HEIT

Imagination and Meaning in Calvin and Hobbes (McFarland, 2012)

EDITED BY JAMEY HEIT

Vader, Voldemort and Other Villains: Essays on Evil in Popular Media (McFarland, 2011)

The Politics of *The Hunger Games*

JAMEY HEIT

McFarland & Company, Inc., Publishers
Jefferson, North Carolina

LIBRARY OF CONGRESS CATALOGUING-IN-PUBLICATION DATA

Heit, Jamey.
　　The Politics of The Hunger Games / Jamey Heit.
　　　　p.　　cm.
　　Includes bibliographical references and index.

　　ISBN 978-0-7864-9658-7 (softcover : acid free paper) ∞
　　ISBN 978-1-4766-2104-3 (ebook)

　　1. Collins, Suzanne—Criticism and interpretation.
　　2. Collins, Suzanne. Hunger Games.　　3. Politics in literature.
　　4. Young adult fiction, American—History and criticism.
　　I. Title.
　　PS3603.O4558Z684　2015
　　813'.6—dc23　　　　　　　　　　　　　　　　　　　　　2015015190

BRITISH LIBRARY CATALOGUING DATA ARE AVAILABLE

© 2015 Jamey Heit. All rights reserved

No part of this book may be reproduced or transmitted in any form or by any means, electronic or mechanical, including photocopying or recording, or by any information storage and retrieval system, without permission in writing from the publisher.

Front cover image of rose in flames © 2015 iStock/Thinkstock

Printed in the United States of America

*McFarland & Company, Inc., Publishers
　Box 611, Jefferson, North Carolina 28640
　　www.mcfarlandpub.com*

For Isla and Annie

Acknowledgments

Though I've never met her (but hope to one day), Suzanne Collins gifted the world with a trilogy that is challenging, engaging, and enriching as both a gripping narrative and a thoughtful reflection on our culture. The Hunger Games series is a gift.

I do not know where exactly this project began in my mind, but I do want to thank the numerous people with whom I have discussed politics over the years. It is hard to capture when and where your influence emerged in this book, but I am thankful for your challenging conversations and support. Jon in particular deserves a particular note of thanks. He is what every good political mind needs: a trustworthy ally who ultimately knows more about the subject than I do.

My dear wife Amy's patience and support have the amazing ability to expand as deadlines near. She continually reminds me that compassion is perhaps the most important characteristic of the truly impactful people in our world and I am grateful that she models this on a daily basis.

My parents deserve my gratitude for every word I write because they were the first to teach me of the power words have. Just as importantly, they showed me through teaching and example that a moral foundation is the key to a transformative politics.

Lastly, I would like to thank my two daughters, Isla and Annie, who remind me daily why all of this matters. I hope that you grow up in Katniss's stead as strong, courageous, and transformative women.

Table of Contents

Acknowledgments   vii
Introduction   1

1. A Political Overview of Panem   11
2. Remembering Rome   26
3. The Social Contract   41
4. President Snow   54
5. Katniss   70
6. Haymitch   87
7. The Rebellion   102
8. President Coin   116
9. The Capitol's Residents   129
10. The Media   145
11. Public Violence   160

Conclusion   169
Chapter Notes   177
Bibliography   185
Index   189

Introduction

Herod I, or Herod the Great, was many things: a caretaker king for the Roman Empire, an architectural visionary who constructed a massive temple complex in Jerusalem, and father to a single son, Antipater. Most people know him as the biblical ruler who ordered the death of all boys age two years and younger in and around Bethlehem.

Herod I also possessed a sly political mind. When circumstances demanded, he was swift in his cruelty in order to protect his power. He was "prepared to commit any crime in order to gratify his unbounded ambition."[1] In this short description one finds two things that surface frequently in the actions of those who pursue political power at any cost. The motivation for Herod's willingness to be cruel is straightforward. His own ambition lies at the heart of decisions that affected those whom he ruled over; his own interests trumped those of everyone else. Fear was his calling card and anxiety about his ruthlessness would have been understandable among those who lived within his shadow. Herod was a king who would kill children in order to achieve ends that he deemed necessary to his own power regardless of what was in the kingdom's best interests.

Heinrich Graetz, a 19th century German historian, accurately summarizes the volatile world during the time of Herod's rule: he was "the evil genius of the Judean nation."[2] Evil rulers rarely work out well for those who must live in the long shadows of a disregard for human life. When those rulers are also adept at pulling on the right strings to strengthen the grip of their rule, the ruled will often suffer in a way designed to strike at the things that they hold dearly. It is not surprising, then, that this evil genius is well known in our world today as the ruler who (despite having an only son) called for the sweeping murder of toddlers in his kingdom in order to head off the rumored threat of a challenge to his power.

Matthew's Gospel relays what happened. Herod first learned about

Introduction

his rival-to-be from visitors: "wise men from the East came to Jerusalem, asking, 'Where is the child who has been born king of the Jews? For we observed his star at its rising, and have come to pay him homage.' When King Herod heard this, he was frightened, and all Jerusalem with him; and calling together all the chief priests and scribes of the people, he inquired of them where the Messiah was to be born."[3] Several details in Matthew's account offer insight into Herod's political mindset. The entire story starts with a rumor; visitors told Herod that a child was born and this snowballs into a ruthless response. For all his evil genius, Herod lacked some way of knowing of potential problems from some internal source. Further, one might also expect Herod to realize that the place where Jesus was born was not a political hotbed. In short, from the outset nothing in the rumor that reached Herod suggested there was any overt political threat.[4]

Still, something gripped Herod's attention as requiring immediate and ruthless action. Matthew's choice of words is telling; Herod was *frightened* when he learned of Jesus' birth. This reaction leads into an important detail that is over overlooked in this narrative. Everyone else in Herod's kingdom was also frightened. This uniform response warrants an explanation. Why would everyone's reaction, which has little grounding in an observable political reality, fall in line with Herod? Perhaps the people did not want someone to overthrow Herod, but, given his subsequent course of action, this explanation would seem unlikely. The other viable explanation from a political perspective is that the people moved in lock step because they understood what was at stake if they were to choose a course of action that ran counter to Herod's desires. There was a political blind spot that the tyrant knew about. His first act was to pull together Jerusalem's leadership and try to ferret out what was happening. Calling on the chief priests and scribes extended the chaos that ensued once Herod accepted the rumor as true. It is worth noting that no one in Jerusalem confirmed the birth; the mere possibility was enough to set the wheels of a violent reaction in motion.

Alongside these public decisions, Matthew reveals that Herod also turned to subversive backroom politics. Herod quietly went to the source to elicit the information he needed for extinguishing the political threat at hand. "Then Herod secretly called for the wise men and learned from them the exact time when the star had appeared. Then he sent them to

Introduction

Bethlehem, saying, 'Go and search diligently for the child; and when you have found him, bring me word so that I may also go and pay him homage.'"[5] Matthew does not reveal the wise men's response during this meeting, but provides enough detail to figure out Herod's intentions. Under the guise of paying homage to a person who was terrifying, Herod asked for information that would allow a quick assassination. The wise men did not need to be overly clever to realize what was at stake in this meeting. They were then involved in a dangerous situation, which was probably why they went see Jesus, and then (thanks to a dream) avoided Herod on their way back home.[6]

Herod did not take the slight well. Once he realized that his plan did not work, he unleashed the full force of his political evil. "When Herod saw that he had been tricked by the wise men, he was infuriated, and he sent and killed all the children in and around Bethlehem who were two years old or under, according to the time that he had learned from the wise men."[7] The response is striking in its brutality. A child from a quiet hamlet who might be a threat in more then a decade had to die to preserve Herod's rule. Just to be safe, Herod went ahead and killed all the children who were two or younger even though the narrative suggests clearly that Jesus would not have been two when this murderous turn occurs. It seems, then, that Herod's willingness to commit any crime was not just the mindset that drove his rise to power. It also describes his total commitment to maintaining that power.

This story is deeply political and through its narrative introduces two important political dynamics. Both are packaged within the edict to kill every child who is younger than two. The first half of the message is clear in its political aim: to kill a perceived threat to power. The second half works alongside the first goal. Herod was decidedly public in his actions in order to remind those under his rule that political threats, real or perceived, would not be tolerated. The emphasis on this second political purpose can be found in an important shift in strategy between the two halves. If the goal were only to kill the political rival, Herod could have been more precise in identifying the children to be killed. He knew the child in question was a boy, so he decided the best course of action was to kill every male child in and around Bethlehem who was two or younger. The result is a broader political message. The specific person was not the main concern; it was the *idea* that someone could

Introduction

challenge Herod that required forceful denouncement. In short, Herod took the opportunity to issue a kingdom-wide reminder that he was in charge and those who threatened his power would be dealt with quickly and harshly.

It would not be surprising if President Snow at least thought of Herod[8] as he watched Katniss undermine his own evil genius at the end of the 74th Hunger Games. When the person with the potential to overthrow a carefully maintained power structure surfaces, a sweeping statement to the ruled can be effective. Following Katniss' public act of rebellion with the nightlock berries, President Snow sets in motion a plan to extinguish publicly and clearly the hope the Girl on Fire kindles. His motivations are, like Herod's, deeply political. There is an important message President Snow is sending throughout The Hunger Games series, just as Herod wanted to be clear that challenges to his authority would be met swiftly and mercilessly. His politics, like Herod's, is built upon sowing fear through any means necessary to sustain his own position of power.

President Snow and Herod share another important similarity in the threat they try to outrun by killing kids. Both men fail because in each instance the target for their violent plan manages to escape. Katniss has the help of her own wise men and women, but at its core The Hunger Games series presents a political world that spins out of control following the failed attempt to kill Katniss. The ruthless steps taken to prevent people from rising up to challenge the rule of the evil genius marks the beginning of the downfall the killing of children is meant to prevent. The wise men gave Herod the slip, paid their deep respects to the baby, and got out of Bethlehem. In their wake they left the first trace of embracing another political possibility. Likewise, Katniss' own survival lays the foundation for the rebellion that will be built through the alternative political possibility her survival symbolizes.

Though there is a clear thematic consistency between Herod and President Snow, there is also an important difference. Though excessive in the brutality of his child killing, Herod was targeted in his motivation for an implementation of infanticide. There would not have been any guessing about how old his victims were going to be. President Snow's kill list, however, expands the parameters of those who can be killed and includes a layer of psychology to his infanticide. The result is to

Introduction

magnify the impact of dead children on the lives of those to whom he wants to send a political warning. The Hunger Games are structured in such a way that so long as a child is alive families are always at risk of seeing their children symbolize President Snow's authoritarian rule. Having one child selected for the Hunger Games in no way precludes another child being selected in a subsequent reaping. So long as a family has children, there is a continual possibility that the family will experience a devastating loss in order to maintain President Snow's grip on political power. Herod's infanticide was quick and complete; President Snow's injects a constant fear into the lives of those he rules.

There is a clear thematic consistency that binds Herod and President Snow together. The point of the comparison, however, is to identify the ways that President is actually a far more unsettling political figure. Herod, though cruel, was not entirely clever. The wise men saw through his plan to get them to reveal where Jesus was. In response, they duped Herod and took a different way out of town (it is worth asking why Herod did not have someone tail them; doing so would have led right to Jesus). President Snow exhibits an enhanced kind of evil in that he exceeds Herod's atrocities. Whereas Herod wanted a kind of insurance policy by killing off male babies, President Snow ensures that dead children who are about to enter adulthood are selected unpredictably and annually. President Snow, in other words, makes infanticide an annual event.

More than anyone else in The Hunger Games series (with the possible exception of Haymitch), Katniss recognizes the role fear plays in President Snow's politics. She is clear in sharing her thoughts with the reader that she does not want kids because of the risk she would invite. Even before her involvement with the rebellion, Katniss understands the political calculus on which President Snow relies. The family, which is the very support system that makes life bearable in the districts of Panem, will always exist within the shadow of the Arena. The cycle is cruel and generational. Should a family avoid having to send an older child as a tribute, there always exists the possibility that a younger child might have to participate in the Hunger Games. Further, children who dodge the reaping entirely will have to endure the possibility of sending their own children to the Arena. The result, as Katniss understands intuitively before the rebellion, is to remove herself from this

Introduction

cycle by deciding not to have children. In doing so, however, she also precludes the chance to raise her own children.

The Hunger Games pose an obvious physical threat to those who are chosen, but the psychological impact they create extends to everyone. When she is running through the Capitol's [sic] sewers as she leads a rebel attack, Katniss articulates the exacting nature of President Snow's politics of fear (by misspelling capital [as would be the correct word for the city], Collins focuses attention on the hollow nature of Panem's government). As she works her way through the sewers in *Mockingjay*, Katniss explains in simple terms how President Snow deals with those who challenge him. She expects: "Whatever Snow thinks will scare me the most."[9] A few scenes later, when Katniss sees the lizards President Snow has released to hunt the rebels, she expands on this psychological warfare that he wages: "the true atrocities, the most frightening, incorporate a perverse psychological twist designed to terrify the victim."[10] President Snow thinks through what matters most to those whom he wants to kill and finds a way to make their suffering as unbearable as possible.

For the families in the districts, this political reality is devastating. Importantly, the role of violence is not just to sow fear; it is to do so *publicly*. As such, political violence is part of Panem's social identity. The violence of the Games affects everyone in different ways, but the political role of this violence is a constant theme throughout the series.

The purpose of this book is to explore this political terrain. Panem has a variety of actors: a totalitarian ruler, rebels and citizens bound by political violence, and the struggle for a moral foundation for a society defined by the absence of moral leadership. The dynamics and decisions that occur within this framework offer deeply relevant insights about human nature, politics, and offer a glimpse of what happens when a society's politics ceases to serve the needs of its members. Echoes of our own politics surface in this exploration. We will find in the fictional world of Panem some uncomfortable reminders both of our own political dysfunction and the consequences of allowing these problems to continue unchecked. The hope is that through an examination of the political themes that affect Panem we can engage a bit more critically in our own political identities.

It is helpful to outline here how I use the term "politics" in this book, as the term is fluid in its nature and broad in its potential appli-

Introduction

cations. One constant, however, is that politics binds an individual to some larger social context. Individual rights and responsibilities take shape within a world where they must live alongside others. In his influential *Ethics*, Aristotle explores what it means for an individual to be virtuous. The goal, for Aristotle, is action in accordance with some good end.[11] Importantly, what is good for the individual must be understood within that individual's broader social circumstances. In Aristotle's words: "the perfect good is self-sufficient. By self-sufficient we mean not what is sufficient for oneself alone but something that includes parents, wife and children, friends and fellow citizens in general."[12] A person cannot, in other words, be *good* if the label excludes the social ties that connect every person to some larger whole. To be good or virtuous requires the exercise of certain qualities in a way that accounts for those around the individual. More simply, politics is about how people can live well with themselves and others.

The emphasis on good moral actions with and toward others is a staple of our culture's political heritage. The idea features prominently in Luke's Gospel, which is one of our most influential cultural texts. The Golden Rule states: "Do unto others as you would have them do unto you."[13] This simple prescription summarizes some particular ways we can be good political citizens. Luke continues: "'Judge not, and ye shall not be judged; condemn not, and ye shall not be condemned; forgive, and ye shall be forgiven. Give, and it shall be given unto you; good measure, pressed down, and shaken together, and running over, shall men give into your bosom. For with the same measure that ye mete withal it shall be measured to you again.'"[14] Our moral identities are formed in how we treat others. The expectation of good treatment from someone else is the basis for treating that individual well. However complex our politics might become, simple moral precepts remain the basis for living a good life.

In the abstract, the moral baseline in politics is easy to discuss. In practice, however, things are rarely this easy. Luke's prescription is not a checklist; it is a goal that might not always be possible. Human life and culture can change in a moment. Sometimes the cause of the change is our own. Other times events outside our control demand a reconsideration of how we will act. In a natural disaster, moral politics may not take the same shape as they would in a society humming along in relative prosperity. Each specific circumstance should recall the ideals of moral

Introduction

action but also recognize that the application of these guidelines can and will change. As such, thinking about politics should remain cautious in its claims. Our goal should be to "achieve such clarity as the subject matter allows."[15]

The result is, for Aristotle, an approach to examining politics that is certainly relevant to the discussion that unfolds in this book. He cautions that political analysis should "never expect more precision in the treatment of any subject than the nature of the subject permits."[16] Throughout The Hunger Games series, we find streaks of gray coloring the characters and their decisions. As such, there is no prescription that will emerge at the end of this book. There are signposts that can be articulated given the dynamics that unfold throughout the themes discussed below, but normative guidelines for "fixing" politics, either in general or specifically, cannot (and, if we follow Aristotle, should not) be the goal.

I am taking the time to limit the scope of this book because of two assumptions that characterize how my ideas have been stitched together. What follows is a discussion that draws on multiple disciplines. There is, then, a creative element that must be acknowledged in how I have read and watched The Hunger Games series. I want to identify patterns in how Collins' characters move within a specific political context. I do not want to claim that these patterns were her conscious intent. My reading is just that: my own. It is one of many possible readings of how politics unfolds within the series. While I will expand upon my ideas with both conceptual support and appropriate examples from the series' books and movies, I am not claiming that my reading is "right" in the sense that it excludes other possible readings. The nature of politics and literature is, individually, something that precludes such a definite conclusion. In fact, as will be discussed, claims to absolutes are a hallmark of damaging politics. If other examples of the themes being discussed come to mind, all the better. The point is to encourage a new way of reading and watching The Hunger Games series, not to finalize a list of political themes that are present.

In Chapter 1, the overall state of political affairs in Panem is examined in order to understand some of the key dynamics that frame life in both the districts and Panem. Chapter 2 looks to the past that preceded this state of affairs by drawing important parallels between The Hunger Games series and the Roman Empire. In Chapter 3, the outlines

Introduction

of our own political heritage is explored by thinking through the key philosophical question of how to balance security and freedom.

With this conceptual background in place, we then take a close look at three important characters: President Snow takes the stage in Chapter 4; Katniss follows in Chapter 5; in Chapter 6, the unlikely political leadership that Haymitch provides is thought through. In each of these chapters particular attention falls on the specific political attributes that define each character.

Chapter 7 examines the shape the rebellion takes in hopes of identifying the things they do well as a political organization and some of the ways they undermine their efforts. On a related point, Chapter 8 looks at President Coin as a leader, and similarly weigh how her presence impacts the rebels' efforts to defeat President Snow.

Chapter 9 turns to an under-appreciated but important part of politics in Panem: the Capitol residents. We know little of their perspective, but as citizens of the same country that sees the rebels emerge, trying to understand their political mindset provides an alternative to some of the questions that emerge in the previous chapters.

The final two chapters look at some of the most important patterns that define politics in The Hunger Games series. Chapter 10 focuses specifically on how the media affects the way politics plays out. Chapter 11, which is the most academic chapter in the book, examines the role violence can play in defining a culture from a philosophical perspective. Those who would rather not dive into this final, denser analysis can move ahead to the Conclusion, where important summary remarks are available.

1. A Political Overview of Panem

The Hunger Games series introduces Katniss while she is in the woods hunting with Gale. Temporarily and partially free from the realities of life in her District, she acts and speaks in a way that hints at a normal life. We quickly learn, however, that *The Hunger Games* is not about a young woman coming of age in an all-to-familiar teenage experience. She is enjoying the one thing in which she finds a measure of freedom before she faces the reaping. To do so she has to break laws, which shows that she is anything but free.

Her conversation with Gale, then, offers a kind of summary of her political experience before the specific effects of the Hunger Games comes into focus. She presents the political outline that informs decisions and actions throughout The Hunger Games series. The setting for the conversation captures the essence of life as a district resident. There is no freedom of movement. Economic conditions are dire. Surveillance is a constant worry and running afoul of the Capitol's rules can result in significant harm to the point of death. In short, her time in the woods reveals that under normal circumstances she and her fellow District Twelve residents live in a state of de facto imprisonment under the constant threat of violent punishment.

The opening portrait that Katniss gives us indicates just how hopeless life in District Twelve really is. The uncertainty that defines life comes directly from the constant threat that the Capitol poses in the form of the Hunger Games. As Katniss explains bluntly, she is "powerless"[1] against the reaping's cold decision to send someone into the Arena. This unavoidable reality stands as a symptom of the underlying disease that characterizes life in each of the districts. Though she and Gale have taken a morning to relax (at least as much as they can) before the reaping, Katniss reveals that life in the district ultimately unfolds within a severely restricting set of rules that are used to smother any and all sense of freedom. The unsettling nature of this life undermines friendships. It brings people to the brink of starvation at the hands of the national government. Even in the woods, Katniss knows that she can never be completely safe. She shares that: "Even here, even in the middle of no where, you worry someone might overhear you."[2] The truth in the statement forces Katniss and Gale to joke about the Capitol accent and the presentation at the reaping. Life in District Twelve struggles to find moments of enjoyment. The meaning of life is a struggle for survival and the greatest obstacle to this goal is President Snow's absolute and ruthless rule over Panem.

At the heart of this dynamic is the Hunger Games, which through its elaborate production serves as a way to reiterate the control the government has over life in the districts. Food and safety may be uncertain, but the cycle of preparing for, participating in, and celebrating the winner of the Hunger Games runs like clockwork. The reaping is the official starting point and everyone must gather to watch two children sent to their likely deaths. Katniss sums up the expectations in chilling words: "Attendance [at the reaping] is mandatory unless you are on death's door. This evening, officials will come around to check to see if this is the case. If not, you'll be imprisoned."[3] The pageantry surrounding the games serves an important purpose in deflating the inevitable anger people feel toward the entire process. The amount of manpower needed to check that no one skipped out on the reaping shows the extent to which the entire process must be managed. This is the world that Katniss finds herself in: a world defined by the carefully scripted process of killing.

In *The Hunger Games* film, Gale suggests an obvious way to undermine the system. He tells Katniss: "What if they did. Just one year what if everyone just stopped watching."[4] Katniss says the plan would not work, but Gale persists because of the underlying emptiness of the whole idea. He continues: "You root for your favorites. You cry when they get killed. It's sick."[5] Though the specifics that emerge from these insights will be developed throughout this book, the key idea at the moment is the simple conclusion that the Hunger Games are "sick" because they manipulate the entire population. Those who play a role in the process that sends tributes into the Arena are forced to participate in a contest that at its core is rotten. Gale, in other words, establishes the framework

1. A Political Overview of Panem

for the political reality that defines the districts. Within this outline, then, Gale's concluding remarks to Katniss on the matter point to the possibility that the Hunger Games can be undone: "No one watches. Then they don't have a game. It's as simple as that."[6] It is not simple, of course, but the sentiment is crucial. The districts can act. They can make a decision within the parameters of the seemingly powerless political terrain in which they exist. In accepting the Hunger Games as a part of life, in other words, the citizens of the Districts are yielding their political identities. Gale reminds Katniss that they do not have to give these up despite the challenges that they face every day.

A further analysis of the rebels' politics will be offered later. For now, the status quo of inaction is worth considering as a starting point for understanding the overall state of politics in Panem. There is, as was discussed in the Introduction, a sustained effort on the part of President Snow to maintain an oppressive power structure through the use of violence. In response, it is fair to ask the following when thinking about the Districts: *what can they realistically do in response*? There are not a lot of viable ways to reassert their identities and basic rights. This does not mean, however, that there are no options available.

Dietrich Bonhoeffer is a name that almost certainly does not have the recognition that it deserves. The majority of his biography reads as a non-descript account of an intellectually capable German pastor who spent time studying in America. The historical context of this basic narrative quickly transforms Bonhoeffer into a deeply important political thinker. In 1939, as Hitler's blitz of Europe unfolded, Bonhoeffer wrote to Reinhold Niebuhr, a leading theologian and public thinker in New York with whom Bonhoeffer was studying. Bonhoeffer had made the decision to return to Germany to challenge Nazi oppression. The explanation he gives for his choice highlights the political importance of action: "I have come to the conclusion that I made a mistake in coming to America. I must live through this difficult period in our national history with the people of Germany. I will have no right to participate in the reconstruction of Christian life in Germany after the war if I do not share the trials of this time with my people."[7] Studying in America while his country sagged under the weight of a dictator was not a tenable political identity. Bonhoeffer knows that something greater than himself— the identity of his country—is at stake. To be a leader means to engage directly with the challenges that are happening in the moment. A failure to do so is a yielding of the right and responsibility of political action. Bonhoeffer did not make this decision when circumstances were convenient. His fellow countrymen and women were suffering under a dictator, a reality demanded his presence.

As a decision based on principle, Bonhoeffer's return to Germany is admirable. He gave up a life of comfort and privilege in New York for a risk that would cost him his life. In his explanation to Niebuhr, though, Bonhoeffer injects a subtle but crucially important qualifier to his brave decision. He continues that he "will have to face the terrible alternative of either willing the defeat of their nation in order that Christian civilization may survive or willing the victory of their nation and thereby destroying civilization. I know which of these alternatives I must choose but I cannot make that choice from security."[8] As a German pastor, Bonhoeffer has competing obligations that seem mutually exclusive. To be a German was to support the elected leader who was willing to kill anyone who opposed his agenda. To be a pastor and to challenge Hitler was to accept that his identity as German must be rejected. In making his decision based on moral principles vis. his identity as a pastor, Bonhoeffer sacrificed himself. The important political point to realize is, therefore, the conceptual basis for the decision. Regardless of what choice he made, he must make the choice within the realities of the political context that determines his options. The lack of an ideal situation does not excuse him from doing something.

Bonhoeffer establishes a difficult but important political consideration: a failure to act is still an active political decision. Bonhoeffer's own decision to engage with a dangerous political reality to the point of suffering in a concentration camp and ultimately losing his life underwrites this claim. We are political creatures, a reality we cannot avoid so we such consider the obligations that come with this marker. The only real question is whether our action will participate in and challenge when necessary politics that do not serve the people, or whether we will fail to act and thus implicitly sanction the political framework in which we exist.

This brief discussion introduces a mindset that is, for the most part, absent in the initial stages of The Hunger Games series. The way that the Hunger Games smother so many basic rights reveals inaction from

1. A Political Overview of Panem

a lot of people. It is important to emphasize that I am identifying this initial state based on the principle as Bonhoeffer discusses it. In its more concise form—not to speak is to speak and not to act is to act—there exists a political obligation to do something within the circumstances that define a person.

In broad terms, the purpose of the Hunger Games is to encourage political inaction by making life difficult to the point of starvation, and then killing children to make sure that no one considers standing up to President Snow. The shared bond across Panem thus becomes not a sense of citizenship but an anxiety driven by the constant threat of violence and fear. The net result of the dynamic President Snow maintains is a lack of political imagination. People are too scared to think of ways to work around the severe restrictions that define their lives. At the same time, Gale and Katniss show by virtue of being in the woods, or, as Beattee explains, there is always a flaw in the system. Even if President Snow puts up fences, there is a way to get in and out of the district. Things might be more difficult given these restrictions but attention to detail and creativity and lead to political action. There is always a possible course of action. It just needs the right people with the right insights to bring about a political alternative.

Gale's response thus establishes the basis for the development of a political response to President Snow. He could try not to watch the Hunger Games, thought the check on attendance at the reaping suggests this strategy would be unlikely to succeed. Refusing to watch the Games would not bring the Hunger Games to a halt. Further, by all accounts the Capitol could easily identify those who were not watching and punish them accordingly. An infantismal impact and/or the threat of punishment are not the right things to think about when considering political action. Bonhoeffer did not return to Germany because he thought he would single-handedly defeat Hitler and he certainly did not return to Germany because he thought there was no risk. He returned to Germany because he knew that political apathy, manifest through inaction, lacked integrity. In suggesting something small, then, Gale takes the first meaningful steps to forming a political response from the Districts.

A further point surfaces when thinking about Gale's comments. At its core, politics is about individual agency, both in terms of the governed and the governing. Singular decisions are the building blocks of what eventually takes a specifically social shape. Localizing politics in this way highlights how devastating President Snow really is. He sows fear in a way that frightens people from the very idea of political agency. In Panem it is very easy to conclude that there simply is not a choice to be made. The constant threat of his violent response is enough to subvert this foundational ability to act. Oppression thrives when small decisions seem impossible.

The point here is not to blame people for thinking there is no way to assert a political identity through small actions. Rather, the point is to narrow the scope of what counts as a political act in order to recover an ability that is perceived as lost. When Gale makes his comments to Katniss, he has no idea what is about to unfold; there is no way to anticipate that he speaks as one of the rebellion's first voices from District Twelve. What he does understand, however, is that he can still speak. The audience is small and sympathetic, but this is perhaps the best place to remember the nature of politics at a basic level: the sum of individual actions. The point, then, is to find political impact in the smallest of things.

Eventually small decisions become big ones. An insight here and the willingness to act outside one's comfort zone there can ultimately lead to breakthroughs in service of some broader political end. Eric Greitens, who through the decision to work alongside those who suffered some of the late 20th century's worst circumstances, recognizes that we can always reconfigure the challenges we face in terms of political action. Greitens writes: "even in the world's 'worst places,' people found ways to turn pain into wisdom and suffering into strength. They made their own actions, their own lives, into a memorial that honored the people they had lost."[9] Greitens saw some pretty bad circumstances as he worked with survivors of genocide in Bosnia and Rwanda as a humanitarian volunteer, so he is not talking about people who decided to act only because it was easy to do so. Rather, action was, perhaps, the most difficult thing to do in response to incredible loss and the difficult of everyday survival. It is in these dark moments that political identities often take shape.

Greitens should know. His humanitarian work eventually leads him to Oxford University as a Rhodes Scholar. When his time at Oxford is

1. A Political Overview of Panem

almost up, he has a clear path to a comfortable material life as a consultant or as an academic. Instead he chooses to become a Navy officer and train to be a Navy SEAL. The story that spins around this decision has become a *New York Times* bestseller, but Greitens ultimately finds the imperative to act in much less grandiose terms. His decision is in large part reflective of a mindset his boxing coach taught him: "every action, even something as simple as washing the strings of your gloves, had a moral component."[10] Moral engagements with one's world do not have to be about sacrificing one's life for a cause; it can start in the smallest details of daily life. It is out of this commitment to a moral end that eventually takes shape as the kind of political leadership that Greitens exhibits in his career as a Navy SEAL.[11]

In *The Hunger Games*, Gale's political influence is largely unseen because the majority of the book is about Katniss's experience in the Arena. However, at the beginning of *Catching Fire*, we can see that Gale's small political acts out in the woods evolve into something more committed to combating President Snow's tyranny. At first, the rebellion seems inconsequential. When the new Head Peacekeeper in District Twelve, Romulus Thread, encounters Gale trying to sell a turkey, Gale thinks quickly to cover his and Katniss's tracks. He just found the turkey wandering around so he killed. Unfortunately, this is still a crime, so Gale's cover leads to being whipped in the town square. *The Catching Fire* movie dramatizes this point by having Gale tackle Commander Thread just as he is about to strike a defenseless woman. In this quick instant Gale's innate rebellion and moral motivation shine brightly. He is no longer an abstract thinker who sits quietly by as things happen once he is back inside District Twelve. He is acting when the stakes are much higher. Gale shows a moral compass that is equally weighty. His accepts the consequences of rebelling against the Capitol despite the pain he will endure. He is willing to protect those close to him for some greater purpose even if in the moment the purpose is relatively minor. Of course, Gale's moral compass eventually points away from moral actions. By the end of the series Gale is complicit with the very violence he struggles against throughout the first two-thirds of the series.

The circumstances in which Gale speaks his mind now deserve attention, as they help to round out the initial state of politics in the districts. Gale and Katniss have the freedom to speak openly because they are literally outside the boundaries of their district. The woods are thus a kind of private sanctuary that provides relief from the Capitol's oppression. This space enables this embryonic political response to form. Jedediah Purdy identifies privacy as a foundational need for developing any kind of identity: "Private life becomes the sole place where we can exercise the trust and care, the sense of good purpose, that seem to have little safe purchase elsewhere."[12] Safety is not a requirement to make political decisions in line with the standard that drove Bonhoeffer's choice, but it sure is helpful. The denial of this security is, therefore, a political consideration in its own right and one that is worth exploring in sketching the basic state of affairs in Panem.

The specific ways that basic rights are denied to the districts provide a helpful starting point for understanding politics in Panem. The fact that Katniss and Gale must sneak away to experience a brief moment of trust and, therefore, the ability to define a good purpose in life reveals the effectiveness of the Capitol's police state in oppressing political thought and action in all of the districts. As discussed in the Introduction, the pursuit of some good end within a social context lies at the core of politics. President Snow's politics are, then, designed to counter an expected response to his use of violence.

In short, to be a citizen in one of Panem's districts is to be denied rights that are considered fundamental to being human. Article One of the Declaration of Human Rights outlines the basis for free political action: "All human beings are born free and equal in dignity and rights. They are endowed with reason and conscience and should act toward one another in a spirit of brotherhood."[13] The right to action is intrinsic and unqualified. Humans have the ability to consider rationally their political choices and should be free to do so with a specifically moral consideration of other free political agents. Here again we see the Golden Rule applies at the core of humanity. We have an obligation to treat one another in accordance with these basic assumptions. Importantly, the Universal Declaration of Human Rights does not just protect action; it *prescribes* action. The default is to be forthright in basing one's political identity in moral choices, small or large, that uphold a moral society.

Politics is, or rather should be, the sum of collective actions that affirm these basic rights and responsibilities. Conceptually, this political equation underwrites much of our culture's political success. As Purdy

1. A Political Overview of Panem

explains, this moral foundation is the reason politics matters: "politics has been among the great sources of inspiration and purpose, giving shape to many lives.... Politics, on this promise, could erase all the foolish, cruel, maddening accretions of history and replace them with fair and human arrangements where for the first time people would live as free as they are born."[14] Purdy accepts that there are bad actors on the political stage, but these figures do not obscure the noble end of politics in general. When people like President Snow ascend to and maintain at all costs political power, there is all the more reason to remember the moral foundation of a healthy politics. Life should be lived freely in accordance with the equality that documents like the Universal Declaration of Human Rights outline.

Based on the assumption of equality, the Universal Declaration of Human Rights then lays out the practical ways this equality is manifest in daily life. There is the ironic balance that we should be totally secure in our freedom: "Everyone has the right to life, liberty and security of person."[15] Among other things, this basic freedom includes freedom from slavery; cruel punishment including torture; fair treatment within a legal framework; recourse when one's rights are violated; and, finally, the right not to be unjustly detained.[16]

President Snow does not just oversee the annual killing of children from each district; his political power structure consistently violates every one of these foundational human rights. Moreover, these violations are based specifically on each district's geographic and cultural boundaries. This, in turn, violates the Second Article of the Universal Declaration of Human Rights, which states: "Furthermore, no distinction shall be made on the basis of the political, jurisdictional or international status of the country or territory to which a person belongs, whether it be independent, trust, non-self-governing or under any other limitation of sovereignty."[17] President Snow's violent program *relies* on these distinctions. By keeping separate the citizens of each district he accomplishes two things. First, he makes it harder for the residents from each district to coordinate a political response. Secondly, he creates an ironic sense of citizenship across all of Panem. The one thing that unites the districts is their shared experience of a life without basic rights. Though some districts hold out longer than others, in the end President Snow's denial of basic human rights allows the districts to rally around this common bond.

Before the rebellion takes shape, however, the reader experiences Panem's districts as a place where there is little, if any, *meaningful*, political identity. The districts have become accustomed to a life without an intrinsic sense of political worth. As a result, there is almost no way the districts' residents can imagine a political alternative to President Snow's way of governing. As Purdy explains, when people lose sight of a politics ground in moral action they enter a vicious cycle. According to Purdy, the result is the kind of robotic existence, oiled with fear, that characterizes the districts: "Public life takes on a quality of unbelievable ritual incredulously performed, like the ceremonies of an aged and failing faith, conducted with the old litanies because no others are available."[18] Purdy's word choice here is telling. Consistency characterizes the litany; culturally, this connotes religious discipline. In our culture, this practice in turn recalls the moral imperative found in Luke's Gospel: the fair treatment of everyone because we expect fair treatment. In Panem, the result is the perpetuation of the Hunger Games. Given enough time and enough oppression, however, it is easy to lose sight of the moral foundation beneath political institutions. This is the state of Panem as President Snow (over)sees it. A politics in service of protecting basic rights gives way to a politics that actively denies those rights so he can rule with impunity.

Reinhold Niebuhr, whom we met earlier in this chapter as the recipient of Bonhoeffer's explanation for returning to Germany, identifies an important symptom of the society that has lost its political way. The absence of basic rights usually requires some kind of policing body to ensure that absence. The actions of this body expose the political class that would turn to violence to keep people from their basic rights. Niebuhr explains: "It proves that the police power of the state is usually used prematurely; before an effort has been made to eliminate the causes of discontent, and that it therefore tends to perpetuate injustice and the consequent social disaffections."[19] The use of force against the citizens the police ought to protect is troubling, but what we should really look for is the use of force preemptively. Shooting first and asking later, so to speak, reveals a systemic absence of a morally grounded politics.

Returning to Gale's whipping at the beginning of *Catching Fire* brings this point into sharper focus. Gale's illegal act was one that reclaimed upheld his right to freedom of movement and the feed himself.

1. A Political Overview of Panem

In the movie version, his actions emphasize his commitment to helping others at the expense of his own safety. His lie is, in other words, justified in our eyes because he was doing something everyone should be allowed to do. Even if going outside the fence is illegal, the desire to have freedom of movement is worth standing up for despite the consequences doing so will bring about. Seeing this right in his fellow citizen tossed aside, Gale rebels against the police state that would treat a person as such. In response, he suffers a vicious beating. Seeing the Peacekeepers react to Gale (who, ironically do keep a kind of peace in that they uphold the withdrawal of basic rights), it is easy to spot the injustice. Behind this overt use force, we find the clue that reveals the character of this political force, as well as another hint at the fragile nature of such force. The crux of this scene actually happens after the whipping has stopped because Katniss, and then Haymitch, intervene.

Haymitch is an important political character in The Hunger Games series and he will be examined in more detail later, but for now it will suffice to think about his response as revealing the Capitol's preemptive use of violence. Thread beats Gale because that is one possible punishment for the crime of holding a dead turkey that is not his. When Katniss intervenes, Thread punches her, then, while she is lying on the ground, whips her once for good measure. Undeterred, Katniss stands up and stands between Thread and Gale. Thread smirks, then tells her: "move."[20] When she refuses, Thread pulls out his gun and points it at her. At this point Haymitch runs up and exchanges some tense words with Thread:

HAYMITCH: You don't want to shoot her.
THREAD: How about I shoot both of you?
HAYMITCH: Look, Commander, you're new here. Trust me. I'm trying to help you. I'm Haymitch. Do you recognize her? Katniss Everdeen? Darling of the Capitol?
THREAD (after realizing who Katniss is): She interfered with a Peacekeeper.
HAYMITCH: I never said she was smart.[21]

Haymitch wisely points out to Thread the downstream consequences of this supposed justice within the political framework that demands Gale's whipping.

As a part of the Capitol's broader political narrative, Thread has become an antagonist because he cut Katniss's face right before a national broadcast. A preemptive use of force gets Thread into a bind that he does not see because of a narrow focus on meting out violence in response to crimes against the Capitol. Violence obscures the ability to think through the political consequences of one's actions. Thread understands this after Haymitch explains and lets everyone go, though not before threatening more violence of course). Importantly, Haymitch manages to ease the tension without showing his allegiance to Katniss. He shifts attention from what she has done to what President Snow will do if someone, anyone, negatively impacts the planned television specials to come.

This exchange is, then, symbolic of the way that political violence will drive the course of events throughout the series. The overt and preemptive use of violence, particularly in the Arena as a way to head off thoughts of rebellion, is actually a bad idea in the broader political narrative that is unfolding. Thread's willingness to use violence as a way of exerting political control ultimately unmasks the inability of that violence to succeed as a default political state. The only difference between Thread's use of force and President Snow's more complex political maneuvering is that Thread pulls back before it is too late.

Violence runs counter to the purpose of a healthy political environment. It kills off, drives out, or sends underground the things in life that we consider part of our intrinsic freedom. A clear result of violence is a limited or impossible way to live a happy life. This is devastating to those living in the districts, but perhaps the worst part of this state of existence is that it results from intentional human action. The *Catching Fire* movie has a brief scene during the televised interviews the night before the Hunger Games begin that illustrates just how pervasive President Snow's reach is. Beattee calmly brings up what should be an obvious question at any point during the entire series: "The Quarter Quell were written into law by men. Certainly it can be unwritten."[22] The Hunger Games are not necessary and they can be stopped through the very processes that created them in the first place. If everyone is unhappy with former victors going back into the Arena, why not just demand a difference course of action? The end of the 74th Hunger Games showed that adjustments could be made to the rules in response to what people want. The original, legal charter for the Hunger Games states clearly (and President Snow subsequently quotes this charter elsewhere; even Effie knows the justification by heart in *The Hunger Games* movie) that there is a "lone victor."[23] Prior to Beattee's comments, then, the precedent

1. A Political Overview of Panem

has already been set to cancel the Quarter Quell. Consequently, Beattee presents a logical and politically sound argument.

Though the film version of *Catching Fire* does a good job of dramatizing Beattee's point, the book offers a further—and more compelling—example of the flaws in President Snow's political calculations. Though we do not hear the specifics from Katniss, she does summarize that Seeder, a tribute from District Eleven, raises a logical question in the same vein as Beattee's remark: "everyone assumes President Snow is all-powerful. If he's all-powerful, why does not he change the Quell?"[24] The question is a strong riff on a classic question about how all-powerful beings (usually the point refers to a good god) allow bad things to happen? If no one wants to see their favorite victors go back into the Arena, then the absolute ruler who relies on the Hunger Games should act in a way that would be truly powerful. The implicit answer, of course, is one that either undermines President Snow's all-powerful persona or exposes the indefensible purpose of the Hunger Games. Either possibility rests on the decisions that President Snow must take responsibility for.

The fact that these questions and suggestions pass quickly shows the extent to which President Snow has undermined a willingness to envision a different political reality than his fear-based rule over Panem. The tributes' points are sound and within the purview of the political system that President Snow has built. However, the reality of violence, both as a consequence of challenging President Snow and as a matter of public expectation, ensures that the sharp responses will fade once the tributes enter the Arena. The Hunger Games must go on.

The impact of violence in Panem emerges forcefully when Peeta and Katniss have a late night conversation on the roof of the training center the night before the 74th Hunger Games begin. Katniss seems resigned to the brutal moral reality the Arena will present and, as such, shows the quickness with which violence can dissolve a sense of what is good. Peeta, on the other hand, refuses to let go of his moral identity. He does not deny the reality of violence; he only states that this norm will not define who he is. He tells Katniss: "when the time comes, I'm sure I'll kill just like everybody else. I can't go down without a fight. Only I keep wishing I could think of a way to ... to show the Capitol they don't own me. That I'm more than just a piece in their Games."[25]

Peeta will stand up for himself and fight, but not to stoop to the violent baseline that the Capitol wants to reinforce through the Games. Peeta will fight because he believes in something greater than the world President Snow watches over. The Games are about a political message, but Peeta refuses to participate in the spreading of that message and, instead, thinks about how he can present a counter-message to the violent world he is about the enter.

The full weight of Peeta's words does not register with Katniss at this moment. It is only later in *Catching Fire* when Peeta and Katniss have another rooftop rendezvous just before entering the Arena that Katniss understands fully how Peeta subverts the political logic behind the Games. Once she realizes the full meaning of what Peeta says as a moral challenge to President Snow, Katniss begins to see her actions as more than survival. She sees herself as a public counterweight to President Snow. The obscene nature of the television Games and the cultural gravity attached to the killing of children can become a way to steer others toward the same mindset Peeta has. Katniss understands that if she can make it clear to those watching that she is resisting the role President Snow has planned for her, she can "give hope to the rebels."[26]

Though violence can be shunned, doing so successfully is essentially impossible amidst the political realities that define Panem. Yes, Peeta can protect his virtuous identity, but Katniss and Gale show different levels of yielding to the realities that come with political action. In her moment of triumph, when she finally gets to kill President Snow, Katniss has a change of heart and assassinates President Coin. Jill Olthouse rightly identifies this point as a singularly important moment in Katniss's leadership: "In her assassination of President Coin, Katniss at last finds a Mockingjay identity that's authentic, one with which she can truly identify."[27] Katniss may come full circle in her role as rebel leader by killing President Coin, but what kind of world does she lead if assassination is the only way to realize fully her political identity? This is not to deny Olthouse's reading of Katniss's actions. Rather, the purpose is to highlight that violence is so pervasive in Panem that even escape from the primary reason for that violence requires violence.

We see of a hint of the silver lining to this vicious cycle in Peeta's resistance to the purpose of the Games. Despite the overwhelming presence of violence and fear throughout The Hunger Games series, in the

1. A Political Overview of Panem

end we realize that a politics built and maintained through violence cannot survive forever. Katniss's assassination of President Coin, though violent in and of itself, reveals the failure of violence as a stable political strategy. In the end, we find that violence hollows out Panem's politics on all sides. The country lacks a collective political stability that can be resilient in the face of uncertainty. Andrew Zolli describes how nonresilient institutions have a terminal flaw: "it's the tendency of most coupled systems to become brittle over time—to lose rather than gain in their ability to adapt. When that happens, a systemic flip—frequently to a less desirable state of affairs—becomes more difficult to avoid."[28] As we will see shortly, this tipping point occurs the moment Katniss volunteers for Prim and ultimately flips the script on a violent politics when the most violent of circumstances, the Hunger Games, begins.

2. Remembering Rome

In *Gladiator*,[1] Russell Crowe's character, Maximus Decimus Meridius, suffers a terrible twist of fate at the hands of a dishonorable and violent tyrant. He goes from being a Roman General tasked with replacing Marcus Aurelius as the head of Rome to a Spanish slave fighting gladiatorial matches on the outskirts of the Roman Empire. In one of the first fights we see, Maximus walks into an arena by himself to face six burly men who have far more armor and weaponry. Maximus proceeds to kill all six men. After decapitating his final victim, Maximus throws his bloodied sword toward the seats where the local elites are sitting. The crowd gasps because it knows the act is brazen.

The decision to throw his sword is rebellious in a variety of ways. First, it is a physical threat to those who are sanctioning the games. Presumably the people sitting in those seats could call in guards to punish Maximus publicly, but they do not. This speaks in turn to the interest these events have generated among the crowd. To kill off Maximus after he has just done something extraordinary in the context of a gladiator match would be deeply unpopular. He has, in other words, inverted the politics of this Roman outpost.

Having neutralized the local political power, Maximus then turns to the crowd. He spreads his arms and yells to those watching, "Are you not entertained?"[2] He repeats the question and hears only silence. What started as a political challenge to local leaders now exposes the crowd's moral bankruptcy. They have been entertained. They cheered as Maximus killed men. The oohed and ahhed when he threw his sword into the stands. They embraced violence that had no purpose.

This scene is worth recalling while thinking about the present day state of these Roman arenas. For the millions of tourists who visit the Roman Coliseum every year, the Porta Libitina may go unrecognized. Within the Coliseum's iconic spiral, this doorway is relatively nondescript. It leads to a passageway that does not stand out from other

2. Remembering Rome

places in the Coliseum that those millions of tourists can explore. During gladiatorial matches, the spectators were probably just as quick to turn their attention to other things within the Coliseum. The Porta was functional; it was the way that dead bodies were removed from the public's eye.

The name, however, marks the doorway's significance. Libitina was the Roman goddess of funerals. Her name stood for death in Roman culture.[3] Naming the passageway through which bodies were away serves as a constant reminder of the Coliseum's purpose. This was a place where many people experienced some pretty terrible things. Few survived. Many more witnessed human suffering as a form of entertainment. They missed the symbolic reality that for those who fought in the arena the only way out was death.

The Hunger Games Arena is a similar mix of violence and cultural importance. As she prepares to enter the Arena for the first time, Katniss shares how the holding room is understood in the districts: "it's referred to as the Stockyard. The place animals go before slaughter."[4] She ceases to be human as she prepares to fight for her life in front of a national audience. The outward grandeur of a room built for her single use contrasts sharply with the absolute disinterest in her life that the room symbolizes.

While Katniss sees the holding chamber as a place where life ceases to matter, for others the room becomes an historical site worth visiting. Immediately after she calls the room the Stockyard, Katniss describes how Capitol residents visit old arenas as tourists: "The arenas are historic sites, preserved after the Games. Popular destinations for Capitol residents to visit, to vacation. Go for a month, rewatch the Games, tour the catacombs, visit the sites where the deaths took place. You can even take part in reenactments."[5] In the context of Katniss's experience, these are difficult words to read, but if we step back and consider the way the arenas are perceived, we notice a striking similarity to the Roman Coliseum. A place designed to kill becomes a part of a shared cultural heritage. People want to experience the world they see on television. They want to relate to what the space represents by reliving what happened. The striking thing is that such visitors do not seem to recognize the disconnect between their recreational interest and the violent purpose of what they want to see. Like so many millions who visit the Roman Coliseum every year, an instrument of violent political power transforms into something that attracts our interest in a recreational way.

What, exactly, is the point of making a show out of excessive violence? When considering the gladiators in Rome, the answer is that violence provided a thinly veiled political message. Rome's rulers could appease political supporters by making an example out of just about anyone. The physical suffering in the Coliseum and other venues was significant, but the psychological layer to these events should not be overlooked. Rome was capable of transforming lives into sport.

Often, gladiatorial events were held to celebrate a significant military victory. Plutarch, a Greek historian, narrates the process Caesar follows to celebrate a victory. First, "Caesar, upon his return to Rome, did not omit to pronounce before the people a magnificent account of his victory."[6] This introductory remark is important because the celebration occurs at home. Caesar uses violence as a way to celebrate in the heart of the Roman world. This location serves to bind the ruler and the ruled in the specific context of violent gladiatorial contests. The seating in the Coliseum was no different than any modern day sporting venue in that the rich and powerful had better seats, but everyone was in the same space watching the same things. Spectators were gathering as Romans to celebrate a Roman victory. In short, the events in the Coliseum offered a reminder, stamped with the blood of gladiators, that those in attendance were all part of the same society, which had been built, in part, through violence.

This shared bond establishes the foundation for a more specific political end to be achieved. Plutarch continues: "After the triumphs, he [Caesar] distributed rewards to his soldiers, and treated the people with feasting and shows. He entertained the whole people together at one feast, where twenty-two thousand dining couches were laid out."[7] There is a cold political logic at work. Multiple events combine to strengthen the unifying goal of celebrating through violence. Caesar honors the soldiers. He provides a great feast for everyone. He makes sure there is plenty of space to relax. Who in attendance would complain? The victims of this calculus will soon be silenced in their deaths, which will ultimately serve Rome's political interests.

Comfortably involved in the celebration, there is now space for Caesar to invoke violence as a commemoration of his triumph. With

2. Remembering Rome

everyone provided for, Caesar then "made a display of gladiators, and of battles by sea."[8] The display exhibits clear intent. The blood spilled in the Coliseum exerts power over those who have to fight to the death and, in so doing, reminds everyone, from the everyday citizens who can afford tickets to the political elite that Rome is powerful enough to reduce life to a spectator sport. The message is implicit but clear. Find yourself on the wrong side of Caesar and you too can look forward to a terrible death. Thus distilled, the political choice presumably would be easy to make for most Romans: support Caesar.

Alongside the role gladiators played as a political message it is important to think about the gladiators themselves. Though their backgrounds varied, a relative constant was that their selection was symbolic within Rome's broader political power structure. Cicero, one of Rome's intellectual giants, asks questions that point to the underlying politics of picking gladiators. Cicero writes: "Just look at the gladiators, either debased men or foreigners, and consider the blows they endure! Consider how they who have been well disciplined prefer to accept a blow than ignominiously avoid it! How often it is made clear that they consider nothing other than the satisfaction of their master or the people! Even when they are covered with wounds they send a messenger to their master to inquire his will."[9] There are two things to think about. The first is the violence the gladiators endured. Surely, Cicero suggests, this should focus spectators' attention on the deeply troubling nature of what they have paid to see. Further, the gladiators were largely representatives of lower classes; the juxtaposition of these disadvantaged social classes with the relative comfort of those watching should similarly give pause to think about what is at stake in this kind of violence. Everything points back to the underling political dynamic that plays out with each swing of a gladiator's sword. This is a showcase of Rome's political power and its ability to do as it wishes to anyone who falls outside the boundaries of what Rome's rulers consider acceptable.

At this point, the language in The Hunger Games series echoes strongly. Those who are chosen at the reaping to participate in the Hunger Games are called tributes. In Rome, then, a tribute had clear political implications. Discussing the language of the tribute in The Hunger Games series, offers a helpful insight: "The Roman emperors viewed the payment of tributes as a sign of respect and a contribution to the well-being of the state, something between a gift and a tax."[10] Paying a tribute was implicit signal—given voluntarily or under duress—that those paying were yielding their political influence. Payment of a tribute was not an official obligation per say. A tax has a legal foundation and is something that one can pay while grumbling. A tribute was understood in a way that did not provide the space to act reluctantly. Finally, because the tribute is not a gift the transaction held open the option for the Roman government to punish those whose participation was not deemed sufficient. Critiquing someone for giving a gift is bad form, but a tribute implicitly constitutes a gesture of respect and/or support. In short, a tribute mandates assent to the political superstructure that allowed Rome's political ruling class to act with relatively little challenge.

A strange tension thus defines the events that occurred in the Roman Coliseum. Within a building that signaled Rome's grandeur, a base, violence spectacle aroused an audience who had paid to witness other people suffer. There is an uncomfortable appeal in these contests. Forcing people to fight to the death for sport contrasts sharply with the outward polish of Rome's political culture. The Empire's political elite were highly polished figures. Imagine the American President or a group of Senators attending an event where people from poor rural communities, urban housing projects, or immigrant communities literally fought until only one or no one was left standing. No matter how divisive American politics may be, the image is difficult to comprehend. If one can imagine this scene, heavy criticism would (and should) quickly fall on the notion that a national leader could allow something like this to exist, much less to organize, subsidize and enjoy in person.

These events had the purpose of bolstering a ruling class through the explicit use of power for those who can, in theory, do something about that ruling class. That is, the citizens who take enjoyment in violent contests are placated because they are the most immediate threat to those in charge. Obviously those who are fighting in public arenas have a more immediate and desperate reason to resist the politic dynamic that threatens their lives. At the same time, the way the games are organized means that those who suffer the actual violence appear to afford almost no political threat. They are unwilling entertainers. It would be a far cry in the minds of those who use these events to further political power for the victims to fight back in a meaningful way.

2. Remembering Rome

And yet this is exactly what happens. The most unlikely source of trouble ends up bringing down the entire political edifice in question because the circumstances of resistance expose the political reality in violence in a specifically public manner. For Tacitus, a Roman Senator who recognized what was at stake in the gladiatorial games, gladiators forced questions to which there could be no answers. He writes: "And indeed there are characteristic and specific vices in this city, which seem to me to be practically born in the womb: the obsession with actors and the passion for gladiatorial shows and horse racing. How much room does a mind preoccupied with such things have for the noble arts?"[11] The spectacle of these events reveals how those who watch are intrinsically detached from the noble ends that politics should serve. Tacitus poses a question that identifies the contradiction that those in power do not want anyone to realize, much less admit it. The use of violence against others precludes the possibility that those using the violence can act morally within politics.

The brazen nature of Rome's gladiatorial contests mirrors the carinvalesque nature of the Hunger Games. The gladiators, then, are a clue to important underlying truths about Roman politics, just as the Games expose the truth of the way that President Snow rules over Panem. Collins makes the connection between the Roman Coliseum and the Hunger Games explicit: "I send my tributes into an updated version of the Roman gladiator games ... which entails a ruthless government forcing people to fight to the death as popular entertainment."[12] We can see clear parallels in the movie version of *Catching Fire*. As Katniss prepares to head out for the tribute parade, the soaring arches, windows where spectators can look down, and generally dark setting echo strongly the feeling of walking through the bowels of the Roman Coliseum. Politically, the tributes from the districts serve the same purpose as the gladiators did for Rome's elite. Transforming human life into sport is ultimately a matter of justifying the political system of those who can enjoy the games as entertainment.

The tributes from the districts can be seen in the same light as the gladiators. Defined as outsiders from the Capitol, there can be in the minds of the spectators (a thought process very much encouraged by President Snow's politics) a justification for the unjustifiable killing of children for sport. In his article "The Joy of Watching Others Suffer:

Schadenfreude and the Hunger Games," Andrew Shaffer explains why this matters: "Although some gladiators were volunteers, many who entered the Coliseum for combat and execution were criminals, runaway slaves, or traitors. The spectators could therefore persuade themselves that justice was being served in these instances, and this belief gave them free rein to cheer as the gladiators fought to the death."[13] There must be *some* moral detachment for those watching the games to accept them as somehow normative. Casting the tributes as *deserving* their fate is about the only way to twist what the Hunger Games actually are into something that can be watched and embraced.

Implicit in this supposed acceptance is a purposeful unwillingness to consider the tributes as fellow human beings. This refusal to see a person as a person is a common way that morally bankrupt things are allowed to happen. From the initial definition of slaves in America as $3/5$ of a person to not allowing women to vote, there is a long tradition in America of claiming liberty for all but, in practice, restricting freedoms to a narrow section of the population. Doing so consolidated power within a specific demographic, a legacy that still more or less determines who makes political decisions at all levels of government. While an expanded discussion of gender, race, or class in American politics is outside the scope of this project, it is important to acknowledge that historically political power was restricted to those who shared common traits: relatively or clearly wealthy, white, and male. Though there have certainly been more women and people of color ascending the ladder of political influence, by and large a representative equilibrium of demographics has not been achieved. Further, it is important to emphasize that for all the progress that has been realized among non-whites and women, lower economic classes are *still* grossly under-represented in American politics.

Finding an example of how this dynamic works today is not terribly difficult. A brief excursus will suffice to show two important points that emerge from a world where political victims are held responsible even though they are not the ones making political decisions. Charles Murray, a conservative sociologist, has uttered several famous lines about the work ethic of those in poverty. Among the poor, Murray explains why he things there is a common denominator: "it will turn out that the population below the poverty line in the United States has a configuration of the relevant genetic makeup that is significantly different from the configuration of the population above the poverty line. This is not unimaginable. It is almost certainly true."[14] The supposed truth here mirrors the logic cited above to justify the selection of lower classes for the gladiators' fights and which President Snow uses in justifying the Hunger Games. The "relevant genetic makeup" implies a cause for poverty that is natural and, therefore, *not* the responsibility of anyone else. Given the disproportionate number of black Americans below the poverty line vis. whites above the poverty line, Murray's argument is meant to "blame" poverty on something other than an economic system that pretty clearly advantages white men.

As a counterweight to Murray's self-serving political logic, Edward Baptist's recent book *The Half Has Never Been Told: Slavery and the Making of American Capitalism*[15] illustrates what should be obvious: there was a clear advantage for whites in early America to build wealth because they did not have to pay labor costs, which, in agriculture and the early Industrial Revolution were significant. Despite this basic economic argument, Baptist's book invited some surprisingly strong pushback. Of note is a review of the book in *The Economist* that critiqued, among other things, the use of the few available slaves' voices as normative: "Mr. Baptist cites the testimony of a few slaves to support his view that these rises in productivity were achieved by pickers being driven to work ever harder by a system of 'calibrated pain.'"[16] The complication here was noted by Hugh Thomas in 1997 in his definitive history, "The Slave Trade"; "an historian cannot know whether these few spokesmen adequately speak for all."[17] Even though *The Economist* subsequently retracted this review,[18] the initial critique of Baptist's work shows the extent to which our culture will justify the social and cultural abuse of a demographic other than the ruling political class. This is, therefore, a clear example of the underlying political dynamic I am exploring in this focused discussion. Blacks were systematically denied education alongside other freedoms, so there would naturally be a dearth of written accounts from this period in history. However the burden of proving a normative experience (despite the fact that the accounts that do exist are pretty consistent) falls on the very people whom the white political superstructure denied the basis and the right to share their stories. Slaves, in other words, had no say in what happened, but, the argument goes, they are responsible for not saying enough.

As a result of this flawed logic and other perceived problems with Baptist's book, *The Economist* initially concluded that his work is not objective. Other historical accounts of slavery—which are based on the ample evidence from white writers per the point made in the previous paragraph—are more balanced. "Unlike Mr. Thomas, Mr. Baptist has not written an objective history of slavery. Almost all the blacks in his book are victims, almost all the whites villains. This is not history; it is advocacy."[19] This statement is equally flawed and equally troubling. If I were to write that existing academic work on The Hunger Games series is biased because it treats all those who died in the Arena as victims and is too quick to blame President Snow for these deaths, I assume that people would line up to point out the absurdity of the statement. When someone is forced to participate in a violent system that denies him or her rights and threatens death for failing to comply, how much choice can they really have?

This political logic walls off both those who would offer legitimate criticism and, in some instances, aligns the ones voicing the critique—often from within the privileged social class—with those who receive blame for their condition. Jeffrey Sachs, who directs the Earth Institute at Columbia University, recounts how American officials argued against providing antiviral medication to combat AIDS in Africa because of the impact poverty supposedly would have on those taking the medication. Andrew Nastios, the recently appointed Administrator of USAID under President Bush in 2001, explained that complicated medical regiments would not be effective because: "you have to take these ... drugs a certain number of hours each day, or they won't work. Many people in Africa have never seen a clock or a watch their entire lives. And if you say one o'clock in the afternoon, they do not know what you are talking about."[20] Nastios then added a broader justification for his comments: "I'm sorry to say these things, but a lot of people like Jeffrey Sachs advocating these things [anti–AIDS drug treatment] have never worked in health care in rural areas in Africa or even in the cities."[21] Nastios's statement assumes two things about Africans who would benefit from medication. First, they lack a skill, telling time, that children understand around the age of 8. The kind of moral detachment necessary to justify violence for sport surfaces in just such a critique. Belittling an adult population's intellect requires a willingness to ignore the fact that "By the end of 2001, over half of Africa's countries—28 nations—had more mobile than

2. Remembering Rome

landline subscribers, a higher percentage than on any other continent."[22] Even basic mobile phones have clocks, a reality that counters directly an already spurious claim. The purpose of an argument like Nastios's is, of course, to justify withholding something that could save lives because of implicit (racial, sexual, etc.) categories that, though never stated, come sharply into focus when read against the backdrop of claims such as these.

As a footnote to this discussion, it is worth highlighting that Nastios also casts Sachs, a respected academic at one of the world's leading universities, as naïve in disagreeing with his argument. A disregard for basic facts is designed to insulate a statement like Nastios's from criticism that is not voiced by those whom he considers unable to do the things necessary to acquire medicine. As Sachs points out, he had worked in rural health settings in Kenya: "The people of Sauri, Kenya, who arrived punctually at 2:30 p.m. for our Monday afternoon discussion, would have been chagrined to know how their lives had been compromised by such profound ignorance of a senior U.S. official."[23] Statements made in a vacuum with no basis in actual experience are precisely the kinds of oppression that justify a politics that will protect its interests at the expense of others' lives. Sachs knows a great deal about what Nastios says he does not (with the added benefit of confirming that those who supposedly do not know what a clock is could turn up punctually for an important meeting). The summary point is clear in this vignette. Reality is filtered through a framework that sets aside the basal truths driving the actions of those in political power. The violence in this instance is not overt, but the resulting consequences are not dissimilar.

The fact of the matter is that in these political dynamics the victim is the one who does not have the ability to make choices and/or counter the narrative that relegates her/him to be a means to a political end. In America, we do not have to imagine blood sport to find an example of this line of thinking. We only need to think about how to make policy decisions that can help people get jobs. Murray's explanation of how to train people makes several telling assumptions: "You want to have a job training program for welfare mothers? You think that's going to cure the welfare problem? Well, when you construct that job training program and try to decide what jobs they might qualify for, you had better keep in mind that the mean IQ of welfare mothers is somewhere in the 80s, which means that you have certain limitations in what you're going to accomplish."[24] Helping mothers in poverty would actually do a lot to help alleviate the acute challenges of raising a family without sufficient resources to meet basic needs. However, a simple solution cannot allow for achievement that would disrupt the underlying bias against those in poverty.

As with the above explanation that there is a genetic basis for poverty, here Murray ties poverty to an intrinsic quality, intelligence, rather than the social and political context in which any intrinsic quality plays out. Murray claims that mothers in poverty are, simply, not smart enough to get out of poverty. In practice, of course, those mothers are probably more resourceful than average insofar as they have to figure out a way to raise their children without the support system that those who are not trapped in poverty have. In this logic, those above the poverty line are considered (a) smarter and (b) not responsible for those who do live in poverty. The result is a trap that justifies a political order that systematically denies a section of the population the same treatment as those who are within the sphere of the political power structure that articulates these flawed arguments in the first place.

Given the echoes between the Games and Rome's own troubling embrace of public violence (as well as the echoes of America's continued willingness to uphold a political class by blaming those outside that class), a close analysis of a conversation between Plutarch Heavensbee and Katniss will bring even more focus to the political realities that come with "blaming" a specific subset of the population. While she is recovering from her gunshot wound, Plutarch explains the reason behind President Snow's political decisions. As someone who ascended as high as anyone realistically can in President Snow's political world, he is as well placed as anyone to shed light on how President Snow goes about governing.

Plutarch's insights establish an important contrast between the rebels and the residents of the Capitol. The former, Plutarch explains, understand what it means to ensure hardship. In the Capitol, however, the de facto motto is: "*Panem et Circenses.*"[25] Katniss is about as familiar with Lain as most of us, so Plutarch explains the phrase: "It's a saying from thousands of years ago, written in a language called Latin about a place called Rome.... *Panem et Circenses* translates into 'Bread and Circuses.' The writer was saying that in return for full bellies and entertain-

2. Remembering Rome

ment, his people had given up their political responsibilities and therefore their power."[26] For all his focuses exercise of power, President Snow ultimately draws on a simple formula to maintain control: dumb down the population. To keep people in the Capitol from noticing the violent reality all around them, President Snow provides two things: food and entertainment in the form of tributes. Katniss realizes that the districts thus play a clear role; they provide both of the things President Snow needs to placate the Capitol.

The outline here is both unsettling and all too common in politics. The expectations for those living in relative comfort are different than those who struggle to survive. The contrast is the not the key point to lift out of Plutarch's history lesson. Rather, the important takeaway here lies in the effect bread and circuses have. These two things are enough to get people to ignore their political identities and thus their responsibilities. President Snow hardly serves the interests of those Capitol citizens, but he does not need to. So long as he meets two needs, he can rest easily knowing that the Capitol remains a benign political place. This allows him to focus his efforts on the districts where he knows political unrest is far more likely to emerge.

The comparison with Rome focuses on the mindset of the Capitol's citizens. Despite the similarities Plutarch describes, there is a deeper critique buried within his outline of how President Snow blunts political action in the Capitol. For Romans, entertainment took the form of those whom Rome's political rulers could cast as true villains. Deserters, conquered enemies, or political rabble-rousers made up the bulk of the people who found themselves fighting gladiatorial matches. In Panem, the entertainers are children. They upend the implicit moral argument that those fighting in the coliseums throughout the Roman Empire deserved their fate. President Snow tries to manufacture this narrative, but when kids are the ones who supposedly deserve their fate, there is a much deeper political problem to address.

Plutarch's outline ultimately raises two moral question marks in a world where people are killed for entertainment. The voices asking these questions are quiet, if they are heard at all. Returning to another Roman thinker will help focus on the implications of encouraging those who see what is happening to call it for what it is. Seneca was one of Rome's most influential thinkers (he also shares the name with Seneca Crane,

The Politics of *The Hunger Games*

the head Gamemaker in *The Hunger Games*). He is known as a Stoic, the school of philosophy that is deeply relevant to thinking about nature of political violence in The Hunger Games series. Stoicism focused on exercising human free will within the context of the natural world. There are certain things that happen in life over which we have no control. If a person suffers a natural disaster, for example, we cannot reasonably place moral blame on that person. What we can change, however, is the choice to act morally or not. An important aspect of Stoicism is thus the ability to exercise one's individual choice in a moral way.

Seneca applied this general philosophical outline to a range of matters, but his comments on the gladiator games in Rome are an important point of focus in this conversation. As with Russell Crowe's Maximus, Seneca raises his critique of the gladiators through questions that ultimately cannot be answered in a moral way. Thinking about Pompey's (a 1st century BC Emperor) decision to mimic the Punic Wars in presenting gladiatorial games, Seneca asks: "Do they fight to the death? That is not enough! Are they torn to pieces? That is not enough! Let them be crushed by animals of monstrous bulk!"[27] Seneca zeroes in on the person who would demand ever more violence in the name of entertainment. There is a one-upmanship here that becomes more troubling as the suffering of those inside the arena increases. This potentially endless increase is, for Seneca, exactly what should cause people to look away: "Better would it be that these things pass into oblivion lest hereafter some all-powerful man should learn them and be jealous of an act that was nowise human."[28] These events are simply not human. There is a moral element to humanity that is absent inside the arena. Only a deep political narcissism can sanction this kind of thing and Seneca is clear in his desire to expose the extent to which popularizing the suffering of others ultimately undermines the basis of what it means to be human.

Not all of Rome's Emperors descended to this state of moral decay. Marcus Aurelius (the Emperor who chooses Crowe's Maximus as Rome's next ruler in *Gladiator*) was clear in his understanding of politics. There must be a moral core to ruling over people. Aurelius wrote extensively about these claims and offers a counterweight to so many of his imperial colleagues who used the suffering of others to preserve and expand political power. In *Meditations*, Aurelius articulates a litmus test for determining what is "right" in the world: "If any man is able to convince me and show me that I do not think or act right, I will gladly change; for I seek the truth by which no man was ever injured. But he is injured who abides in his error and ignorance."[29] Several key standards emerge from this short saying. First, we should be willing to change in the face of evidence that proves wrong action. An implicit critique is thus leveled against those are presented with evidence of a broken politics and refuse to change their behavior. If President Snow were watching kids kill one another in the Arena, surely he would recognize the unjustifiable nature of the Hunger Games.

President Snow is happy to let the games continue because in his political mindset he misses the next important part of Aurelius' statement: what constitutes truth. For President Snow, this term is defined in a way that justifies his own political position. The truth Aurelius is talking about, however, is a moral truth that remains *independent* of any specific circumstance. This is the standard against which we should measure our actions, political or otherwise. The failure to do so results in the "injury" that cannot be outrun. Underlying moral truth will, in other words, eventually reveal the reality of using violence as a way to pacify and manipulate a populace.

Given this moral argument, there should be a clear symbiotic balance between political leaders and those whom those leaders govern. Aurelius explains: "That which does no harm to the state, does no harm to the citizen. In the case of every appearance of harm apply this rule: if the state is not harmed by this, neither am I harmed. But if the state is harmed, thou must not be angry with him who does harm to the state. Show him where his error is."[30] The crucial issue here is to recognize that the Hunger Games, like the gladiatorial games in Rome, expose a broken social and political system. Killing others to entertain the masses does not strengthen a political ruler in a meaningful way. Rather, it masquerades as strength in the eyes of the public. The truth is that harming people will weaken the state by exposing its moral bankruptcy.

Aurelius forces us to confront the political realities of The Hunger Games series in a way that simultaneously invites us to consider our own political context. In a changing world, we should look to the depths that a bad politics will reach in order to recognize the importance of a morally sound social contract. Purdy offers helpful guidance in this effort: "We [should] strive to eliminate certain sorts of inconsistencies, revising principles to account for strongly held views about cases, using principles that have so far withstood scrutiny to shed light on new and uncertain cases."[31] Importantly, Purdy is not claiming that aligning politics in our world with a moral baseline is an easy task. The world is a messy place and we must continually work to define our politics given the challenges we face. There will be shortcomings, but this is different than refusing to try in the first place. The challenges we face do not justify a retreat to a political system that privileges absolute and exclusive statements. As we have seen in this chapter, this approach begins by blaming those harmed at the hands of a political ruling class, which can extend to the extreme nature of the violence we see throughout The Hunger Games series.

As we work to build a cultural mindset that can think about politics in this way, we cannot overlook the importance of taking responsibility for our own politics identities. Again, Purdy is helpful in thinking about this point: "the moral language we use in daily life has much to do with what that life is like, with what we are like. To belong to a society in which the language of honor is dominant and the language of human rights has no place is to be a certain sort of person."[32] We have to take seriously what words like value, moral, freedom, and humanity mean because we co-exist with others whose experiences may demand different definitions. Finding common ground will require at times the ability to translate divergent moral dialects into a shared definition of a moral politics. In other words, we must recognize the impact rigid definitions within politics can have; we have to admit the ways that our definitions and decisions have cast people into terrible suffering. We do not currently pay to watch gladiators battle to the death, but we are also a culture that has seen the justification of proxies for this kind of violence. In admitting that we can be entertained when we see those whom we consider outside the parameters of our political class suffer, we can take an important political step. We can do what Gale suggests. We can stop watching.

3. *The Social Contract*

Following 9/11, President Bush requested that the amount of the federal budget devoted to homeland security be roughly doubled from $19.5 billion to $37.7 billion.[1] The introduction to the budget which established the Department of Homeland Security highlights two poles that defined America's post–9/11 approach to national security. In the President's language: "There are two inescapable truths about terrorism in the 21st century."[2] Framed within the specific context of the attacks on 9/11, those two truths—security and freedom—are probably the definitive considerations of modern political thought. Finding a good balance between the two remains one of a politician's greatest challenges.

The language in the budget conveys this very point. On the one hand, "the characteristics of American society that we cherish—our freedom, our openness, our great cities and towering skyscrapers, our modern transportation systems—make us vulnerable to terrorism of catastrophic proportions."[3] If politics is about individual choice, then one of the core functions for a government to do well is protect that freedom. Freedom, however, has a price, which President Bush captures in these introductory remarks. The very things that follow freedom, the innovation and the opportunity to transform lives at the local or national level, require a measure of insecurity. The ability to communicate easily and to travel across the country provides opportunities for bad actors to bring about terrible things. More freedom, in other words, requires that we assume a measure of insecurity.

In addition to these vulnerabilities that are intrinsic in a free society, President Bush also called attention to the specific ways freedom can be exploited. There are increasingly sophisticated ways of leveraging the vulnerabilities embedded in our freedom into acts of terror. In President Bush's language: "the technological ability to launch destructive attacks against civilian populations and critical infrastructure spreads to more and more organizations and individuals with each passing year. This trend is an unavoidable byproduct of the technological, educational, economic, and social progress that creates jobs, wealth, and a good quality of life."[4] Ironically, the better off we the more vulnerable we are in terms of security. Free email is a mainstay of personal and professional life. The Internet gives us instantaneous access to information. These tools also make it easy to research and coordinate violence against civilians. To counter these possibilities, a measure of security thus becomes necessary. The cost to those who enjoy the privileges of freedom is to accept that at times the government needs to infringe upon that freedom to keep us safe.

A very practical example of this trade off is well known to most of us in the post–9/11 world. Traveling by plane now includes multiple inconveniences that did not exist before 9/11. Before the attacks, everyone had the freedom to go to the departure gates or carry liquids in carryon baggage. The ability to do so is a freedom that has since been revoked in the name of security. With few exceptions, liquids are prohibited when passing through security and only ticketed passengers can access departure gates. This is a loss of freedom. However, we understand the rationale. These restrictions serve to provide increased security while traveling as they attempt to reduce the chance of a future attack.

Jean Jacques Rousseau is a giant among modern political thinkers. The opening lines from his most famous work, *The Social Contract*, capture the fundamental tension that defines an individual. "Man is born free," Rousseau claims, but "everywhere he is in chains. One thinks himself the master of others, and still remains a greater slave than they. How did this change come about? I do not know. What can make it legitimate? That question I think I can answer."[5] There exists an intrinsic freedom that defines humanity. The problem is that this freedom exists within a world that restricts freedom in a variety of ways. Our freedom is not a blank check to do what we want in life. Everywhere we turn, someone or something constrains those choices. Rousseau is not out to trace the history of a disappearing freedom. His point in establishing this contradictory freedom is to address the second point here: how to recover the freedom at the heart of who we are and what our culture should be.

The starting point in Rousseau's thinking is important to emphasize. The reality of political life is movement from freedom toward the chains that Rousseau finds everywhere. In the air travel example above,

3. The Social Contract

we have moved from relative freedom to enter and exit airports carrying just about anything to a state where we can do far less than we used to. Our initial freedom is something that within the context of the world we inhabit must be compromised. The reason that freedom must be compromised and how to limit the consequences of the things that end up restricting what we can lies at the heart of *The Social Contract*.

Importantly, Rousseau does not lay out a plan for unchecked freedom to do whatever we please. He recognizes that this is not a viable intellectual journey or a practical social paradigm. The implicit point is that at least some of what we have given up cannot be recovered. Much like President Bush states in creating the Department of Homeland Security, the complexities of our world demand vigilance. The question, then, is how we can legitimize the parameters within which we give away some of our freedom.

In order to legitimize the process of accepting limits on freedom, we have to accept that some social reality is necessary in our lives. For Rousseau, this is an important assumption: "the social order is a sacred right which is the basis of all other rights. Nevertheless, this right does not come from nature, and must therefore be founded on conventions."[6] Several important things happen in this outline. First, there is a difference between our inherent freedom and the exercise of that freedom. We are part of a broader world—a social one—and this is, like our freedom, something deeply important. Our rights must align with this sacred social order. At the outset, then, Rousseau establishes a balance between the individual and society that ultimately underwrites the decisions that limit freedom.

A follow on point must be emphasized here. Rejecting society in the name of personal freedom is not how things work. Our participation in society frames our freedom and we should uphold the good that society provides. This does not, of course, mean that society can erase our freedoms (a point that will be discussed at length below in thinking about Panem). It does, however, protect against the extreme political argument that life can or should be lived entirely on one's own.

The broader social context in which our successes (and failures) occur often gets set aside in our current political discourse. There exists across the political spectrum an overemphasis on the individual. Libertarian ideology is the most pronounced form of articulating a politics that is often divorced from a broader social context. A particular point in Libertarian thought that deserves discussion is the idea that taxation should not occur. The vision outlined on The Future of Freedom Foundation's website is clear on this: "No more income taxation and Internal Revenue Service. Everyone would be free to keep everything he earns or inherits (and would decide for himself what to do with it)."[7] This sounds great in a time of economic strain. Why should anyone pay taxes to a government if s/he does not support or trust the government? If money is tight, the thinking goes, then the government is the first thing that should be prevented from reaching into our pockets.

This argument has clear appeal, but the appeal blocks an intellectually honest assessment of the implications that follow. On both a personal and social level, no taxes would have clearly harmful consequences. A former colleague who worked in the federal government would often tell me that taxes should be abolished. The irony of taking a paycheck from the government but arguing against funding that government never seemed apparent. On a national scale, without taxes funding an army would be very difficult, as would securing our borders. Absent security infrastructure we would be deeply vulnerable to a variety of bad actors.

The problem, in other words, is that the foundation for wishing the government away is the government itself. Senator Elizabeth Warren made this point recently in a campaign speech that garnered much attention, both positive and negative. Warren pointed out the obvious: no one who is successful within our culture can divorce her/his success completely from that culture: "There is nobody in this country who got rich on his own—nobody. You built a factory out there? Good for you. But I want to be clear. You moved your goods to market on the roads the rest of us paid for. You hired workers the rest of us paid to educate. You were safe in your factory because of police-forces and fire-forces that the rest of us paid for."[8] Warren continues: "You didn't have to worry that marauding bands would come and seize everything at your factory—and hire someone to protect against this—because of the work the rest of us did."[9] Warren's point here is not to take credit for another person's success and thus to undermine the rewards that come to those who take risks, build businesses, and create economic growth. Her point is that success occurs against a specific backdrop that is communal.

The person who succeeds with the help of that social context has

3. The Social Contract

an obligation to participate in it. Warren concludes: "Now look, you built a factory and it turned into something terrific, or a great idea. God bless—keep a big hunk of it. But part of the underlying social contract is, you take a hunk of that and pay forward for the next kid who comes along."[10] Her language here is telling. The social contract that enables so much is so easily forgotten when someone outpaces her/his fellow citizens. To encourage this kind of thinking is to undermine the very basis of *shared* success at the level of providing security while protecting everyone's freedom. After all, those innovators make most of our lives better and yes, they contribute a lot in the form of taxes. The point is that they are not excused from doing so. We cannot and should not sanction people who would reject the society that gave them the advantages they have drawn on to succeed.

This lengthy discussion frames a closer examination of the social contract—or lack thereof—that characterizes Panem. The government's role should be, in Rousseau's thought, a kind of scale that weighs security and freedom based on particular circumstances and assures the balance achieved is fair to everyone the result will affect. Things change and as they do the social contract should be revisited to ensure that the citizens are content with the political foundation that frames their lives. The problem throughout The Hunger Games series is that there is very little active political action in either the districts or the Capitol. President Snow is hardly good news for anyone but (presumably) a few elite members of his circle (though Seneca Crane shows that being a part of the inner sanctum is anything but enviable). The outline we find in *The Hunger Games* speaks volumes about the political apathy that allows President Snow's abuses to run rampant across the districts.

One-way political streets are a problem. Yielding the right to negotiate the social contract is enabling poor governance. As the 2014 Congressional elections approached, America was overwhelmingly dissatisfied with its elected leaders. Congress' approval rating was a mere 14 percent.[11] One of the few things partisans can agree on, in other words, is that America's government performs horribly. At the same time, voter turnout in non–Presidential election years averages less than 50 percent.[12] Thus, despite a clear statement regarding the quality of political leadership getting half of eligible voters to the polls counted as "major"[13] turnout. The quality of the leadership should not determine whether someone votes in the first place. In fact, this enables the very dynamic that drives people away from their role in the social contract. This is a key point in this chapter. When citizens disengage from the political process, they hand the political ruling class a de facto vote to carry on as is.

In a stable democracy, it is easy to look the other way from this continued poor performance. However, when this process extends to the extremes of political possibilities, we begin to see how evil geniuses can consolidate their rule. In fact, they often assume and/or enforce disinterest and non-participation. Still, there is a way to demand accountability, but this requires active participation in the political process. Whether one is talking about a democracy or throwing off an authoritarian regime, this requires a choice to reject the status quo from one's political reality. Arguing that there are no good choices and therefore there is no reason to vote is not responsible civic behavior. If the choices are that bad, then there are other steps to take (e.g. running oneself or recruiting a candidate worth voting to run). Katniss's struggle to assume the role of the Mockingjay is the significant example of reversing this dynamic, but those who play their small parts—Prim's support before the victory tour and Joana's partnership to get Katniss in shape despite her own dark secrets are two of many examples—to reclaim their obligation to correct the political imbalance that smothers their freedom.

A government administers the rights that protect our freedom and this government is not something that possesses an inherent permission to exist. The right comes not from nature; it is something that we build with one another. We establish a government that will keep our freedom secure through this shared process and ask us to share in the outcome. This is the dynamic that serves as the title for Rousseau's contribution to political philosophy: the social contract. The agreement that outlines what we have negotiated regarding what we can and cannot do within the legal—and implicitly moral—terms that characterize how we mutually agree to balance security and freedom. This is the binding agreement that should uphold both our intrinsic freedom wherever possible and the social structure that will protect this freedom. Freedom remains the basis for a good social contract, but the very language of the contract—something that stipulates terms and conditions between two interests—sanctions the reality that at times individuals must yield to the social reality that they are part of. Citizens have an obligation and a freedom

3. The Social Contract

to participate in negotiating the contract, especially if that contract ceases to or neglects to protect their freedom.

Revisiting how Rousseau defines the government will explain what is at stake in holding the government accountable. "What, then, is the government?"[14] asks Rousseau. The answer: "An intermediary body established between the subjects and the sovereign for their mutual communication, a body charged with the execution of the laws and the maintenance of freedom, both civil and political."[15] Two salient points stand out. First, the government is a communicative medium; those involved in the social contract should be able to communicate with one another openly about the parameters of their agreement. Second, the government's specific function is to uphold laws and the maintenance of freedom. The qualifier here casts out all claims that a society's laws are just merely because they are on the books. The laws must serve to preserve both civic and individual freedom.

Given these qualifications, we can see exactly how President Snow fails as an arbiter of a social contract. Though there is no firsthand account of his inner political workings because Katniss is not privy to them (we do get some insight when Katniss and President Snow speak at the end of *Mockingjay*), it seems safe to conclude that President Snow does not offer an open office policy to the Capitol's citizens. Further, the laws of Panem fail in their moral focus: to protect freedom. In short, the distance between President Snow's obligation and the political reality in both the districts and the Capitol is stark. Quite simply, there is no freedom on either count.

Just how bad does President Snow make things? If we look at some of the signs Rousseau identifies as indicating a strong social contract, things look pretty grim. One specific litmus test for Rousseau is how often citizens are punished: "In a well governed state, there are few punishments, not because there are many pardons, but because criminals are rare; it is when a state is in decay that the multitude of crimes is a guarantee of impunity."[16] By this standard, President Snow's rule over Panem is very troubling. There are frequent and excessive punishments that range from executions to mutilation (Avoxes are a constant and silent testimony to this) to infanticide to starvation. Interestingly, the basis for these punishments does not actually map to crime. Rather, punishment is a preemptive tool President Snow implements in order to maintain a sense of fear among Panem's citizens. Ironically, then, criminals are rare in the strict sense of behavior that is truly wrong. At the same time, everyone is treated as a partial criminal given the severe restrictions on just about every aspect of life in Panem.

The extensive use of punishment signals an underlying problem in President's Snow's actions. Rousseau explains: "In any case, frequent punishments are a sign of weakness or slackness in the government. There is no man so bad that he cannot be made good for something. No man should be put to death, even as an example, if he can be left to live without danger to society."[17] Are any of the tributes who die in the Arena unable to live without danger to society? The supposed danger is entirely the byproduct of President Snow's program to maintain his grip on power. There is no sense of restorative social practices; fear, suffering and often death are the only punishments we see President Snow mete out over the course of The Hunger Games series. There is, in other words, a clear message that he sees citizens as intrinsically threatening and therefore not valuable components given his understanding of what society should be. The hidden weakness that Rousseau mentions thus emerges from within President's Snow's abuses. He relies on fear and suffering to stay in power, which ultimately calls attention to the bankrupt relationship between himself and Panem's citizens.

Among modern political philosophers, Thomas Hobbes provides the counterweight to Rousseau's political thought and his understanding of government's role will help fill out the social contract in place throughout Panem. Unlike Rousseau, Hobbes foregrounds the government's responsibilities as the basis for politics. The basis for government is in the intrinsic instability that comes from desire. Hobbes claims: "For there is no such thing as perpetual Tranquility of mind, while we live here; because Life itself is but Motion, and can never be without Desire, nor without Fear, no more than without Sense."[18] People are forever uneasy either because they seek more than they have. Alongside the desire to acquire we find a fear of others who want the same thing. The world in such a conception is zero-sum; for one to benefit, another must lose. Fear of loss is a well-known psychological dynamic that allows suspicion to set up shop in our minds. As a result, there exists in society an inherent distrust that can quickly manifest itself in negative ways.

Freedom, in other words, can be a real problem. Played out to its logical conclusion the human mind's state as described above will inevitably lead to conflict. In a well known passage from *Leviathan*, Hobbes summarizes this point: "When all the world is overcharged with inhabitants, then the last remedy of all is war, which provideth for every man, by victory or death."[19] If the end result of human action will be victory or death, then everyone has an interest in a government that will make sure things do not get to the point of war. There is no guarantee who will win or lose, so to hedge our bets we should accept a government that limits our freedoms to protect us.

The way Hobbes' thought can appeal to President Snow is obvious. Government isn't the problem; it is the proactive, protective solution to our inability to keep ourselves out of trouble. Once this framework has been established, it becomes very easy to justify actions from the government's perspective. Specific threats require the government to act in a way that prevents a descent into war. As we saw in the introductory discussion of Herod, the potential for someone to usurp Herod's position becomes a justifiable (in Herod's mind) reason to preempt an insurrection through blanket infanticide. Because someone other than the government is the root cause of potential warfare, rulers can always fall back on the explanation that a particular course of action was the only option.

When President Snow goes to Katniss's house at the beginning of *Catching Fire* for a one-on-one chat, we get some clues as to the similarities between President Snow and Hobbes regarding the role of the government. President Snow essentially outlines this argument, but he also admits that his political calculation is based on some tenuous assumptions. In admitting these, however, he also tells Katniss that he is willing to scorch Panem's earth if a rebellion takes hold. He explains: "Do you have any idea what that [a rebellion] would mean? How many people would die? What conditions those left would have to face? Whatever problems anyone may have with the Capitol, believe me when I saw that if it released its grip on the districts for even a short time, the entire system would collapse."[20] There is a roundabout logic here. President Snow acknowledges that rebellions could undo his choreographed control over Panem. If that happens, however, there exists a consequence that will be severe. The script requires in some way restraint. If, however, a rebellion were to diverge from President Snow's plan, his restraint in controlling the districts would cease to exist. He would do whatever would be needed to win the fight.

War is messy, costly, and dangerous to everyone. This is precisely why everyone should want the government to prevent war. President Snow may as well be quoting Hobbes here: "To this war of every man against every man, this also in consequent; that nothing can be unjust. The notions of right and wrong, justice and injustice have there no place. Where there is no common power, there is no law, where no law, no injustice. Force, and fraud, are in war the cardinal virtues."[21] If war breaks out, chaos reigns and there will be no safety for anyone. Yes, there are restrictions when living under the current state of Panem for the districts, but the (self-serving) point in the exchange is that order in society is worth the costs. Security is necessary, so citizens must accept the limitations that enable security.

President Snow's message is subtle, manipulative, and straight out of *Leviathan*. In his eyes, responsibility for government action rests on the shoulders of the governed. This is because: "For to accuse requires less eloquence, such is man's nature, than to excuse; and condemnation, than absolution, more resembles justice."[22] Citizens are the problem because they cannot be trusted. As such, the very notion of a social contract negotiated between citizens and the government is untenable. There must be a mediator within society to preclude—not just oversee but be prepared to engage—the possibility of war. "Covenants, without the sword, are but words and of no strength to secure a man at all."[23] Force, in other words, is part of freedom.

Problematically, an emphasis on security through the use of force does not necessarily exclude a moral foundation in politics. Greitens, whose own participation in the military reflected a sincere desire to do good for the world, highlights this point. There are times when people are simply unable to protect themselves and if we take the notion of equality seriously, then, Greitens argues, we must protect those people. Force, in other words, can serve a moral end.

In our own, the discussion here forces a question: can we accept risk knowing there are people who are devoted to violent action against our society or do we need a government that will sticks its arms into the muddy reality of geopolitics? There is, of course, no definitive answer, but the conversation in this chapter considers the implications of tilting

3. The Social Contract

our society toward liberty or security. Historically, America sides with the latter. Benjamin Franklin's famous dictum conveys this mindset: "Those who would give up essential Liberty, to purchase a little temporary Safety, deserve neither Liberty nor Safety."[24] Franklin's point is not that we have to pick either liberty of security. Rather, the emphasis is that, much like Rousseau, liberty must be the foundation of thinking about security. We should not assume that people would inevitably find themselves in a zero-sum game with their fellow citizens. This assumption easily leads to victim blaming that undermines the notion of liberty. Franklin's claim has to do with approaching the balance between liberty and security in a way that foregrounds freedom. The failure to do so will enable a politics that preserves neither liberty nor security.

The Hunger Games series ultimately arrives at the same conclusion. The limits of Hobbes's thought become apparent when considering the way defaulting to government as the basis for society can lead to serious problems. By handing control of political discourse and action to a narrow few, the opportunity to abuse everyone becomes manifest. While not a guarantee that the government will abuse its power, we should be cautious of the possibility as the line between possible and actual can be crossed very quickly.

Our shared humanity lies behind the caution I am sounding in thinking about the connection between Hobbesian thought and politics in The Hunger Games series. When distrust is part of our social identity, very few will benefit. Politics should smooth out differences. Purdy explains why: "Rousseau proposed that these psychic agonies might be overcome through politics.... By creating a civic realm in which every citizen is absolutely equal to every other, and making this the primary site of moral identification, politics brings us what we need most: every man has the regard of every other, which he earnestly reciprocates."[25] Our social contract is the moral framework that governs our interactions with one another. This is not a prescription for a society without distinction. To argue from a classically liberal political philosophy is not to posit an ideal along the lines of Ayn Rand's Twentieth Century Motor Company. Rousseau's equality as Purdy describes it does not argue for a uniform culture with respect to success and failure. Rather, the argument seeks an admission from everyone that everyone else has equal moral and political standing within a society of infinite differences.

There can be rich and poor; those who risk can and should expect reward. However, those who are successful should recall Warren's speech and, moreover, the biblical caution to a society's elite members: "From everyone to whom much has been given, much will be required; and from the one to whom much has been entrusted, even more will be demanded."[26] This is not a prohibition against wealth. In context, this is a reminder that there is a broader moral paradigm that affects how each individual lives her/his life.

Purdy echoes this point. He, too, turns to biblical language to underline the moral imperative of a healthy politics: "Because so much as at stake in the unity of the political community, it must not be divided against itself."[27] The reference points to the famous biblical passage: "Every kingdom divided against itself becomes a desert, and house falls on house."[28] The image too often overshadows the particulars of the process that will unfold. A divided house does not necessarily fall apart in an instant. The point is that over time collapse will occur. Deserts are not pleasant places to be and the realities of such a harsh existence affect everyone.

Division is troubling. We see the rebels struggle continually to align their respective interests as they orchestrate the war against President Snow. A politics that embraces division implicitly and explicitly loses sight of the moral ties that bind us together. When political unity no longer exists, an opening occurs for a politics to become a tool of the powerful few. As we have seen thus far and will see moving forward, President Snow shows just how troubling abuse of this tool can be. The political strategy *Divide et impera* (divide and conquer) is a well know approach to maintaining power (Caesar and Napoleon both ruled with this saying in mind). The weaker everyone else is, the more powerful a dividing leader can be.

In the end, the divided political body will suffer the consequences of discord. Urgent problems may fester when a solution is readily at hand. In America, for example, investment in infrastructure lags well behind other countries. Monetary policy makes borrowing large amounts of money a relatively cheap proposition. Despite a seemingly clear reason to start repairing our roads and bridges, or modernizing our air travel system, political gridlock ensures we will continue to drive and fly in less than ideal (and in many cases dilapidated) circumstances. Importantly, the long-term consequences of these near-term political

3. The Social Contract

choices threaten everyone. A bridge will not discriminate between luxury cars and worn out sedans if it collapses.

Psychologically, we are similarly at long-term risk. When liberty gives way to overwhelming security, we lose sight of the intrinsic goodness that defines in part what it means to be human. Purdy summarizes our condition well: "We are fragmentary, even masters of fragmentation, and we hunger for wholeness."[29] Conflict is a risk for Hobbes that justifies strong governments, but the real conflict we should worry about is our search for meaning in an apolitical sense. Why not proactively seek to avoid a social context that refuses our attempts to find wholeness? If the answer is because of a political affinity that denies our shared humanity, then we are engendering social division and lose sight of our role in creating and upholding a social contract.

4. President Snow

If we could sit down at the breakfast table with the President and listen to him (or her) talk to his (or her) grandchild, perhaps we would be able to set aside politics and see the person at the table as normal. Stripping away the pressure of navigating difficult political waters might just reveal that once all of the criticism and hyperbolic praise cast upon a senior political leader is removed, we can catch a glimpse of who that person really is. Making serious decisions, often as the result of intense negotiations, is a politician's job. At the table with a grandchild, weighty matters might escape our attention and allow us to see President Snow in some kind of sympathetic light.

Thinking about President Snow in a way that differs from the man we read about in The Hunger Games series is a difficult thing to do. What the books reveal about him is filtered through Katniss's perspective. He is the tyrant who happily sends her to the Arena, and then haunts her for the better part of two books until the rebellion ultimately ends and he is dead. He is not someone who can be untangled from his unwavering commitment to being a tyrant.

The movie versions of the books, however, allow for the slight bending of this perspective. There are a handful of scenes that cannot be based on Katniss's experiences because they occur where she could not be present. In addition to being an important reminder when evaluating the citizens of the Capitol, this window into President Snow helps us to think more clearly about how his actions affect Panem.

Early in the *Catching Fire* movie, we actually see a domestic moment involving President Snow. For an instant, it appears his political mind is not always on. He is eating breakfast with his granddaughter and watching television. The news, unfortunately, is not upbeat. President Snow watches the riots in District Eleven after Katniss's speech during the Victory Tour with a clear look of concern on his face. He then turns to his granddaughter, realizes she is wearing her hair in the same braid

4. President Snow

that Katniss prefers, and remarks casually: "Your hair looks lovely, darling. When did you start wearing it like that?"[1] Clearly happy he has noticed, she replies: "Everyone at school wears it like this now Grandpa."[2] The movie shows a close up of President Snow's face as his granddaughter's response registers. He says nothing, but the implication is clear, if subtle. Katniss has become known in a positive way. Though she is innocent in wearing her hair like Katniss, President Snow's granddaughter gives him the first clue that a rebellion is taking shape and the movement has a clear symbolic leader that has seeped into the Capitol's social consciousness.

Like most school-age girls, she wears her hair in a way that falls in line with current trends. In a city obsessed with what is considered fashionable, one can easily perceive President Snow's granddaughter as slowly absorbing her city's hyperawareness of the in-crowd's appearance. He recognizes immediately that an innocent hairstyle among children also signals trouble (a fact made clear in the *Mockingjay* movie when, after President Snow bans all symbols relating to Katniss, his granddaughter quickly takes out the same braid). Later, we catch another domestic glimpse of President Snow and his granddaughter watching Katniss hug Peeta after Finnick revives him in the Arena. President Snow leans back, deep in thought. The spark he so desperately wanted to extinguish is no longer contained. The power of love is apparent. Even his granddaughter recognizes what is going on. She tells President Snow: "Someday I hope I can love someone that much."[3]

To understand the problem that unfolds in this brief exchange, we need to return to a scene from *The Hunger Games* movie where President Snow and Seneca Crane have a meeting about how things are going. Their conversation offers a window into President Snow's mindset regarding Katniss and explains why his granddaughter's hair is a significant problem. President Snow asks Seneca Crane: "Why do we have a winner? If we just wanted to intimidate the districts why not round up 24 of them at random and execute them all at once? It would be a lot faster."[4] Seneca Crane looks perplexed and do not answer. President Snow quickly answers and an important exchange follows:

PRESIDENT SNOW: Hope.
SENECA CRANE: Hope?
PRESIDENT SNOW: It's the only thing stronger than fear. A little hope is effective. A lot of hope is dangerous. A spark is fine as long as it's contained.

The Politics of *The Hunger Games*

SENECA CRANE: So...
PRESIDENT SNOW [interrupting]: So contain it.[5]

There is a delicate psychological balance at work in how the Hunger Games are managed. There must be enough of a narrative to distract those watching from the brutal reality of the entire story. A little hope is fine because it accomplishes this goal. Too much hope, however, and what starts as an aside can become an established mindset. The spark of hope, then, must be smothered in order to accomplish the larger political purpose of the Hunger Games.

A more revealing exchange occurs when President Snow and Plutarch discuss strategy at the beginning of the *Catching Fire* movie. The topic is the same—hope and fear—but the implications we get to see are far more serious from President Snow's perspective:

PRESIDENT SNOW: She's not who they think she is. She's not a leader. She just wants to save her own skin. It's as simple as that.
PLUTARCH: I think that's true.
PRESIDENT SNOW: She's become a beacon of hope for the rebellion, and she has to be eliminated.
PLUTARCH: I agree she should die, but in the right way, at the right time. It's moves and counter-moves, and it's all we gotta look at. Katniss Everdeen is a symbol. Their Mockingjay. They think she's one of them. We need to show that she's one of us.
PRESIDENT SNOW: What do you propose?
PLUTARCH: ...Sow fear. More fear.
PRESIDENT SNOW: It won't work. Fear does not work as long as they have hope, and Katniss Everdeen is giving them hope.[6]

The problem is that people are starting to realize that Katniss is a leader and, therefore, she presents an alternative to the image President Snow wants to cultivate. Hope has escaped the Arena and it needs to stop. Plutarch agrees with the premise, but he puts forth a more subtle, patient idea. In time all that needs to happen is to show that she is just as self-interested as the Capitol. In other words, he encourages President Snow to double down on fear and let the impact be felt as it has in the past.

The films provide an opportunity to round out our understanding of how President Snow understands his role in the political narrative throughout the series. A common theme emerges clearly: fear is the core thing President Snow relies on when using his power. This is the primary way that President Snow is able to build and maintain a culture where

4. President Snow

the Hunger Games can exist. It is also creates the weakness that ultimately creates space for Katniss and the other rebels to bring down President Snow's dictatorship.

The idea that fear provides an effective political weapon stands as a frequent political idea in the midst of our culture's (i.e, a Western) politic history. Though it appears in various forms, perhaps the most well known comes from Niccolò Machiavelli's *The Prince*. Machiavelli offers clear advice on fear for the political mind: "it is much safer to be feared than loved because ... love is preserved by the link of obligation which, owing to the baseness of men, is broken at every opportunity for their advantage; but fear preserves you by a dread of punishment which never fails."[7] Fear gives those who live within a strongman's (or strongwoman's) shadow reason not to challenge the rules that can make life miserable. Few would argue that life in District Twelve is desirable, yet based on the books there appears to be resignation to this way of living. Fear obscures the truth of President Snow's motivations and actions.

Another specific thing that goes unnoticed but should be obvious is what kind of person President Snow is. Donald Sutherland's portrayal of President Snow in each of *The Hunger Games* films thus far captures his unsettling and mechanical nature. He does not show any overt satisfaction in the violence he perpetuates and he certainly does not appear to regret it. Violence is just part of the world he runs.

A brief video exchange with Katniss in the *Mockingjay* movie captures the reason that President Snow can inject fear so effectively. He threatens her with a smirk on his face: "Ms. Everdeen, it's the things we love the most that destroy us. Did you think I didn't know your friends are in the Tribute Center?"[8] The message to Katniss hits on all the points one should expect from President Snow. He knows what she values and the certainty of how he will target those close to Katniss (or torture those whom he has captured) hits her where she in vulnerable. He understands that Katniss knows how he operates, but the way almost everyone else perceives him guarantees (in his mind) that she must unwind a tangled narrative about who he is. There is no indication in this exchange that he is worried because he knows how fear affects the districts. Fear unsettles people. Even if Katniss knows the truth about President Snow's actions in the war, he sticks to his bet that the reality of his actions—which, if widely acknowledged, would be fatal to his political power—

will not override the fear he works so hard to instill in everyone's minds through the liberal use of violence.

President Snow's smirk reveals what is at stake in his conversation. It signals the dual nature of his political position. Machiavelli describes the paradox at work in the politician who consolidates power through fear: "Everyone sees what you appear to be, few experience what you really are."[9] We see yet again in this exchange President Snow's willingness to be transparent with Katniss for precisely the reason Machiavelli states. Through the effective use of fear President Snow has accomplished a position where he can trust two things. First, almost everyone fails to see the truth behind his actions. There is, then, very little risk in being honest with Katniss because she knows what he is doing and what he wants to achieve. This second point rests on the strength of the public image President Snow has cultivated. When he is seen or heard in public, his message is starkly different than this one shared in private. The distinction Machiavelli presents thus explains to a large degree how President Snow can perpetuate this dual image. Perception counts for a lot more than experience so long as almost no one realizes the truth behind his actions.

Unfortunately for President Snow, perception can be manipulated. The 74th Hunger Games is full of surprises. Toward the end, Seneca Crane announces an unprecedented rule change: two winners are possible if the final two contestants hail from the same district. The basis for this decision is, of course, to allow Peeta and Katniss to embrace one another as the star-crossed lovers who also survived the Arena. When Peeta and Katniss actually pull off this improbable result, Seneca Crane subsequently announces that the change has been revoked and only one winner is possible. What follows is one of the crucial political moments in the entire series.

Before considering how Katniss and Peeta respond to the revocation, it is worth rewinding to series of events that preceded the initial change of rules that allowed for two victors. In the film version of *The Hunger Games*, Haymitch is seen lobbying Seneca Crane to alter the rules.[10] Haymitch suggests the possibility of two victors with political delicacy. He appeals to an underlying purpose of the Games from the Capitol's perspective: embrace the story of love and give people the chance to root for a story they have already embraced. Implicit in this

4. President Snow

argument is the risk that the audience will set aside the narrative of the Games as entertainment and justified. In doing so (and the look that passes across Seneca Crane's face when Haymitch makes his appeal suggests that he quickly follows the chain of events to this concern), the audience might start thinking about the fact that two kids in love are about to die.

Haymitch takes advantage of the veneer that defines the Hunger Games. He knows perception can be manipulated. He knows that the Hunger Games to protect the interests of a powerful few in the Capitol because they use the same kind of misdirection. To do so they must be perceived within the Capitol as more than a fight to the death. In the districts, what unfolds in the Arena must reflect the Capitol's control. In both cases, the particular events within the Arena do not matter per say so long as these dual ends are achieved. As a tool of political exertion, the Hunger Games can take many forms. Haymitch astutely plays this card to alter the specific calculus in the 74th Hunger Games to expose what is an overt and indefensible slaughter. In so doing he can not only call attention to President's Snow's political program, but also create in that exposure the possibility of overcoming the political reality the Hunger Games enable. In short, Haymitch's appeal to Seneca Crane complicates the role that the Games are supposed to play in the broader context of Panem's politics.

Though Seneca Crane temporarily reverts back to the strict rule of one victor only, Haymitch's initial appeal eventually becomes manifest because Katniss similarly complicates an otherwise simple set of rules. Once the possibility of two victors has been revoked, Katniss and Peeta face an impossible choice: they must decide, together or on their own, who is going to live. The Games are back to a zero-sum game among the contestants. However, in returning to that state, Katniss, like Haymitch, recognizes an opportunity to undermine President Snow and what the Games stand for in service of his power. She hands Peeta some of the nightlock berries and suggests a mutual suicide. Peeta objects, but Katniss knows exactly what will happen. She responds to Peeta simply: "Trust me. Trust me."[11]

The plan works exactly as Katniss anticipates. As soon as the berries hit their mouths, Seneca Crane's voice breaks into the Arena and announces that there will be two winners. The movie is helpful in thinking about this moment because the desperation in Seneca Crane's voice is clear. The equation that requires a winner now takes a slightly different form. Yes, the Capitol must have a victor, but in the wake of Katniss and Peeta's mutual willingness to deny a victor this requirement is a bit more specific: the Capitol needs *at least one victor*. Zero victors would be far more damaging than two victors, so Seneca Crane knows he has to reinstate the updated rule. Thus, the 74th Hunger Games must have two victors.

Having survived the Arena, Katniss knows firsthand how fear and violence come together in President Snow's world. She must contend with a well-structured narrative the President Snow serves Panem's interests. President Snow recognizes this risk (a point discussed above when we explored the conversation between President Snow and Seneca Crane), so it is important to see this exchange with Katniss not just as an honest exchange, but also as a move within the continued chess match that unfolds after Katniss survives the Arena. What she accomplishes, however, is to give President Snow a taste of that same fear. The problem, as Haymitch makes clear at the end of *The Hunger Games* movie, is that she is too successful. He tells her simply: "They're not happy with you."[12]

Machiavelli again provides a roadmap to understanding how fear plays out in practice. He writes: "There is no other way to guard yourself against flattery than by making men understand that telling you the truth will not offend you."[13] Alongside hiding the truth from almost everyone, using fear requires that one guard against the person does know the truth. To do so, one needs to state the truth openly to those who can recognize a politics of fear for what it is. Katniss would like nothing more than to expose President Snow for what he is, but the threat of doing so is blunted when President Snow tacitly admits that she could do this. In other words, the threat Katniss poses requires to some extent that President Snow be worried but what she knows. By stating this point for her, President Snow ensures that he guards against her efforts to subvert his political thinking The truth, then, serves to extend the public image that very few understand. As such, Katniss can be direct in telling him what she thinks about his use of fear, but doing so will not bother President Snow because he has in effect encouraged her to speak by making clear that the truth of her words will not offend him in the slightest.

4. President Snow

There is more. President Snow actively encourages Katniss to be truthful in their conversations. The clearest example of this dynamic occurs at the beginning of *Catching Fire*. When Katniss returns from a hunt in the woods, she quickly realizes that something is abnormal. Her mother and Prim greet her with obvious edges in their voices. When two Capitol representatives (strangely, they do not seem to be Peacekeepers based on what they are wearing) ask Katniss to follow them, she understands that something serious is unfolding. The film does an excellent job of capturing the subtle changes in emotion that cross her face as she realizes her home has become an unsafe place.

The reason to be on edge is that President Snow has made a personal visit to District Twelve to stop by Katniss's house for a one-on-one conversation. It is important to note that there seems to be no awareness of his presence outside the home; the visit is covert, which, in the context of this discussion makes sense. Direct communication is an exception, not a rule, so President Snow's decision to be discreet in visiting Katniss makes sense. The framework for his visit, in other words, affirms the dynamic discussed above. His public persona is detached and built on deception. In Katniss's house, however, we encounter a different President Snow.

When Katniss enters the room, President is calm. He sips a cup of tea. Before long, however, he issues a severe warning during a tense exchange:

> PRESIDENT SNOW: You fought very hard in the Games, Ms. Everdeen. But they were games. Would you like to be a real war?"
> KATNISS: No.
> PRESIDENT SNOW: Good. And neither would I.
> KATNISS: What do I need to do?
> PRESIDENT SNOW: When you and Peeta are on tour, you need to smile. You need to be grateful. But above all you need to be madly, prepared to end it all, in love.[14]

The threat is precise. The act of rebellion at the end of the 74th Hunger Games becomes the standard for saving the lives of those whom Katniss cares about. She now has to maintain a lie that is at odds with her feelings toward Peeta and Gale. In short, she faces an impossible task and violent consequences wait if she fails. This is all established in the comfort of her home.

The underlying commonality that his persona reveals—which is a marker to watch out for in thinking about the way politicians abuse power—is deception. President Snow is clear in his desire to lower Katniss's guard, and then to scare her. He wants to discourage her bubbling rebellious attitude because he knows that she understands his actions and, moreover, is willing to call them for what they are. She will not uphold the narrative he has worked so hard to create. Consequently, he must threaten her subtly but unmistakably.

In response, Katniss exposes even more about President Snow's underlying character. She provocatively and accurately points out that his entire political superstructure is actually pretty flimsy. If a girl from District Twelve can blow apart the entire lie with a single act of refusal to follow the proper script that produces a winner in the Games, then does he have any power at all? President Snow tacitly admits this, but he then reverses yet again the power dynamic. Of course she might have won with her "stunt," but if she continues the stunt during her victory tour—and draws public attention to the truth of the politics at stake in the Arena—then things will be far worse. She must therefore decide whether to grudgingly buy publicly affirm the narrative President Snow relies on, or whether to repeat her rebellious act.

There is in this exchange another echo of a common dynamic between the villain who would profess to be virtuous and the person who will identify the villain's true character, a fact evident in President Snow's follow on threat (he may be honest, but he is being honest about killing far more people than a yearly crop of tributes). Specifically, Katniss finds herself negotiating with a shrewd kind of character who under the guise of some virtuous mindset seeks to destroy someone's life. The old phrase making a deal with the devil rings loudly in this scene. There appears to be a better choice in the matter; for Katniss this would be continuing her role as naïve lover in the political narrative President Snow wants everyone to see. The truly better choice, the one that labels the villain for what he is, will result in a lot of suffering for a lot of people. The decision is excruciating in its impossibility.

The decision is also incredibly deceitful. In presenting the options as he does, President Snow effectively (though temporarily) transforms Katniss into an unwilling supporter. Katniss's ability to see and articulate the truth is precisely what President Snow needs to overcome the episode

4. President Snow

with the nightlock berries. He does not ask her to go back on her act; he *encourages* her to continue how the act of rebellion was perceived. Her performance must be convincing and she has every motivation to try because she knows the damage a failure to convey a public, undying love for Peeta will cause. Her commitment to something good thus relies for the initial part of *Catching Fire* on a conscious lie. In other words, President Snow's best counter to what she reveals is to get her to be outwardly deceptive in a way that is similar to his own deception.

Her perceived virtue across Panem is crucial to this inversion. In his *Analects*, Confucius articulates the strange but effective logic at work. Confucius writes: "Raise up the straight and apply them to the crooked, and the people will submit to you. If you raise up the crooked and apply them to the straight, the people will never submit."[15] If he is not virtuous (and he is not), then President Snow can use Katniss's moral identity to cover up his deception. By applying her goodness (i.e. her willingness to rebel) in a way that supports his own political end, President Snow accomplishes what Confucius says will happen: the people will submit. Importantly, this strategy requires the underlying moral commitment that Katniss never quite shakes throughout The Hunger Games series. If she were flawed at her core, this plan would work. A crooked person cannot convince straight people to abandon the truth of their individual and corporate identities.

At the same time, relying on truth necessarily leaves open the possibility that the real purposes for President Snow's actions will be exposed at some point. His rule remains unstable because he lacks the underlying moral foundation for begin accepted as a leader through a means other than fear. There is no moral component to his politics and the steps he takes to cover up this weakness enable the rebels—led by Katniss—to win the war with the Capitol.

This exchange illustrates just how complex the political game between President Snow and Katniss really is. The psychological wrestling for control over what one another's actions mean in the context of the rebellion requires a difficult and intricate plan. In this early encounter, we see the extent to which Katniss is outmatched in playing this political game when the stakes are as high as they are. President Snow not only presents an image of himself that hides his use of fear. He also does so over a long time frame. This requires keeping the lie straight which is hard to do. The ability to speak the truth to someone is in some ways a significant psychological help because he allows him to state what he really things without risking what is at stake if people recognize the truth *en masse*.

There is a second component to consider in this tense relationship between President Snow and Katniss: everyone else. Katniss does not yield to the fear President Snow injects through Panem. Others, however, are not as strong in their resistance. In fact, almost everyone is a direct or indirect victim of fear. Further, their experience with the violence President Snow uses and its intended psychological impact is almost impossible to unwind. This is, for Machiavelli, the sign of fear put to good use: "If an injury has to be done to a man it should be so severe that his vengeance need not be feared."[16] Katniss may not be breakable, but everyone else is, so President Snow can put a good safety policy into effect. He can double-down on the violence he uses in order to remind the citizens of Panem that he is willing to be swift and cruel in response to any perceived rebellion.

Importantly, the practical application of this approach is manifest in District Twelve almost immediately after President Snow's visit to Katniss's home. A new Peacekeeper Commander arrives in District Twelve to tighten up the security after President Snow has become uneasy with the tension he sees bubbling up. Whereas the Commander whom Katniss knows as a young adult will look the other way on some thing, Thread, the replacement, brings the kind of injury Machiavelli is talking about. Corporeal punishment and the threat of execution are effective ways to hedge against the idea of revolution that might be percolating in the minds of Katniss's fellow district residents.

The notion of committing to any means necessary in service of maintaining one's grip on power recalls the discussion in the Introduction about the political purpose of killing children. The impact must be totalizing in its ability to extinguish any idea in those who experience violence of pushing back. President Snow councils Seneca Crane to smother hope that Katniss and Peeta will win the games because even the slightest space to rebel exposes the leader to revenge. As Machiavelli explains: "Men ought either to be well treated or crushed, because they can avenge themselves of lighter injuries, of more serious ones they cannot; therefore the injury that is to be done to a man ought to be of such

4. President Snow

a kind that one does not stand in fear of revenge."[17] There are two possibilities for a politics built with fear. A person can either be in the good graces of the tyrant or be exposed to the tyrant's fear. There can be no middle ground and, as such, once a ruler commits to the kind of politics that characterizes President Snow there can be no exceptions. Everyone must live in fear if President Snow is to resist experiencing fear himself. The damage must be so severe that there is no possibility of reprisal because he knows that if those wronged will fight to the end to avenge those who have suffered.

Absolute commitment to violence against a group of people echoes some of our intellectual tradition's darkest moments. President Snow justifies overt violence against those he governs by sowing a narrative that creates the basis for seeing the tributes as deserving their fate. It is important to recall in this dynamic that the victims here are children who had no role in the initial violence cited as the basis for the Hunger Games much less the specific experiences of specific children in the Arena.

As we have seen, President Snow relies in part on a population that will either fail to recognize or, more effectively recognize and set aside, the way he exercises control across Panem. There are dangerous echoes to another dictator who similarly would kill with no discretion: Hitler. A chilling passage from *Mein Kampf* could be an excerpt from President Snow's political playbook. Hitler explains how to subdue a population in order to carry out a campaign of totalizing power: "When the propaganda work has converted a whole people to believe in a doctrine, the organization can turn the results of this into practical effect through the work of a mere handful of men."[18] Once the population accepts the reality of President Snow's mercilessness, it becomes strangely easy for him to deploy violence as he sees fit and not encounter and resistance. Numbing a population to the truth of what they see blinds that same population to the truth of what is happening. When the truth is obscure in politics, a handful of people can then act with impunity.

It does not take much, in other words, to adopt and act on the political mindset that we see in President Snow. The "practical effect" Hitler mentions is consonant with President Snow's willingness to use the Hunger Games as a way to instill fear in those outside of the Arena. If we think through the number of people who are needed to put on the

Hunger Games, there are relatively people who carry out a yearly tournament of infanticide. How can so many people not see what they watch for what it is? In the case of the districts throughout Panem, the answer would seem to be a deep and paralyzing fear that President Snow nurtures at the expense of anyone.

The "practical" nature of a fear-driven politics finds more support in the words of political fear's architect: Machiavelli. In the lesser-known but more expansive political tract, *The Discourses*, Machiavelli expands on the practical steps rulers should take in building and consolidating political power. President Snow no doubt recognizes the key ingredient Machiavelli requires for success: "security for man is impossible unless it be conjoined with power."[19] Two key terms come together and help to explain why President Snow is ruthless in his treatment of Panem's citizens. Security is the goal, though it is worth noting that President Snow is not after security of person; he is after security of his own power. To achieve this, he must bet on the use of power and, consequently, he spins his violent cycle. Security requires power, which brings about security. The obvious thing missing from the process is the kinds of rights security should protect.

Though Machiavelli would no doubt like President Snow's approach to ruling Panem, he would also sound a clear warning. The game President Snow plays has a weak spot. Machiavelli includes an important caution to the person who would pursue security through power: "a warning to all princes that they can never live secure in their principality so long as those live who have been despoiled of it."[20] Those who suffer while a ruler pursues power will always remain a threat to that ruler's position. People have long memories and if denied security for the benefit of another they are primed to rebel. President Snow seemingly knows this, which is why he takes steps to fold the victors into the Capitol's culture while also providing rations to the victor's district.

While the approach of pacifying those who are denied security of rights would seem to make sense, Machiavelli extends the warning to the specific impact violence and fear have on a population. He offers a second important caution: "a reminder to all potentates that old injuries are never cancelled by new benefits, least of all when the benefits are of less importance than the injuries previously inflicted."[21] Though steps can be taken to soften the ways people suffer, the impact of the suffering cannot be erased fully. This point is particularly important when aligning specific benefits to specific wrongs as the rewards for a victor and her/his district do. The worse the suffering, the longer the memory will remain. In a systemic pattern of abuse like the Hunger Games, there will always exist resentment toward the Capitol and thus President Snow must always guard against the possibility of rebellion.

The legend of Robin Hood is one that holds a lot of appeal in a culture defined and directed by a powerful few. If people perceive their lives as unjustly required to support the interests of the elite, then they will feel justified in an expanded set of options to respond to the rulers who benefit from a feed-the-powerful arrangement. Niebuhr provides a helpful way of thinking about the dynamic captured in the legend of a Robin Hood: "When power is robbed of the shining armor of political, moral and philosophical theories, by which it defends itself, it will fight on without armor; but it will be more vulnerable, and the strength of its enemies is increased."[22] Katniss serves this kind of role. She first unmasks President Snow's conceptual foundation that is required to justify his politics of fear. Absent this framework to support his rule, it must continue with the narrative that has been established. The difference is that the person who is now isolated will be increasingly vulnerable to the responses and desires for revenge that previously were not a concern. As we have seen throughout this chapter, President Snow ultimately relies on the citizens of Panem showing a continued unwillingness to push back against all the suffering President Snow causes.

The initial unmasking constitutes a core point in the rebellion that Katniss leads. Alongside Niebuhr, Foucault argues that what passes as strength is ultimately something where success is proportional to an ability to deceive. Niebuhr explains: "Power is tolerable only on condition that it masks a substantial part of itself. Its success if proportional to its ability to hide its own mechanisms."[23] The political corollary to this point is that once power can no longer hide its mechanisms, power will wilt as those who suffer under power reclaim the moral and political boundaries of their own lives.

President Snow, in other words, has lost an important battle as soon as Katniss pulls out the nightlock berries at the end of *The Hunger Games*. Though his days are number, he shows one final political dynamic: he has to stick to his own script. His addiction to power will not be given up voluntarily; he will fight to the end no matter the cost of doing so. Niebuhr summarizes well the reason for the last stand that the immoral political leader makes: "Men will not cease being dishonest, merely because their dishonesties have been revealed or because they have discovered their own deceptions. Wherever men hold unequal power in society, they will strive to maintain it. They will use whatever means are most convenient to that end and will seek to justify them by the most plausible arguments they are able to devise."[24] In short, President Snow will do what he has always done: sow fear to preserve his political power regardless of how ineffectual that influence has become. Even when the political arguments cease to be plausible he will still try—he has no other choice but to try—so only his death at the end of *Mockingjay* will allow Panem the chance to rebuild a healthy political identity.

President Snow's strength is ultimately his weakness. By his rules, political success begets political failure. The logic of his political actions requires an endless and total commitment to suffering among those he rules over. He is, like Herod, capable of incredible evil, but these plans only work if they are wholly successful. When so long as there remains a single rebel, President Snow cannot rest easily in his power. Machiavelli summarizes the impossible task facing the ruler who would build an empire on fear: "a warning to all princes that they can never live secure in their principality so long as those live who have been despoiled of it."[25] The very acts that consolidate power by instilling fear in a population continually create the possibility that someone somewhere will finally say enough is enough. President Snow encourages Seneca Crane to allow a flash of hope, but to extinguish it quickly. The real advice he should give to Seneca Crane—and to follow himself—is to make sure sparks never happen if he continues to rely so heavily on fear.

Further, a single violent action against the population is all that is required to commit a ruler to this continual and impossible politics of fear. Once the initial step in this strategy is taken, the damage is permanent. Again, Machiavelli emphasizes the irreversible course. He offers "a reminder to all potentates that old injuries are never cancelled by new benefits, least of all when the benefits are of less importance than the injuries previously inflicted."[26] The pain the culture experiences when it watches children fight one another to the death can never be erased fully. Any effort to redress this kind of violence will fail because it creates

4. President Snow

a psychological scar that will remain present in cultural memory. Is anything ever more important than watching your child die a violent death on TV? Even if an answer to this question were possible, the fact remains that President Snow would not attempt to redress his wrongs.

The broader takeaway from thinking about President Snow's willingness to use fear is twofold. First, the benefits this approach to politics help a ruler or an elite class to realize will create a liability that cannot be met. This kind of politics, in other words, requires decisions that necessarily alienate the very people the government should be representing. This introduces a second important point: the ruler class that is responsible for the wound cannot then claim that the wound should be forgotten. Those who suffer at the hands of the one or the few who would use fear to build and maintain a power base should remember, always, the source of their pain and hold those responsible accountable. In Katniss, we see this mindset manifest clearly in its simplicity. In the moments when she is most aggravated with the events that are unfolding, she falls back on a singular desire to kill President Snow.

5. Katniss

For all of her influence across The Hunger Games series, Katniss is not the most likeable character, at least as determined by those with whom she interacts. Haymitch is forthright in pointing this out soon after they meet in *The Hunger Games* movie: "To get sponsors, you have to make people like you. And right now, sweetheart, you're not off to a real good start."[1] Given her prickly nature when interacting with others, Katniss's specifically political identity is a challenging and rewarding topic to explore. In our own culture, where popularity counts for a lot with respect to political influence, the frequent lack of personal appeal that characterizes Katniss invites our attention.

As we explore Katniss's specifically political role in The Hunger Games series, it is helpful to think about the sacrifice she makes for Prim during the reaping. We learn a lot about Katniss when she volunteers to take Prim's place in the Games. At the time she makes the decision, Katniss essentially gives up her life so that her sister could live (at least for another year; the sacrifice is tragic in part because it does nothing to guarantee Prim would not end up in the Arena in subsequent years). The odds of Katniss surviving in the Arena at the outset are low, though perhaps she does take solace in the fact that Prim's name being called was the least likely outcome possible during the reaping.

Several important themes emerge during the reaping that will frame Katniss's political identity throughout The Hunger Games series. First and foremost, the decision is ground in a clearly moral commitment to someone else that is dangerous to act upon. There is a sacrifice, yes, but the contours of that decision reveal a lot of how Katniss will grow into the role of the Mockingjay. She accepts a likely death that will include a great deal of physical suffering. Further, the substitution is done publicly, which means the act takes on a specifically political significance, which in turn invites the attention of those who will be responsible for that likely suffering and death. In short, the sacrifice announces to all

5. Katniss

of Panem that Katniss is different in a way that threatens the very nature of the Hunger Games.

The reaping requires choreography that is meant to obscure what is at stake in randomly sending two children to their deaths. As Katniss relays Effie's response to her volunteering for Prim, we find a distance from what the reaping represents. Effie gushes: "That's the spirit of the Games!"[2] Effie's remarks illustrate the friction that the Hunger Games program causes when it is treated as a "festivity."[3] A carefully scripted event that encounters an unexpected twist reveals the meaning of the event. Nothing about Katniss's decision is in the spirit of the Hunger Games. Volunteering for Prim goes announces the kinds of virtues and beliefs in human nature that the Hunger Games are supposed to erase. This is about a political superstructure that cannot accommodate the person who rejects the conclusion that President Snow intends and most of Panem assumes. In other words, Katniss reverses the power dynamic in that she ceases to be a passive victim. She acts and in so doing recovers her ability to reject the parameters of the governing social contract in Panem. The implications are that others can (and will, as we see in *Catching Fire*) deny the premises that justify the Hunger Games. The result is the breakdown of the fear-based politics the Hunger Games are meant to support.

Though she is inconsistent as a political actor throughout The Hunger Games series, Katniss does consistently refuse to follow the established way of doing things. In this respect she establishes an unknown and therefore uncontrollable factor in the political dynamic meant to devastate and terrify the district becomes the basis for resisting everything that the reaping normally signifies. Katniss inverts fully the expectations that everyone brings to the reaping. For the residents of Panem, a death sentence becomes the basis for saving one life and, in so doing, giving hope to many lives. For President Snow's architecture of fear, Katniss exposes that some things simply cannot be erased despite the risks involved.

If upending an established political order through sacrifice sounds familiar, it is because this theme has been etched into our collective memory throughout Judeo-Christian culture. In the Introduction, we looked at the parallels between President Snow and Herod and the thematic comparison continues in reading Katniss's decision alongside

Jesus's execution. Crucifixion was a Roman punishment designed to send a very public and very political message: those who seeded unrest in the Empire would be punished in a way that maximized suffering.

As it lies at the heart of Christianity's theological narrative, the political implications of Jesus's death often get pushed to the side or ignored altogether. However, a brief re-reading of what how events unfold will highlight the ways that Jesus is an explicitly political victim. The Gospel of John offers an account of Jesus's death sentence that gives us important clues as to the specifically political nature of crucifixion. John makes clear that a death sentence was a Roman punishment. Having questioned Jesus, Pilate is unclear about what Jesus has done. He asks those who brought Jesus in for clarity: "Pilate went out to them and said, 'What accusation do you bring against this man?' They answered, 'If this man were not a criminal, we would not have handed him over to you.' Pilate said to them, 'Take him yourselves and judge him according to your law.' The Jews replied, 'We are not permitted to put anyone to death.'"[4] A little trickery and a clear explanation help clarify what unfolds. There is no explicit statement as the reason Jesus was handed over to Pilate, but there is a clear request for a summary execution (and, importantly the Jewish leaders make clear that they cannot execute Jesus because they cannot make this decision within the context of Roman law). The request is, then, for political ends. Further, the political objective looks past the legal innocence of Jesus. As Pilate says before sending Jesus to his death, "I find no case against him."[5] In a context where fear can be a valuable political tool—a legacy Pilate no doubt understood given Herod's infanticide a few decades earlier—innocence is not enough when there is enough political motivation.

At this point, a quick look at Matthew's Gospel will expand on the specifically political dynamic that leads to Jesus's death. If Pilate really thought Jesus was innocent, then why did he go ahead and have Jesus crucified anyway? Pilate attempts to dissuade the crowd from asking for Jesus's death,[6] but they do not back down from their request. At a crucial moment, the crowd turns and Pilate has to do something: "Pilate saw that he wasn't getting anywhere and that a riot was developing. So he sent for a bowl of water and washed his hands before the crowd, saying, "I am innocent of this man's blood. The responsibility is yours!"[7] Pilate does not give in to the crowd because he is concerned about Jesus's innocence or even because he cares why the crowd wants Jesus to die. The narrative turns because Pilate perceives that the situation is about to become disruptive. As the crowd simmers, he takes the decisive step of acceding to their request because the situation now has political implications from his perspective. Just as the Peacekeepers appear when restlessness is about to turn into active protest, Pilate turns to violence to quell political unrest. As is often the case with those who resort to violence for political ends, he makes his decision in a way that claims to push responsibility onto someone else. Despite the lingering claim that the Jews killed Jesus in our culture, Pilate's claim to wash his hands does not really work because as John makes clear in his account only Roman prelates could execute people.

In these biblical narratives, multiple themes emerge that link Jesus and Katniss as political figures. First, there is the authoritative ruler who turns to violence in order to maintain order. Second, the violence occurs despite the victim's innocence. Third, the violence occurs publicly, which ultimately allows for those responsible to undermine their own political power. The death or threat of death thus transforms the target of political violence into a symbol that exposes the use of violence for what it is.

The comparison here may invite some skepticism. Even if Collins did not intend to map Katniss's decision at the reaping to Christianity's key narrative, the echoes are obvious enough that they appear clearly in the film version of *Catching Fire*. Once Katniss has shot her electrified arrow into the roof of the Arena, the camera looks up at the sky from Katniss's perspective. Bright light frames the rebel hovercraft that appears to take her to safety. The clamp lowers to the ground, encloses her body, and pulls her out of the Arena and into a rebel world where she will become the Mockingjay. The Hunger Games have destroyed and she will eventually lead the campaign that ultimately liberates Panem. If this were all that happened, perhaps we could ignore the parallels to Jesus. However, the film offers an unmistakable clue as to how we should understand what happens in these moments. As Katniss is pulled toward the hovercraft, her back arches slightly and her arms spread out to her sides (the hovercraft's clamp luckily closes just far enough down her torso to allow this posture). Her limp body is cruciform and, therefore, an indication that she has become not just a sacrifice but also a savior for Panem.

The Politics of *The Hunger Games*

Despite the strong biblical echoes we hear in reading and seeing Katniss volunteer as a tribute point to Jesus, other biblical figures expand the way Katniss thinks about her political role. While it is tempting to see her as a bold leader, she is actually somewhat hesitant to become the rebels' symbol. At the beginning of *Mockingjay*, she withdraws from the rebel leadership as she wrestles with the role she wants to play in the fight that is unfolding. In this respect she mirrors figures such as Moses and Jeremiah, both of whom respond to God's leadership request with overt skepticism.[8]

This initial uncertainty plays an important role in that it contrasts sharply with the commitment to leading that emerges once things really get going. For all her hesitancy at the beginning of *Mockingjay*, once Katniss steps forward to be the rebellion's symbol she exhibits a fearless nature. Despite the constant risks, the low chance of success, and the continued harm those around her experience, Katniss plods on in her political role. Though this characteristic plays an important narrative role, within the political examination this book undertakes her fearlessness may be the most important trait for success. The equation to explain this claim is simple. If President Snow relies on fear and extends fear through violence, then Katniss's fearlessness is the perfect antidote.

Given the ordeal she experiences throughout The Hunger Games series, Katniss's claim not to be afraid is remarkable. She has many, many reasons to yield to President Snow's tactics, yet she somehow resists. She is able to endure tremendous hardship and, in so doing, she maintains her focus on the goal at hand (be it surviving in the Arena or leading the final charge to President Snow at the end of *Mockingjay*). The combination of success and focus point to an important characteristic: resilience. This label captures the way Katniss manages to thrive despite the number of reasons she should not survive, much less become the foundation for the rebellion.

Zolli offers a helpful framework for understanding how Katniss overcomes the political fear that defines Panem. He summarizes what makes someone and/or something resilient. They "have the ability to reorganize themselves to maintain their core purpose, even under radically changing circumstances."[9] The key idea here is reorganizing because it assumes events that forever shift and thus make it every difficult for someone to retain a clear sense of purpose. This variability reflects a successful strategy for responding to a politics based on fear. So long as the population is uncertain it will have difficulty organizing a response to the source of that political fear. As we see throughout The Hunger Games series, President Snow's swift use of violence to quell any hint of disagreement goes a long way toward discouraging anyone from trying in the first place.

Katniss, however, continually adapts to her surroundings. At the reaping, she makes a quick decision to protect her sister despite the probable outcome that she will die. Faced with a likely death that would cast significant harm on Prim—the one whom her sacrifice is meant to keep safe—she stays ahead of the other tributes in the Arena and not only survives, but does so in a way that keeps Peeta alive as well. If we recall the various things that happen in the Arena that are specifically designed to neutralize Katniss's advantages and ultimately kill her, we can appreciate her adaptability. In *Catching Fire*, she continues to adjust (albeit with a bit more help from those within and outside the Arena) in a way that defies the odds of actually surviving.

Though suffering has been discussed elsewhere in depth, it is worth returning to this point briefly in light of examining the ways Katniss is resilient. She does more than survive; she redefines the rules of the political game with President Snow in the process. Her resilience allows her to define a terrible situation as something other than President Snow intends. This ability to reorganize what events mean points to an important concept that arises in Viktor Frankel's *Man's Search for Meaning*. Amidst suffering, there may be better options for defining what is good. However, this is not the same thing as claiming suffering as something that does not allow meaning to be defined. Frankel explains: "Is this to say that suffering is indispensable to the discovery of meaning? In no way. I only insist that meaning is available in spite of—nay, even through—suffering, provided ... that the suffering is unavoidable."[10] Having touched on some of our history's darkest moments and how to assert a political identity in spite of a politics that would maximize suffering, Frankl's claims offer an important second layer of what it means to recover a political identity. Suffering is not intrinsically a good thing; we should not hope for suffering. At the same time, when we experience the kind of suffering we see in The Hunger Games series, meaning can be found within circumstances that are designed to erase meaning.

Through his own suffering, then, Frankel recognizes an important truth about the nature of that suffering that in turn helps us to understand the impact Katniss's resilience has. For those who wield power in a way that is supposed to make people afraid, the assumption is that suffering will be a destructive thing. No one wants to see a child die in the Arena; President counts on this as the conclusion people will arrive at when thinking about what the Hunger Games mean. What Frankel argues for, however, is a new way of thinking about the kind of suffering that tributes experience. They can create meaning in their suffering. Katniss's trials allow her to grow into a symbol of hope. From the Girl on Fire to the Mockingjay that defines the rebellion, she continually recasts President's Snow's political world as something other than he intends. Importantly, this allows her to recover her own political agency and influence. In doing so she refuses to play the role she is supposed to play as one of tributes. She ceases to be a victim of bad luck and violence in the Arena and becomes someone capable of creating an entirely new political order in Panem.

In the beginning of this chapter, the biblical echoes that characterize Katniss were clear. Here, similar notes sound that undermine the broader political narrative that relies on violence to achieve its goals. The story of Joseph is one of suffering.[11] His brothers sell him into slavery to cover up their plans to kill him. Through his own adaptability, however, he becomes an indispensible mind for Pharaoh. More specifically, Joseph is able to redefine a political course of action because he can interpret Pharaoh's dreams. By cautioning Pharaoh to store up food when the harvest is plenty, Joseph creates a hedge against the suffering that descends when seven years of famine begin. Lacking Joseph's insights, his brothers end up leaving their home and traveling to Egypt because they have heard about the stores of food that were set aside during the good times. The narrative climaxes when Joseph's brothers stand before him, broken and hungry. Joseph could have responded in a way that magnified his brothers' suffering, but instead he inverts the narrative. He tells them: "Even though you intended to do harm to me, God intended it for good."[12]

Resilience conveys the qualities that lead to these inversions. Frankel describes the process whereby resilience reframes a context defined by suffering: "the priority stays with creatively changing the sit-

5. Katniss

uation that causes us to suffer."[13] Creativity is something that we might not associate with Katniss, but, in the context of her suffering, she frequently does exactly the thing that Frankel describes. One of the most striking examples of this occurs when Rue dies toward the end of *The Hunger Games*. Katniss's friend and ally dies a death that captures the essence of the Games: cutting down a young life that has done nothing wrong to remind everyone that Panem is a country ruled with a devastating disregard for its citizens. Cradling her dead friend, Katniss would seem to be at a breaking point. However, she does something completely unexpected. She holds a kind of memorial service for Rue and gives us one of the most striking images from all of The Hunger Games series. She covers Rue's body with flowers and sings a song in her honor. In the context of the Arena, this act exposes Katniss to significant risk. She lets her guard down when we know that at least one of the Careers is close by. The implication is that the others might be near. To stop and eulogize Rue is to put herself at risk, but Rue's death demands the risk to show that the rules of the Arena do not erase the value of human life.

Katniss, then, creatively changes a situation designed to make her suffer. Everyone probably assumes that she will get back to the Games having seen Rue's body. With the eyes of Panem on her, Katniss sees a chance to challenge the circumstances that led to Rue's death. Rather than cast her friend aside as meaningless, Katniss reminds everyone that the Hunger Games are the thing that should be cast aside because every life has value. Her friend has died needlessly, so she will reclaim meaning for Rue even if within the context of the Games such meaning has no place.

Through her memorial for Rue Katniss not only reveals her resilience, but also the failure of the Games as a political event. This effect clarifies why Katniss's resilience is a specifically political quality. When she visits the District Eight hospital in *Mockingjay*, we see how her ability to adapt despite disheartening events begins to rally others to her.[14] Every eye watches as she slowly walks to the center of the room. We can see uncertainty on Katniss's face. However, when those in the hospital raise their arms in unison with the same three-finger salute that Katniss saw at the reaping after she volunteered, we can see on her face that she understands what is at stake in the role she has adopted. The Mockingjay gathers people together amidst desolation.

The film version of *Mockingjay* thus adds a further layer to this point through is visual portrayal of Katniss development. The film broadens our awareness of how others respond to Katniss as she speaks of a hope that seems impossible amidst President Snow's bombing campaign. As she encourages the wounded (and as the cameras roll), Katniss establishes herself as a moral leader. Importantly, this leadership comes into focus in a way that contrasts Katniss's adaptability with President Snow's destruction. The result is a distinctly moral choice that binds the people who are suffering to a message of hope.

As the Mockingjay, Katniss takes on a gravity that Confucius recognizes as the sign of a true leader. In the *Analects*, Confucius writes: "One who rules through the power of Virtue is analogous to the Pole Star: it simply remains in its place and receives the homage of the myriad lesser stars."[15] In Chapter 1, we looked at the importance of a moral compass for a healthy politics. Here, it is helpful to add a further layer from Purdy's discussion. He, too, emphasizes the importance of defining a positive meaning from within suffering that threatens the ability to speak for oneself. Those who can encourage others to resist the impact fear can have tie moral recovery and hope together. Purdy writes: "The full response to despair is not just to invoke hope, but to generate it."[16] In this dark, dank hospital, surrounding by suffering, Katniss plants herself at the moral center of a new political world. Fear need not be the foundation of Panem. Those who cannot or will not find meaning in suffering—the hope that President Snow wants to extinguish as explained to Seneca Crane—can recognize in Katniss a leadership that makes sense of their suffering. The ability to convey this message provides a clear example of how Katniss's resilience enables her to become an effective political leader.

Katniss's presence in the hospital reminds others of their own need to engage the political movement she embodies. They have become immobile in the midst of fear; she is there to give hope by pointing to a way that political fear can be overcome. Purdy's description of a dormant politics is helpful to understand what is at stake in this hospital scene. Purdy writes: "the turn away from politics is not just a response to what public life has become. Instead, both the indifference to politics and, in lesser measure, its stagnation are symptoms of a lack in the culture."[17] We have seen what public life has become for those living in the districts. The key point Purdy wants to emphasize is the way political stagnation results in a loss of culture. If we recall the discussion about the social contract, the specifics of this loss become clear. The districts have lost their ability to understand politics as protecting freedom.

Narratives based on a single leader guiding an entire population to freedom stretch across our culture. Two examples echo strongly with the role Katniss plays as the Mockingjay. The first has been discussed already; Katniss, like Moses, leads an oppressed people to freedom. The second cultural echo is more explicitly political and it comes from Plato. In his *Republic*, Plato tells the story of a group of men who are chained inside of a cave.[18] On the wall in front of them, they see shadows from objects that pass by behind them. The objects are not real; they are merely representations of a thing. For example, the men might see the shadow of a dog on the wall and the shadow would be the result of something like a puppet passing in front of the fire. There is no living dog in the cave.

Eventually one of Plato's prisoners manages to turn around and see the reality of the cave. Having seen the truth of the shadows he previous took as real, he continues to explore the cave. He eventually realizes that there is a world outside of the cave. There he finds real versions of the objects he has seen in the cave. To continue with the example from the previous paragraph, the person who emerges from the cave would see a living dog. With an understanding of the real world outside of the cave, the person returns to his friends who are still trapped to share what he has learned. Unfortunately for the person who returns, those still in the cave do not accept his explanation of what he saw. They respond to the knowledge he shares by killing him.

Plato's analogy of the cave speaks to the limited understanding we have of our world. When new information arrives that disrupts what we are used to, we often react negatively and forcefully. Importantly, the Allegory of the Cave must be understood not just as a reflection on knowledge, but also as a specifically political narrative. The Allegory occurs in a work that sets out to describe the ideal political state. The role of the one who escapes and learns the truth of things assumes a political responsibility to others. The one who learns the truth must return to share this truth in order that everyone might live a more informed life.

This summary describes pretty closely the experiences Katniss has throughout The Hunger Games series. She knows the truth of President Snow's use of fear in ruling over Panem. She knows that the Hunger Games are designed to cow the population into a fearful state that smothers any ideas of pushing back. Her knowledge is dangerous and she has an obligation to share it with others. Her role, then, is to recast political perception in line with the way things are, which in turn rejects basing politics on the way things appear through the world President Snow maintains.

Once this knowledge disperses through a population, the ability of those like President Snow to sustain a politics based on fear breaks down as people realize there are other ways to build a liberating political identity. Further, this realization enables people to act in a way that embraces the moral responsibility to live alongside their fellow citizens. Purdy describes this bond as a culture and describes why it matters: "One thing that a culture does is to give people ways of thinking about what they are doing. They can see the connections among their work, their talents, and the needs of the world. They perceive their work as belonging to a whole, some of whose possibilities are good, which they help to sustain."[19] Katniss's role is not to oversee the liberated population; like Moses, she will fade into the background eventually. Her goal is to initiate the process of recovering a politics that others will fight for. She encourages people across the districts to connect political dots in a way President Snow works hard to keep apart. She helps everyone see the needs of their world independently of fear and violence.

Katniss is by no means perfect. Throughout her journey she has moments where she shies away from her role as a leader. However, when things matter, she consistently stands up to the world of fear that President Snow presides over. When she stands in the hospital in District Eight she does not utter hollow words. She acts as she speaks. In doing so she crosses a line that sets her apart as a leader who can make a difference. Greitens suggests that the ability to differentiate oneself in this way is the true mark of leadership. He explains: "there was a great dividing line between all of the speeches, protests, feelings, empathy, good wishes, and words in the world, and the one thing that mattered most: protecting people through the use of force or the threat of force. In situations like this, good intentions and heartfelt wishes were not enough.

5. *Katniss*

The great dividing line between words and results was courageous action."[20] Katniss wants a better world and she articulates in the hospital how President Snow prevents that world from becoming a reality. She is willing to use force—she will fight if she must to defeat President Snow—and this strength backs up her message of political actions. The wounded, the fearful, and those who doubt look through the dark hospital at Katniss and see someone who will protect them. She is courageous because she is willing to stand in the middle of the room and absorb those skeptical gazes and speak of a better world.

Katniss's message in the hospital combines two important things that define her political leadership. The first, as noted in the previous paragraph, is her courage. She has survived the Arena twice. She can endure a lot and keep going. She is, in other words, outwardly virtuous in a way that convinces people she will fight for them. These qualities reveal a deeper characteristic that truly sets Katniss apart as the rebels' leader. She is authentic in her leadership. She does not try to be perfect. She can withdraw or complain or lash out at those who are trying to help her (a tendency Haymitch certainly understands). However, these inconsistencies never mask the strength that shows up when it really matters. Katniss stands up. She survives. She protects those who cannot fight for themselves.

Though it is hard to define fully, the authenticity that characterizes Katniss's leadership is a key part of her political identity. In particular, her strength and her willingness to act can be trusted. She does not immediately default to the use of force in leading the rebellion. When she has to, she will resist the urge to use force. In a powerful scene in *Mockingjay*, she puts this different kind of strength on full display. Having stormed District Two, Katniss finds herself confronting a man who is unsure how to react to her presence. She is his enemy, but she talks to him instead of shooting. Importantly, he processes his reaction while keeping his gun pointed at Katniss. Vulnerable, she acts by not acting. She puts down her weapon and tries to reason with the man

The conversation heats up when he asks a fair question given the military context in which they are speaking. He challenges Katniss: "Give me one reason I shouldn't shoot you."[21] Her answer makes explicit the political purpose of the Hunger Games as someone who was inside the arena: "I am [a slave] ... Its just goes around and around, and who wins?

Not us. Not the districts. Always the Capitol. But I'm tired of being a piece in their Games."[22] They have been tricked into thinking they are enemies. She lays bare the reality that the districts are all pieces in President Snow's self-serving game. Everything he does ultimately benefits a few in the Capitol at the expense of everyone else. She assumes she has answered his question, so Katniss punctuates her speech to the man (and to all of Panem) by asking for him to fight alongside her against the true oppressors: "Please! Join us!"[23] We expect the man will stand up and say yes, but instead we get a surprise. On the public screen Katniss "watch[es] myself get shot."[24] The argument is unconvincing. The rules of force that this man knows cannot be undone by setting weapons aside. He knows only the rules that President Snow enforces and responds to Katniss in the only way he realistically knows how to: through violence. At this moment, we are still in Plato's cave.

Katniss could have used force and, in so doing, perpetuate the violent cycle that this solider knows all too well. In strictly military terms, she would seemingly be excused for protecting herself through the use of violence. In opting to put her weapon down, however, she upholds a long tradition of non-violence as a political choice. In "Letter from Birmingham Jail," Martin Luther King, Jr., outlines the basic steps for a nonviolent campaign. He explains that: "In any nonviolent campaign there are four basic steps: collection of the facts to determine whether injustices are alive, negotiation, self-purification, and direct action."[25] These steps identify several important points that bring a discussion of Katniss into the orbit of King's thought. First and foremost, nonviolence is ground in a clear injustice. It responds to a significant immoral reality. As we have established throughout this book, there is a clear and consistent use of violence to extend injustice across Panem. Few would argue that injustice is not alive throughout the events that underwrite the rebellion. As such, Panem's political state meets King's first criteria.

King's second point applies to Panem. Katniss very much goes through a process of preparing herself to stand as the rebels' symbol in the face of President Snow's political machine. She spends most of The Hunger Games series following the path King describes for purification: "we would present our very bodies as a means of laying our case before the conscience of the local and national community."[26] Purification accomplishes two things. It prepares for the rigors that a commitment to nonviolence will bring in the context of a struggle that poses significant risk. Second, it establishes the public (i.e. political) basis for the campaign in specifically moral terms. King appeals to the conscience of all those who witness nonviolent actions because at some point they cannot deny the damage that violence causes. In these terms, Katniss is an exemplar of King's mandate in that she presents her body to the conscience of an entire national both inside and outside the Arena. Her suffering at the hands of President Snow makes clear the effect his politics has on her life, both as an individual and as a representative of Panem's citizens.

Having made this case, Katniss, like King, is justified in action and this is where King's breakthrough as a political leader is relevant to The Hunger Games series. In turn, the point at which action is justified helps us understand what is at stake when Katniss lays down her weapon. The act reveals the secret to nonviolence as a powerful political statement. She is not being passive in doing so; she actively chooses to set aside power in the form of violence for power in the form of the moral appeal that emerges in the second step of King's paradigm. In other words, the solider (like so many others) expects Katniss to shoot him. In the face of these expectations she surprises by showing him (and everyone else) that another course of action is possible. Nonviolence is, then, the power of deliberate restraint, which King tells us is the hallmark of nonviolence: "Nonviolent direct action seeks to create such a crisis and establish such creative tension that a community that has consistently refused to negotiate is forced to confront the issue."[27] In this immediate exchange, Katniss presents a choice to this soldier. He can do what he expects and has been trained to do: act violently. Or he can do nothing and break the pattern of violence and fear that frames this entire encounter. He still chooses to shoot her, but the *choice* has been broadcast countrywide. The contrast with Katniss is unmistakable. Of the two people involved, who occupies the high moral ground? Those watching must wrestle with the answer to this question. The result is that the community must now wrestle with the choice they have seen. The moment is tense and the creativity lies in the way Katniss undermines the expectations that govern in and through President Snow's actions. In watching this exchange everyone must now ask the same question Katniss presents this soldier: are you going to shoot or are you going to realize the pointlessness of shooting?

This is not to say that shooting is *always* a bad choice. Katniss is more than willing to use force when necessary. She kills in the Arena. She shoots down Capitol bombers. Her breakthrough as a political presence in The Hunger Games series is to evaluate whether violence is the only option. In this effort she mirrors Greitens' own journey through the ways force can and should be a part of an effective politics. Greitens became a member of the pointiest part of America's very big military spear. Implicitly, then, violence remains a viable option when he makes the following comment: "Warriors are warriors not because of their strength, but because of their ability to apply strength to good purpose."[28] At times, the warrior may deem violence justifiable because it is part of some good purpose. The importance distinction here is that strength and force are not necessarily the same thing. The ability to apply force well—to recognize in an unclear and complex set of circumstances—is the mark of a true leader. Further, the defining quality for using force is a good end. Beneath questions of power and violence we find yet again the importance of a moral framework for effective leadership and we see, therefore, why Katniss's role as a political leader is one that can lead a successful rebellion.

Part of the impact this moment has comes from the broader political game that occurs throughout The Hunger Games series. Haymitch explains this to Katniss during the victory tour at the beginning of *Catching Fire*. The Games are ongoing. Thus, any action Katniss takes will be perceived as a move in a contest with serious implications. The crisis she creates when she lays down her weapon in District Two is to undermine the assumptions President Snow makes about all those who are aware of the continuous nature of the Games. He fully expects that at some point she will devolve into the same mindset that drives his own decisions.

We see this clearly at the end of the *Catching Fire* movie when Katniss winds Beattee's wire around her arrow. Finnick returns to the tree frantically looking for her. She pulls her bowstring back and aims her arrow at Finnick. President Snow, who is watching this tense moment in the safety of the Capitol, leans forward eagerly. This is the moment he has been waiting since his conversation with Plutarch that we saw in Chapter 4. Plutarch suggested that President Snow allow the Games to unfold without proactively killing her off and the advice is about to

5. Katniss

pay off. The implication is clear; at some point she will have to kill those she calls her friends. When she does, Plutarch explains, everyone will see that she is no different than the Capitol's power-hungry leaders. President Snow assumes this is true, which is why his heart must sink when Katniss decides not to shoot Finnick and instead sends her arrow into the ceiling of the Arena. As she does when she chooses not to shoot the soldier in District Two, she shows all of Panem that an alternative to violence and fear exists and that she has the moral strength to follow this different path.

It is important to note that the choice need not be given to everyone at once. Questioning violence can be just as effective in a singular instance. To make the point, a brief excursus to another fictional character involved in a broader political narrative will be helpful. Jason Bourne is a decidedly violent person; anyone who has watched the Bourne trilogy starring Matt Damon will know the body count at Bourne's hands is pretty high. As someone who has literally been brainwashed into a violent default, Bourne follows in Katniss's footsteps at the end of *The Bourne Ultimatum*. Following yet another spectacular car chase, Bourne advances toward the assassin sent to kill him who hangs out a car window in a barely conscious state. Bourne aims his gun at the assassin and we know what should happen next. Bourne, however, does not fulfill his obligations to kill his opponent. He lowers his gun and walks away. Later, this same assassin confronts Bourne on the roof and is poised to kill his assigned target. Bourne does not fight back, but, rather asks a simple and powerful question: "Do you even know why you're supposed to shoot me?"[29] For someone whose job is to shoot without asking questions, this is probably the last thing he expected to hear. For the audience, the question recasts the entire framework that contains this interaction in a new light. Perhaps violence does not have to be the only option. Further, if we really stop to think about an answer to this question, we find rather quickly that there is no answer. A politics of violence lacks an underlying foundation to justify its presence in moral terms.

In the end, Katniss presents a choice to those who would opt for violence. She does not coerce those to whom she shows an alternative politics to President Snow. Rather, by rejecting violence she allows both options to linger in the minds of those faced with a choice. As someone deeply involved in a violent game, her impact is outsized. In asking rather than answering or forcing, Katniss exposes the moral bankruptcy of violence as a political tool. In doing so she follows in the footsteps of other cultural figures—real and fictional—who help us take the first step toward recovering a moral politics.

6. Haymitch

For the person who has just been selected to be a tribute in the Games, knowing that Haymitch Abernethy is your mentor would have to seem like a cruel trick at first. The initial description Katniss provides of Haymitch suggests he might actually make the reality of the Hunger Games worse for the District Twelve tributes. She summarizes his appearance at the reaping: "[He is] a paunchy, middle-aged man, who at this moment appears hollering something unintelligible, [who] staggers onto the stage and falls into the third chair. He's drunk. Very."[1] Inappropriate and ineffectual are two adjectives that come to mind. If Haymitch cannot stay sober long enough to give the tributes at least an initial sense of confidence in their mentor, then there would seem to be little, if any, redeeming value in the person who stands alongside the Effie and the Mayor as the tributes are selected.

In a very public and and very political moment, Haymitch plays the fool. Having served as District Twelve's only mentor for years, he knows the parameters of the reaping. He knows the cameras will be watching. He knows that all of Panem will see what he does and no doubt laugh (or cry) that he is the man who is solely responsible for helping Peeta and Katniss in the Arena. We do not get Peeta's initial reaction to Haymitch's appearance and actions, but Katniss's response can serve as a reliable proxy for what just about everyone is probably thinking. Haymitch is a liability in a situation where even the smallest disadvantage is unacceptable. He reflects the nationwide perception that District Twelve is hopeless.

Based on his drunkenness, his seeming disinterest in his job, and the relative scarcity of specific guidance to Peeta and Katniss, we cannot help but feel sorry that Haymitch will be the one helping out the District Twelve tributes. He is almost invisible as the events of *The Hunger Games* take shape. This initial outline of his character is as discouraging as we can imagine. He lacks the virtues we associate with our great political leaders. He certainly cannot moderate his alcohol consumption. He shows no outward commitment to Peeta and Katniss much less some higher moral ideal. It is hard imagining that his gruff exterior and social isolation can be the basis for building the social support needed to help his tributes in the Arena. In short, there does not seem to be a single political bone in his body that can do anything in the face of President Snow's calculating mind.

We start to get a sense there is more to story once Katniss has volunteered and the entire District Twelve crowd gives her the three middle fingers salute as a sign of solidarity. Suddenly, the normally stoic Katniss is in danger of bursting into tears on national television and, in the process of doing so, marking herself as weak in the eyes of the other tributes who will see a reply of the reaping in District Twelve. In this moment, Katniss explains how something unexpected happens: "I am truly in danger of crying, but fortunately Haymitch chooses this time to come staggering across the stage to congratulate me."[2] He sputters on about how much he likes Katniss, which has the effect of distracting the cameras from Katniss. At the end of his verbal outburst, Haymitch tumbles off the stage into a drunken heap. Katniss can only look on with mixed emotions and conclude: "He's disgusting, but I'm grateful."[3]

Katniss reads the situation as we assume everyone else in Panem does: Haymitch is a classic fool and a disgrace given his responsibilities. At such an important moment, he launches into an outburst that seems out of place. Katniss, though, mentions a clue that she does not recognize in the moment when she emphasizes that Haymitch *chooses* to act this way at *this* moment. She perceives the choice as an extension of his drunken demeanor, but in reality, the choice is well timed. Haymitch recognizes that Katniss is about to cry on television and he knows this will be bad for her. Thus, he does the best and only thing he can do: act in a way that gets the cameras off of Katniss to protect her image.

The fool turns out to be an invaluable ally who is playing a long political game. Though we could dismiss Haymitch's timely outburst as pure coincidence, we see repeatedly that he does the thing Katniss needs at just the right time. In these opening scenes of *The Hunger Games*, Haymitch echoes a long tradition of the seeming comic relief speaking more truth than anyone else. In Shakespeare's *King John*, the Fool speaks wisdom that reflects a political approach that summarizes well the sum total of Haymitch's actions: "Have more than thou showest, / Speak less

6. Haymitch

than thou knowest."[4] We know very little of Haymitch's background (I discuss what we eventually learn later in this chapter). He knows an awful lot about how to navigate dangerous political waters, but he speaks relatively few words to this effect. When he needs to, he will surface to influence events at hand, but for the most part he aligns clearly with the Fool in *King John*. There is a lot to the drunk who will humiliate himself on television in order to protect his mentees. In short, from the vantage point of the person whom no one considers relevant in a broader political narrative, we find the outline of how to maneuver through a dangerous game while accomplishing two things: surviving and influencing the outcome.

The tradition of the fool's outsized impact appears clearly and consistently in Haymitch's character, which explains why he is one of the most influential characters in terms of political impact throughout The Hunger Games series. For all of his outward shortcomings, he does several things very well. First and foremost, he reduces politics in the context of the Hunger Games to a simple and constant goal: survival. In fact, this is his first comment to Katniss when she asks for his advice on what she should do. She may feel extreme frustration with this response as the train speeds toward the Capitol to face what she knows will be a likely death. However, this reaction masks the relevance to advice's precision. If death is all but certain, then she should focus on the only thing that guarantees she will avoid that outcome. She has to stay alive. Moreover, in the broader political context of what the Games do in President Snow's political calculus, the advice continues to echo as the series unfolds. Haymitch frequently returns to this advice and it is always applicable.

His second redeeming quality is tied tightly to the first. He works very well within the context of the Hunger Games to succeed in his simple goal. In *The Hunger Games* movie, there is a short vignette of Haymitch as he watches the Games in the Capitol. He sits, drink in hand, watching Katniss suffer a serious burn on her leg after the gamekeepers herd her back to the Careers with a stream of fireballs. We watch him think through the situation, put his drink down, and go chat with some of the sponsors in the room. We do not get to hear what he says, but we quickly see the results. The drunk who is the laughing stock of the reaping in District Twelve is an efficient negotiator. In very little time he is able to secure sponsorship to get Katniss the medicine she needs.

This is one example of many that exhibits Haymitch's ability to adapt to the particulars of the moment. In a dangerous political game, he always seems to be one step ahead of everyone else. This skill emerges clearly when Katniss and Peeta are watching tapes of previous Games as they head back to the Capitol for the 75th Annual Hunger Games. When they watch the 50th Annual Hunger Games, they get to see one of the most important backstories through the series. Haymitch won the second Quarter Quell despite facing double the number of tributes. The way he did this is reveals much about his mindset when it comes to the Hunger Games.

As soon as the countdown hits zero and the Games begin, Haymitch gets his weapons and goes in the opposite direction of the Cornucopia. Once he starts moving, he does not stop and the reason is that he is probing his surroundings. Katniss notices his focus. Despite his troubles in the arena, "he persists in moving forward, always keeping the mountain at his back."[5] He understands that the Arena is a constructed space and, therefore, that there are particularities that may be helpful down the road (in this way he foreshadows Beattee's own insights in the training room when he explains to Katniss about the weak spot in the force field). Eventually he figures out that the Arena is circular and at the boundaries the mechanisms in place to keep tributes in can be used to his advantage. In understanding the specifics of the Arena he also realizes (even if not consciously in the moment) the truth of the entire political system of which the Hunger Games are a part: "it has to end somewhere.... The arena can't go on forever."[6]

A final quality is worth mentioning about Haymitch's political skills. For all of his prickly moments, Haymitch tends to keep his poker face on. He maintains an outward ambivalence about whatever he is doing. His outward disposition, then, keeps his calculating nature hidden from everyone. Even Katniss is usually unaware of his next move. In this sense he embodies the Fool's advice by ensuring that the way people perceive him disarms their expectations regarding his actions.

This, in turn, enables him to be deeply effective within a political game framed by fear. If President Snow is overt in his use of force in order to instill fear across Panem, Haymitch's approach to politics takes a different angle from Machiavelli's playbook. Force is not the only and certainly not the best way to succeed. In fact, it is always a second choice.

6. Haymitch

Machiavelli cautions: "Never attempt to win by force what can be won by deception."[7] Force might appear to be the most effective way of achieving a political end, but in the messy world of politics deception is far more effective. Those who would rule with fear rely on simplistic assumptions about what will be most effective. Haymitch recognizes the power of manipulation against a political opponent who is obviously stronger. Being clever and precise in his actions enables a continued run of political influence outside of the purview of President Snow who continues to look for the overt political threat.

More broadly, these examples speak to the long tradition in our culture of the underdog who comes from nowhere to secure an unexpected victory. Our own history follows this narrative; the American Revolution was a long shot in many ways. In each case, the baseline assumption of the ruling power is that its strength cannot be overcome. Further, any conflict with those who would challenge that power occur within a framework that blindly assumes outward power will always win out in the end. However, this mindset can give way to a devastating alternative when the clever opponent manages to exploit one of the weaknesses that power creates.

Haymitch consistently shows himself to be one of the most influential political figures in terms of his practical ability to navigate the tricky politics throughout The Hunger Games series. Importantly, his success goes beyond his simple advice to Katniss. He does not succeed just because he helps to keep Katniss alive; much of his success emerges from his deeply moral commitment to both Katniss and the broader rebellion. Yes, the man who drinks far too much and appears to care for little—including himself—is a moral signpost. It is fair to ask on the heels of this statement: how can such a claim be justified? Haymitch is moral? Articulating an answer to these questions will help to identify not only the basis for this claim, but also to recognize that in difficult political terrain the person who is adaptable will often be the most successful.

Haymitch's virtue does not lie in aligning with some abstract moral good. Rather, he is virtuous because his actions continually bring about good results for those fighting against the Capitol. The condition in which he often appears does not, in other words, preclude him from being a moral force in The Hunger Games series. To understand Haymitch's particular kind of virtue an exploration of Aristotle's concept of *phronesis*, or practical wisdom, will prove helpful.

From the outset of his *Ethics*, Aristotle locates goodness in *doing* rather than simply *thinking*. Simply put, Aristotle holds that "The virtue of a thing is related to its proper function."[8] Things have particular purposes for which they exist. Banks hold our money. Brakes stop our cars. A good bank is one that makes sure our money is still there when we want it. A good set of brakes will help us avoid slamming into the car that stops suddenly in front of us. Likewise, the failure to do these things would make a bank or a set of brakes bad. Humans are no different. There is a specific purpose that defines who we are and to be good humans is to do that function well.

Two things are important to emphasize at the outset of exploring how Aristotle defines virtue. First, thinking about doing something does not count as actually doing that thing. If we return to the bank example, we could receive endless assurances that the bank is doing everything possible to protect our money. If, however, the money is not actually available when we want it, then the assurances will mean very little. When we have a friend who routinely assures us that s/he will do something but then fails to do so, we will not take seriously that person's claims that s/he is always there for us.

The second point to emphasize here is that actions outside the scope of the main function do not count as virtuous with respect to the situation in which a decision is made. Virtue, in other words, cannot be a matter of luck. Goodness requires conscious and consistent action to bring about good ends. A bank may be very good at maximizing profits on the money it loans out, but if the purpose is to keep our money secure, then maximizing profits is tangential to what we ultimately want and need the bank to do. If we ask our partner to pick something up at the store for us, but s/he returns with the wrong thing, then s/he has not really done what we needed to do.

Virtue, then, is a particular kind of action that is focused on achieving a particular end. For humans, Aristotle ultimately concludes that human purpose is to use our reason in accordance with virtue. We have to think through our actions and choose to do something in accordance with a guiding moral principle. Aristotle emphasizes the importance of choosing to act in accordance with this moral standard: "moral virtue

6. Haymitch

is a state involving choice, and choice is deliberate."[9] There is a subtle but important point of emphasis here. While the moral standard in question helps to determine whether we have chosen well, the actual choice precedes any specific outcome. Being good is a label that applies first and foremost to our willingness to act in the right way. The particulars in which the action unfolds are secondary considerations.

A willingness to choose the right course of action has a better chance of bringing about a good result if we are able to use our rational decisions to act in the right way given the circumstances at hand. Aristotle explains: "if the choice is to be a good one, both the reasoning must be true and the desire right; and the desire must pursue the same things that the reason asserts."[10] In other words, being moral requires that we are able to apply choice in the right way. We must reason through the context given our circumstances to arrive at the best choice. This requires the ability to tolerate ambiguity across competing influences in a difficult moral situation. In other words, we are, Aristotle tells us, "speaking of intellect and truth in a practical sense."[11]

Practical impact is Haymitch's calling card (a fact evident in his clever messages that he sends on the cards that come with gifts from sponsors). As he is about to part ways with Katniss and Peeta before they enter the Arena in *Catching Fire*, Haymitch offers a concise goodbye to Katniss. Katniss's perspective is telling: "'Katniss, when you're in the arena,' he begins. Then he pauses. He's scowling in a way that makes me sure I've already disappointed him. 'What?' I ask defensively. 'You just remember who the enemy is,' Haymitch tells me. 'That's all. Now go on. Get out of here.'"[12] For such an important exchange, this seems unnecessarily tense and terse. Katniss takes the pause and the expression as signs of disappointment, but in fact Haymitch is making sure he says as much as he can in as few words as possible. The simple caution to remember who the enemy is will be all Katniss needs. She just does not realize this yet.

Once she is in the arena, Katniss hears this phrase again at a crucial decision point. She has returned to the tree that Beattee wound with the special wire. She frantically looks around to figure out what to do. When Finnick crashes through the brush, she pulls her bow and looks him down. Finnick, who has already shown Haymitch's gold bracelet to her in the arena (when they both reach the Cornucopia at the beginning), echoes his parting advice. "Katniss, remember who the real enemy is."[13] Only after she hears this does Katniss piece things together as far as the purpose of the advice. These words signal a plan that Haymitch had in place from the beginning. He is always a step ahead in the game.

Haymitch's plan in *Catching Fire* helps to show us what we should do in order to identify the best (in a moral sense) course of action. The parameters of being good cannot and should not be contained within a singular event. According to Aristotle: "it is thought to be the mark of a prudent man to be able to deliberate rightly about what is good and advantageous for himself; not in particular respects, e.g., what is good for health or physical strength, but what is conducive to the good life generally."[14] Goodness can be understand in localized terms, but the way we should think about goodness is much broader than any single event. In the bank example above, it is good when a person can withdraw money at the ATM for a specific need, but the continued ability to provide money at ATMs while also protecting your account from those who should not have access to your account is what makes a bank good in our eyes. We can see the clear connection to political goodness in this respect. Good political figures will be the ones who continually make decisions with our best interests in heart. This means, obviously, then they will not put us at risk (much less kill our children as President Snow does), but more important it also demands more than a single beneficial act. The politician who achieves a single victory that proves beneficial is not necessarily a good politician. We should expect a sustained record of service that continually protects our freedoms before we speak in terms of goodness in politics.

This mindset contrasts sharply with the current state of our political system, which in turn speaks to the political themes being discussed in this chapter. We live in a country where short-term political contests trump long-term interests. Senator Mitch McConnell can propose legislation he then filibusters in search of acute political gains and hold on to his leadership position.[15] This is but one example of many; how many national political figures routinely make news for bringing about positive results? What is lacking—and what defines Haymitch as a strong political figure—is a sustained record of getting things done that benefit people when it matters. The result of singular decisions like giving Finnick a sign to help Katniss past her distrust within a context that almost

6. *Haymitch*

demands paranoia gradually produces a political breakthrough because they occur repeatedly. A simple test helps to prove the point. If we ask how many scenes Haymitch is a part of that do not have a positive impact, we come up with very few, if any answers (the test requires that we keep in mind his necessarily sly decisions given the risky political environment in which he moves).

We know a lot about Haymitch by the time we figure out what he did in the Arena. He survived a particularly difficult Hunger Games by staying alert and thinking through the options he has while in the Arena. When he serves as a mentor to Katniss and Peeta, his ability to choose well has been honed. There is, in other words, a dynamic whereby successful decisions lead to more good decisions; success begets success. Aristotle agrees when it comes to develop the specific ability to identify and follow through on the correct course of action: "we call people prudent in particular respects when they have calculated successfully with a view to some serious end ... so that in general also the man who is capable of deliberation will be prudent."[16] There is no more serious end than survival and Haymitch achieves this end through his close calculations. The mere fact that he survived a stacked Hunger Games in the Second Quarter Quell signals that he understands how successful calculation pays off. He has proven himself capable of deliberating in a way that enables him to stay alive and this is the benchmark for continued success. He is clearly deliberative when he continues walking around the Arena in his own experience, which is ultimately the reason he is able to help Katniss navigate some of the hardest challenges she faces in the Arena and as the Mockingjay. As a result, she can trust him because his mere presence (by virtue of survival) speaks to his skills as someone who understands and can navigate the political realities that frame the Games.

Because politics is ultimately about acting and interacting with other people, how a person handles her/his interpersonal relationships is a point of particular importance in the current discussion. Aristotle is clear that moral action cannot be the result of isolated choices: "nobody deliberates about things that are invariable, or about things he cannot do himself."[17] If we return to the Arena, we see Haymitch embodies this point as the normative basis for action. He does not concern himself with invariable things. The outcome of the Games is fixed and he cannot change the rules (though, as we have seen elsewhere, this does not prevent him from lobbying for a chance of rules to help Katniss and Peeta). What he can do is examine his surroundings and make the best possible decisions within the rigid world of the Arena. In doing so, he succeeds because of his ability to recognize the best course of action with respect to the variables of the environment in which he finds himself. Further, while is isolated from others in his success in the Arena—and even here he is an outlier because alliances are considered part of the early stages of the Games—he still knows how to engage other people when it matters. He relates to Katniss better than anyone else by speaking to her strengths and weaknesses. The result is that despite her occasional anger she comes to trust Haymitch. He also balances other stakeholders, from Peeta to President Coin, while simultaneously staying mostly out of view. In short, he knows what he can do and he effectively finds help when he encounters a situation that he cannot handle on his own.

The ability to identify the best course of action requires an ability to work without a definitive signpost as to the possibilities and consequences of one's actions. Life is not a fixed equation that can be predicted with enough effort. Rather, as Haymitch shows so clearly, life is terribly difficult and at a base level coping is often good enough. As someone who lives in District Twelve, this particularly seems to be the case. In fact, the constant pressures of emerging from and descending into a place where drunkenness gives way to unconsciousness provides a good kind of practice for Haymitch to be nimble when the stakes are high (and he is sober). The person who possesses phronesis is able to adapt continually because s/he encounters a world that is unhinged from the notion of a safe and stable place.

Keeping in mind the way President Snow doles out violence and fear, this adaptability is doubly valuable. Politics is about acting prudently; Aristotle explicitly aligns individual choice and political standing: "Political science and prudence are the same state of mind."[18] The course of action and eventual goal, then, are the same kind of thing and, therefore, require the same skill set. The ability to adapt, to keep moving when the stakes are as high as they can be, serve Haymitch well when he finds himself in a much bigger political narrative. He does what he is best at; he adapts in a way that advances what is important to him. In the midst of constant change he perhaps more than anyone else stays on an even keel as he combats President Snow.

6. Haymitch

Haymitch illustrates how Aristotle situates individual virtue firmly within the broader context of corporate life. That is, individuals may exhibit virtue in their own particular circumstances, but in so doing that advance a public sense of moral identity. Prudence is the ability to use our reason to achieve a desired end. For Aristotle, this skill ties individual desire and political welfare together: "People do in fact seek their own good, and think that they are right to act in this way. It is from this belief that the notion has risen that such people are prudent. Presumably, however, it is impossible to secure one's own good independently of domestic and political science."[19] We see here the balance between the individual and the collective that underwrites the social contract. Individual desires can and do coexist alongside social good when people realize that their own desires run parallel to a collective good. This mutually beneficial dynamic lies at the heart of a good politics. Prudence will enable all parties within a social contract to thrive.

Importantly, the relationships that form in the Arena tend to exhibit this mutual benefit. Despite the parameters of the Hunger Games alliances form that extend the survival of both the individual and the small group. The exception, of course, is the Careers who rely on brute strength in a way that mirrors President Snow's politic actions. Everyone with whom Katniss befriends converges on the use of prudence that Aristotle describes. Peeta likewise keeps the benefit of those to whom he is close at the heart of his actions. Neither Katniss nor Peeta kill in the arena in a manner that puts themselves or their allies at risk. In fact, Katniss's direct kills in *The Hunger Games* occur when she is trying to protect Rue and when she mercifully kills Cato.

For all of his shortcomings, then, Haymitch excels in guiding his tributes through their experience in the Arena not only because they survive, but also because they do so in a way that upholds a prudent politics. Prudence, Haymitch understands, requires the ability and a willingness to act in concert with the interests of others. In the *Catching Fire* movie, we see this social awareness in action as Haymitch helps Katniss and Peeta network with other victors prior to the 75th Hunger Games. As he laughs with old friends, there is no vestige of the drunk who falls off the stage at the reaping before the 74th Hunger Games.

There exists in Haymitch's seeming randomness a calculated ability to be in the right place at the right time. This is not a consequence of

The Politics of *The Hunger Games*

randomness. The ability to have access to key people when needed is a hallmark of what Malcolm Gladwell calls the connector. The summary description of this person should sound familiar: "Connectors, people with a special gift for bringing the world together."[20] On a surface level, this seems obvious. People who know a lot of people collapse social circles so that they can get to the person who has what is needed. There is, however, a more subtle point to the connector that Gladwell brings to the surface: "when it comes to finding out about new jobs—or, for that matter, new information, or new ideas—'weak ties' are always more important than strong ties."[21] The connector does not look to a best friend for what is needed. Rather, the connector can move quickly across a group of people because s/he has weak links to many people. This dynamic fits nicely with the contrast we see between Haymitch's public drunkenness and social adaptability. Particularly when he needs to network to get Katniss a sponsor during *The Hunger Games* movie we see this softer side at work. When everyone knows of Haymitch he can skip past introductions. His notoriety provides the basis for those numerous weak links that Gladwell says are crucial to getting things that are needed.

Practically, the connector can accomplish a lot, but there is a more important conceptual point at stake. Alongside the ways Haymitch can help Katniss's interests through his wide-reaching connections we see a focused approach to advancing the broader political movement of which he is a part. He provides a clear example of what Albert-László Barabási calls the breakdown of randomness in networks. Barabási explains that: "Accounting for these highly connected nodes [i.e. people] requires abandoning once and for all the random worldview."[22] This is particularly true of social networks and supports the earlier claim that Haymitch's drunken persona is, in part, a calculated pattern of behavior that ultimately produces significant help to a lot of people working against President Snow.

As a well-connected person, Haymitch plays a necessary role as an invisible political leader. Because he is not outwardly attempting to influence the political games at hand, he is easily overlooked as influential in a given situation. This, in turn, provides space to maneuverer within very difficult circumstances. He is what Zolli calls a "translational"[23] figure. According to Zolli, these individuals: "must be connectors, mediators, teachers, behavioral economists, and social engineers. They must carry out these duties with candor, transparency, generosity, and commitment. They must also embrace the key principles of social network creation: Build your network before you need it. Build direct relationships so that, in a pinch, reconfiguration and collaboration can emerge quickly, but not so many relationships that things become densely overconnected."[24] As a summary of those who can alter a political landscape, this is an impressive list of characteristics. As a summary of Haymitch's role in The Hunger Games series, it forces us to consider that he acts with incredible precision. In a pinch—and he encounters several of these—he can draw on his social networks to bring about a solution that does not seem possible.

A final point from Zolli's description deserves specific attention. Haymitch has the foresight to build relationships that he might need. In *The Hunger Games* movie, we get access to an exchange that the books cannot provide by virtue of Katniss's inability to be aware of what is going on behind the scenes. Haymitch realizes that he can find a way to bring both Katniss and Peeta home from the Arena. The film shows Haymitch having a one-on-one conversation with Seneca Crane. Haymitch suggests that Seneca Crane should allow Katniss and Peeta to be potential co-victors because everyone in Panem wants to see the star-crossed lovers make it out of the Arena.

Several things stand out in how this exchange. The first is that Haymitch can get a private audience with the person running the Hunger Games while they are going on. This speaks to the networks he puts in place along the lines Zolli establishes. As the old saying goes, the best time to build the ark is before it rains. We can assume that Haymitch built up the relationship with Seneca Crane well before this conversation just in case (and if he did not, then we should be impressed that he was able to convince Seneca Crane to give five minutes of time to someone whom he never met prior to the conversation). The second point to highlight is the pitch Haymitch gives. He presents a value proposition that is wholly self-serving but also has clear appeal to Seneca Crane. Finally and most remarkably, Seneca Crane follows through on the idea. For the first time ever, the Hunger Games can have co-victors because Haymitch presents the idea in a way that does not appear to run counter to the overall purpose of the Hunger Games.

Haymitch's subtle awareness of human interests and his ability to build relationships ties back to his constant ability to focus. While he no doubt enjoys the relief alcohol brings (and he probably does need it to make it through some days), the outward actions we see when comments about his stupor appear do not align with the reliable political mentor he is when the chips are down. He understands, in other words, the power of deception in a political game where fear can quickly erupt. It is easier to survive if he is perceived as a public fool rather than as an incisive political mind. Outwardly, he is smoke and mirrors, but when it comes to the few to whom he is close, he shows nothing but a morally upstanding character.

Katniss often fails to realize the scope of Haymitch's virtue, particularly when it comes to the decisions he makes that suggest he is not on her side. She frequently accuses him of lying. On one level this is certainly true; he is lying, just not to her. Rather, he is communicating in subtextual ways in order to guide her while also maintain the appearance he has developed over the years. In the moments where Katniss reaches the edge of her ability to keep herself together, Haymitch inevitably appears to provide support. One of the most telling examples of this practical wisdom occurs when Katniss sees the wedding cake at Finnick and Annie's wedding. She immediately recognizes that the frosting is Peeta's work, which tells her that he has not gone completely crazy. At such a crucial juncture, we should not be surprised that she finds in this moment "As if anticipating my reaction, Haymitch is at my side."[25] As with the intervention at the reaping, we could chalk his presence up to luck, but the timing is too good. Haymitch anticipates what Katniss needs and he makes sure he stands by her when she sees something that will cause a strong reaction. Importantly, his presence is not simply a matter of political action; it is also a sign that he knows her well enough to provide emotional support.

If we recall the two primary features of Aristotle's notion of virtue, we begin to understand the claim that Haymitch is not only a good person, but also one of the most influential political figures throughout The Hunger Games series. The first quality needed to be a good person is a willingness to act in the best possible way given the circumstances. When he needs to Haymitch steps out of his drunken persona to protect people. When Gale is being whipped in *Catching Fire*, we see (in the movie ver-

6. *Haymitch*

sion) this courage displayed in full effect. Katniss already took up a spot between Gale and Thread, but her intervention only aggravates the situation. Haymitch, on the other hand, is able to do the same thing and talk Thread down from punishing Katniss.

This exchange with Thread characterizes a politics based on practical wisdom. There is the ability to act decisively in a very tense situation. Haymitch does not claim abstract reasons as the basis for Thread to ease the tension of the situation in the main square. He is deeply practical in explaining why it is in Thread's interest to stop. President Snow's plan requires that Katniss be seen in a particular way and harming her will directly counter this need. As such, there is clear self-interest in stopping that also serves everyone else involved. Further, he does not defend Katniss as having the right to escape physical harm. He publicly critiques her intelligence, which implicitly lays responsibility for the situation at her feet. Virtue is not abstract; he does not defend a friend at all costs. Rather, he says exactly what needs to be said to pacify Thread and thus achieve his political goal: getting everyone out of the problem without any further harm.

Haymitch, then, plays a smart political game within the parameters that President Snow has set. He deceives his way to significant influence. Machiavelli would no doubt congratulate Haymitch on succeeding in a context defined by fear. For Machiavelli, political "Wisdom consists of knowing how to distinguish the nature of trouble, and in choosing the lesser evil."[26] When he acts, he knows both the reason a problem has come about and he is subsequently able to find the best way through the challenge. He does not cling to an impossible moral foundation for his political actions. He does what Machiavelli and Aristotle would both suggest. He opts for the best solution given the situation at hand.

This conclusion points to the second characteristic at the heart of how Aristotle describes virtue. Haymitch is precise in his actions. He does just enough to succeed. He does not overreact. The sum of these small actions illustrates how accurate Haymitch is in calculating and acting within a political context. Crucially, the outcome of his intervention is a good result for everyone, even Commander Thread. This is exactly what politics should be, particularly in a context defined by fear. Everyone walks away better off for a leader's action.

7. The Rebellion

The Declaration of Independence offer some of history's most powerful words in thinking about what politics can and should be. Its introductory remarks represent a vision of government that can serve everyone: "We hold these truths to be self-evident, that all men are created equal, that they are endowed by their Creator with certain unalienable Rights, that among these are Life, Liberty and the pursuit of Happiness."[1] The basis for the American Revolution is, the Declaration makes clear, a self-evident set of rights that all citizens should enjoy. The core of these rights includes an understanding of humanity that we saw earlier in the Universal Declaration of Human Rights. People are equal. They have an intrinsic life to pursue happiness while remaining secure. Finally and fundamentally, these rights exist at the core of who we are as individuals and as members of a society.

Any legitimate government rests on the foundation of these principles. Though not quite as well known, the passage in the Declaration that immediately follows this famous introduction is also crucial in understanding the basis for revolution. The outline of any government's obligations is worth quoting in full: "That to secure these rights, Governments are instituted among Men, deriving their just powers from the consent of the governed,—That whenever any Form of Government becomes destructive of these ends, it is the Right of the People to alter or to abolish it, and to institute new Government, laying its foundation on such principles and organizing its powers in such form, as to them shall seem most likely to effect their Safety and Happiness."[2]

Protecting freedom is the government's first priority and a failure to meet this responsibility is grounds for a new government. The political dynamic here is powerful if a bit subtle. When a government ceases to be effective in protecting rights and preserving freedom, the government is the problem. Failed governments are not the responsibility of the citizens whom the government serves. Further, in the case of failure

7. The Rebellion

the people have a "Right" to get rid of the problematic government and establish a new political presence that will better serve our intrinsic rights. The agency for political change rests with people who perceive that their rights are not being met. They determine, always, who and what will best lead to their safety and happiness. The principle of self-governance emerges forcefully from this right. Governments should be defined by the terms the people deem best suited to their circumstances.

Based on these principles, there is little doubt that the rebellion in The Hunger Games series is justified. President Snow very clearly fails to provide the safety and happiness of anyone outside his own personal interests. The only reason he might perceive consent (though it is doubtful President Snow actually believes he has the consent of those whom he rules over) is that any right to abolish the government has not been exercised. This argument rests on inaction, which ultimately follows from the fear and violence President Snow uses to silence any critics.

In short, President Snow's track record in Panem mirrors the circumstances that led to the American Revolution. The Declaration announces clearly that a breaking point has been reached: "But when a long train of abuses and usurpations, pursuing invariably the same Object evinces a design to reduce them under absolute Despotism, it is their right, it is their duty, to throw off such Government, and to provide new Guards for their future security."[3] President Snow's train of abuses is long indeed and his role in Panem certainly qualifies as establishing absolute Despotism. As such, the rebels who sign the Declaration claim their right and duty to create a new political order independent of the English King.

The same argument could flow from Katniss. President Snow must be thrown off so that future security might be realized. The principle at the heart of the rebellion echoes strongly the basis for democracy as fought for, achieved, and nurtured in America's history. There is a deep moral component to be reclaimed in establishing a political order based on these principles. We know that the Founding Fathers meant it when they signed their names—thus committing treason—under the Declaration's final words: "we mutually pledge to each other our Lives, our Fortunes and our sacred Honor."[4]

Benjamin Franklin recognized what was at stake in this political revolution. The rebel collective would succeed by working together or suffer a great deal. Of Franklin's many quotable moments one of his most poignant sayings occurred at the signing of the Declaration and highlights what is at stake in claiming a new political order "We must all hang together, or assuredly we shall all hang separately."[5] Thomas Jefferson speaks similar words of advice during his First Inaugural Address despite the deep philosophical differences that existed among the Founding Fathers: "But every difference of opinion is not a difference of principle. We have called by different names brethren of the same principle."[6] The ability to unite supersedes the inevitable variations that emerge when individuals start speaking about their freedoms to pursue happiness. Success depends on mutual respect and a deep commitment to everyone involved in a political rebellion.

In other words, rebellion demands that individual principles remain bound to some collective good. People must work together to bring about the freedom from despotism that the Declaration speaks about. Protecting everyone's freedom meant setting aside differences and working toward a common fate by assuming common risk. This deep commitment to principle constitutes the legacy of politics that the Founding Fathers left the world. As a baseline for evaluating what unfolds throughout The Hunger Games series (as well as reflecting on our own political state of affairs), this unwavering pledge of solidarity actually reveals a rebellion that surprises because it probably should not be successful if unity is what success will demand.

If unity and commitment are hallmarks of what it takes to throw off an oppressive government, then the frequency with which division, distrust, and betrayal surface among the rebels demands attention. Once she has been rescued from the Arena at the end of *Catching Fire*, Katniss finally learns that a rebellion has been underway for quite some time. Serious back channel conversations were going on that she had absolutely no idea about when she entered the Arena a second time. Once in there, she remained ignorant of an elaborate plot to rescue her (and others, if possible) to build on the rebels' momentum. A positive reading of these different examples would accept that there were extenuating circumstances at each turn, but added up this seems like either an incredible coincidence or a pattern of keeping Katniss out of the loop. It would be helpful to conclude that the rebels have a unique mix of bravado, virtue, and clever insights to combat President Snow, but they actually have some clearly dysfunctional tendencies.

7. The Rebellion

When Katniss reacts, however, a much different picture emerges. Once she has been brought up to speed, she shares her thoughts: "It's an awful lot to take in, this elaborate plan in which I was a piece, just as I was meant to be a piece in the Hunger Games. Used without consent, without knowledge. At least in the Hunger Games, I knew I was being played with."[7] The very thing the rebels are fighting is in some ways *better* because at least Katniss knows President Snow's game. Here, those who stand on principle and desire a society that throws off his abuses actually deceives her in a way that she likens to the oppression she experiences in the Arena. Most importantly, Katniss calls attention to the lack of the things that are supposed to underwrite a legitimate government: freedom and liberty. Instead of embracing these noble political goals, the rebellion really kicks into gear by actively denying some of these rights to the person who will become their leader.

The exchange gets worse. Plutarch tells Katniss that deception was necessary to serve the rebellion's goals, even if those goals did not align with Katniss's individual right to choose who she is or wants to be. He tells her simply that the rebel leaders his the truth from her because "We had to save you because you're the mockingjay…. While you live, the revolution lives."[8] The notably absent component in this supposed honor is the lack of agency Katniss has in deciding if this is a good thing or not. The political leaders at the head of the rebellion make a very important decision about Katniss's life without her knowledge, much less her input. As a result, Katniss draws an important conclusion about how those with whom she will fight think of her. She muses that they deceived her "Because I obviously can't tell a friend from an enemy."[9] Katniss has just come from a devastating experience in the Arena and her first thoughts are that the rebels have acted in a way that is the same as the person they are fighting against. Amidst this sudden change of events, she does not know who is on her side.

These introductory remarks show a rebel cause defined by something other than a cohesive, mutually reinforcing commitment to political freedom. These rebels are not the Founding Fathers. Their purpose is, of course, legitimate in the sense that they want to oust a despotic ruler who has systematically abused his power by sowing fear and inciting violence across Panem. At the same time, they tend to drift in both their moral calculus and their internal cohesion.

This final point offers a good way to introduce this chapter's examination of the political identity these rebels exhibit. Rather than focus at first on their eventual success, thinking about the rebels' political identity will be better served by examining how they are prone to failure. The surprise occurs in their eventual success. Why this is the case is a far more interesting question to ponder than to consider the deeply troubling things they do as exceptions to a consistently noble effort. Importantly, just about every rebel leader is guilty of some serious infraction when measured against the principles we saw outlined in the Declaration of Independence.

Given our own history, our cultural willingness to treat rebels kindly makes sense. However, a more critical approach to the rebels in The Hunger Games series is a helpful exercise in a specifically political discussion. Morals still matter (and we will return to them before the chapter is done), but as noted above they do not constitute the definitive part of the rebels' campaign against President Snow. As such, it is worth considering some of the reasons and consequences that accompany the rebels' shortcomings.

Lincoln B. Krause offers a little known but foundational basis for critiquing these rebels. His article "Playing for the Breaks: Insurgent Mistakes" highlights the ways that insurgents fighting against an established power often go off track. The reason for this consistent misdirection lies in the nature of an insurgency: "An insurgency is a risky and highly complex human activity susceptible to a range of mistakes by its protagonists. It is safe to say there has never been a mistake-free insurgency."[10] Quite simply, rebels begin with a significant disadvantage. More often than not, this starting handicap will inevitably lead to problems, many of which can prove fatal to the effort. While we celebrate the success of the American Revolution, we should consider what the Founding Fathers accomplished to be exceptional in that their campaign was similarly risky, unlikely to succeed, and lucky at times to overcome its mistakes.

Krause outlines two key ways that insurgents mess up and these categories will help us understand what unfolds in The Hunger Games series. The two general areas are "original sins" and "situational miscalculations."[11] The former category is straightforward in its effects. When movements start with intrinsic flaws, there exists a significant likelihood

7. The Rebellion

that problems will materialize later in the campaign. The mistrust Katniss expresses on the hovercraft at the end of *Catching Fire* offers a good example of this point. She continually wonders (rightfully it turns out) at what point her role in the rebellion will cease to matter. This is a strange place for the face of the movement to be and at multiple points only Katniss's adaptability saves the rebels from falling apart.

For Krause, situational miscalculations warrant particular attention because they exhibit particularly damaging tendencies. Krause explains that these mistakes: "principally involve decisions regarding intermediate objectives and tactics to be employed."[12] Whereas original sins indicate decisions made prior to engaging the cause against which the insurgents fight, situational errors happen during the conflict and, therefore, can pose a more immediate roadblock to success. Krause clarifies why this is the case: "Most mistakes in this category have a common root in overreach. Simply put, insurgent leaders overestimate their own capacity.... These mistakes often stem from impatience or are driven by hubris built from initial success."[13] When fighting an uphill battle, overreach can be especially costly. All the careful planning that waits for the perfect moment can go for naught when leaders make decisions that ignore their own (often obvious) shortcomings. Further, these mistakes are in Krause's conception *avoidable* and not contained within the parameters of the conflict. Rather, they result from personal miscalculations. To return to the manipulation Katniss realizes, the decision to keep her out of the loop reflects the perception among rebel leaders that Katniss must remain ignorant. This is a curious choice, especially when we think back to the meeting between Katniss and President Snow at the beginning of *Catching Fire*. He realizes Katniss's capabilities, so he decides to be wholly honest with her about his plans. The enemy, in other words, measures Katniss's strength more precisely than those she is supposed to lead into battle.

The distrust the rebel leaders show toward Katniss impacts the initial military endeavors we see in *Mockingjay*. Katniss's prescribed role is to be a prop, not to engage in actual military matters. With Katniss on the sidelines, Capitol bombers inflict significant damage on important resources. Once Katniss throws off her instructions and fights back, she is able to shoot down some of the Capitol's planes and thus save further destruction of District Eight.

At the core of this initial military foray we find a miscalculation of Katniss's abilities as the Mockingjay. The rebel leaders prefer that she step aside when the fighting begins, yet she shows pretty quickly that this decision is wrong. Thus, she reveals what Krause identifies as one of the crucial mistakes insurgents make. He writes: "insurgents who misjudge the strength of their movement, the impact of their initial actions, and the government's capacity to respond often result in a government counteraction they are not prepared to withstand."[14] Katniss's strength is clearly misjudged when she is sent to District Eight. Her ability to neutralize the Capitol's air power proves invaluable in the moment, yet it is only through her defiance of the leaders' expectations that she prevents further harm. Keeping her on the sidelines of the fighting thus constitutes a serious inaccuracy in deploying the military resources at the rebels' disposal. Further, the Capitol's capacity to respond would have multiplied the mistake to keep Katniss away from the fighting had she not decided to disobey orders.

Without Katniss, the rebels in District Eight would likely not have been able to repel the Capitol attack. We know that the Capitol can raze an entire district, a fact we see in the ruins of District Twelve. The initial decision from the rebel leaders thus comes very close to realizing the impact misjudging strength has. Krause explains that these "miscalculation[s] will doom a movement or hamper its growth."[15] Absent something to reverse the initial decision, we should expect the rebel leaders to experience a significant loss in District Eight. Had this occurred, this crucial early fight would have actualized the kind of thing Krause notes rebels cannot afford: "[not only] a military disaster, but also a major psychological blow."[16] While the rebels retreat, Krause notes we would expect that the Capitol's "morale soared."[17] In short, the rebels' initial military decisions mirror a common trajectory that frequently halts any momentum that has been built. Katniss is able to stop the slide, but only through a decision that aggravates the sense of distrust that defines her relationship with the rebel leaders.

This initial discord spills over into the rest of the military campaign the rebels mount. Even as they experience more success and push toward the Capitol, we see simultaneously the emergence of greater internal discord. Rebels start taking sides as the chess match between Katniss and President Coin intensifies. This is precisely what Krause says we

7. The Rebellion

should expect when an insurgency manages to last past its early stages. He explains how insurgencies mature and he could easily be describing the rebels' campaign in *Mockingjay*: "Insurgencies by their very nature are fractious affairs, and the stress and discord generated by decisions at strategic junctures can bring to the fore internal disagreements or variances over the direction that the insurgency is moving. Disunity can produce or exacerbate these situational miscalculations as insurgent leaders work to outmaneuver rivals or advance personal and ideological agendas."[18] At seemingly every strategic decision from the moment Katniss is lifted out of the Arena at the end of *Catching Fire* we see the discord that Krause mentions.

Perhaps the most telling way this tension appears is the way Gale and Katniss drift apart as the rebellion takes shape. When it comes time to figure out how best to confront and defeat President we see two best friends and political allies take very separate routes. The final scene involving between President Coin and Katniss obviously speaks to a climactic difference. Even Haymitch, who more than anyone cuts Katniss some slack, shows frayed nerves during crucial conversations. Boggs eventually turns his back on President Coin to whom he is fiercely loyal. In fact, the only relationship that seems to get better in *Mockingjay* is the one that is most fractured at the outset of the third book. Peeta and Katniss gradually come around to the bond they share during *The Hunger Games*, but there are significant moments of the kind of discord Krause describes before that reconciliation is possible.

Personal agendas warrant a specific look at how the rebels ultimately conduct their war against President Snow. Gale in particular stands as an example of how a shared goal can take on a different shape as the rebellion unfolds. As we have seen from the first moments of The Hunger Games series, he and Katniss share a strong bond in their awareness of and consequently their anger toward President Snow. Despite the shared perspective, by the halfway point of *Mockingjay* the two have adopted irreconcilable attitudes toward their common enemy.

As the rebel leaders consider how to overtake the command center in the mountain in District Two known as the Nut, Gale is the one who comes up with a solution to what seemingly constitutes an insurmountable problem. The defenses the Capitol has around the command center make a frontal attack almost suicidal. The Nut, however, is a nerve center so the rebels eventually have to strike an important blow by rendering the Nut inoperable. Gale is the one who offers a new way of thinking about the problem. Rather than try to overtake the Nut, he suggests blowing up the mountain in a way that would kill everyone inside.

Katniss describes the reaction in the planning room in a way that makes clear how agendas have diverged. As different people consider the implications of Gale's plan, a variety of responses surface. Beattee states ambivalently: "The majority of the workers are citizens from Two."[19] Though they may be complicit in helping the Capitol, Beattee also acknowledges that the majority of the people inside the Nut are not Capitol residents and therefore could have affinities with the rebels. He does not resolve the tension between these two allegiances, which is why he does not take a stand on whether the plan is a good idea. In short, he recognizes that the leaders face a serious moral question.

Lyme is a bit more pragmatic as a fighter. Perhaps because she is a military leader she recognizes that within the context of war slaughter of this kind may be extreme. She cautions that those inside the Nut should have the opportunity to surrender. At this point, Gale interjects with his understanding of the situation and his opinion marks the point at which he and Katniss suffer an irreparable split. He tells Lyme that surrender is "a luxury we weren't given when they firebombed Twelve, but you're all so much cozier with the Capitol here."[21] Two points stand out in Gale's remarks. First, he does not think about the people inside the Nut any differently than his fellow District Twelve residents were treated when the Capitol obliterated everything. While we can understand the logic Gale uses here, the implications of that logic are troubling. Though he justifies killing the workers inside the Nut based on what he suffered as a District Twelve resident, his actual argument is that they can act in the same way President Snow has acted. As such he sets aside a moral compass in his decision-making and instead reveals his true motivation. The result is, ultimately, to align Gale's moral approach the final stages of the war with the very person he is fighting to defeat.

Gale wants revenge. This second key point immediately sets him at odds with the political goal of ousting President Snow and rebuilding a healthy political society in Panem. The war for Gale is no longer about justice. It is about getting even. Further, he wants to be the one who car-

7. The Rebellion

ries out the revenge. Lyme flashes anger in response to Gale's initial claim, which only intensifies his desire for revenge: "We watched children burn to death and there was nothing we could do!"[21] We see the same slanted logic at work again. Though he bases his anger on those who died at the Capitol's hand, he is really thinking about playing the role of the Capitol in the suffering blowing up the Nut will bring about.

Katniss takes her time before responding, but when she does, she calls out Gale for thinking as he does. Importantly, she makes explicit the connection between what the Capitol did to District Twelve and the plan he proposes. She tells him: "The Nut's an old mine. It'd be like causing a massive coal mining accident."[22] Katniss then shares her thoughts by adding as the narrator: "Surely the words are enough to make anyone from 12 think twice about the plan."[23] The loss of a father, brother, or friend in the coal mines of District Twelve would seem to be enough to pull Gale back from the edge and help him remember the moral basis for his actions that occur before he becomes a rebel leader.

In the thought she adds, Katniss shows that despite her justifiable anger toward what President Snow has done, she does not lose sight of the underlying purpose of fighting a war against him. Revenge undermines the basis of what she and the rebels want to accomplish. For Gale, maximizing the suffering counts as an improvement on that cause. He yells to the room: "Is that everyone's problem? That our enemies might have a few hours to reflect on the fact that they're dying, instead of just being blown to bits?"[24] The foundation of a legitimate political system has disappeared from Gale's mindset about what the war is based on. He no longer worries about protecting others. In fact, considering the other side as fellow humans is a problem, not in the moral sense but in the sense of being an impediment to his goal in blowing up the Nut. If the end result of his plan is the death of those inside, then strictly speaking the answer to Gale's question would be yes. Suffocating slowly, then dying, would probably be a worse death than the immediate loss of life that occurs in an explosion. Gale thus reveals that revenge requires more than a simple eye-for-an-eye trade of lives. He wants his enemies to suffer as much as possible before they die. He reiterates in essence that he wants to act in the same way President Snow does: to maximize fear through the use of violence.

Katniss realizes the gravity of the moment. She narrates the change she perceives in Gale's words in telling language: "Back in the old days, when we were nothing more than a couple of kids hunting outside of 12, Gale said things like this and worse. But then they were just words. Here, put into practice, they become deeds that can never be reversed."[25] Gale does not speak in hyperbole and abstract ideas. Katniss knows that he is serious in his desire to inflict maximum pain on people whom others say should have the chance to surrender. Katniss's reminder of their childhood and the loss the experienced as a result of the mindset driving his insistence on revenge cannot puncture the way Gale has drifted apart from the other rebel leaders. We can hear the language from the Declaration of Independence fading. For Gale, the rebellion means something different than the standards he upheld when he promised to watch over Prim and Katniss's mother and when he covered for Katniss knowing full well that doing so would result in being whipped.

With this kind of divergence, we see a campaign against a tyrant regressing into anything but a unified effort based on honorable principles. The outward commitment to justice becomes an explicit desire for revenge in the minds of a moral stalwart through most of The Hunger Games series. If this exchange regarding the attack on the mountain were the point at which we had to decide if the rebellion is going to succeed, we would be justified in suggesting that the rebels were simply falling apart. The bonds that brought them together clearly fray as they move closely to the realization of their goal. Importantly, amidst that discord we see the decay of the moral basis for their rebellion in the first place.

Aristotle identifies how the mindset Gale reveals in this exchange aligns his goals with those of President Snow. More specifically, Aristotle explains how the glimpse we catch of Gale's anger signals an important shift in what the fight is about. Aristotle explains: "Men turn seditious when they suffer dishonor themselves and when they see others honoured."[26] They decision about the mountain should be compared to the explosions that occur so often in the District Twelve mines. The problem lies in the different way Gale and Katniss (along with the others) think about the similarities. For Katniss, the suffering this kind of experience will bring cannot justify the military goal at hand. For Gale, suffering is due to those who we should recall are residents of District Two, not the Capitol. We do not know their motivation for fighting alongside

7. The Rebellion

President Snow—perhaps they have no choice—but we see in Gale a refusal to consider this as relevant. He suffered through the death of his father who experienced what a collapsed mountain would bring, a risk he faced for a short while himself as a mine worker (and this is after the frequent and increased risk of being cast into the Arena as a tribute). In short, Gale understands very well what is means to suffer dishonor. He sees the mercy that others want to extend to the people in the mountain as an honor that ignores his own experience. As a result, he exhibits the sedition Aristotle claims will often come about when someone in Gale's circumstances must think politically and morally.

The tragic thing in Gale's anger is that we can sympathize with his desire. He has suffered, just as those whom he cares about have suffered. Why should he act mercifully toward others when those people are complicit (at least in terms of the military campaign of which both sides play a part) in his suffering? While there is no easy answer to this question, voicing what seems fair ultimately points toward the need to recover a specifically moral foundation for building a new political order through rebellion. Greitens once again provides a valuable insight on this kind of matter from the perspective of someone who can sympathize with Gale. Greitens lost many friends and fellow soldiers at the hands of those committed to sowing terror. However, as he reflects on his experience as a Navy SEAL, Greitens finds that there must be some collective moral goal to military action: "when people serve a purpose beyond themselves, they have a remarkable capacity for resilience."[27] Suffering exists in the world and often this suffering comes at the hands of those who abuse their political power. The response that breaks the cycle we see in Gale's anger is to remember that individual freedom is about protecting everyone's rights. Force should serve a moral collective that recognizes the humanity we share with one another.

Greitens, then, hints at the way that Katniss is able to prevent the rebellion from completely breaking down. Throughout the challenges she faces, she shows the resilience Greitens describes. The term is worth clarifying, as doing so will indicate how the fractures we have examined in this chapter eventually heal. Zolli adds an important consideration by recognizing that, at their core, resilient things: "have the ability to reorganize themselves to maintain their core purpose, even under radically changing circumstances."[28] A couple of features stand out in Zolli's definition. First, resilience as a quality surfaces when circumstances are particularly challenging. This is not a quality that everyone has and those who have it do not use it just because they can. Resilience indicates a deeply rooted ability to adapt to the most difficult of circumstances. We certainly see Katniss show this adaptability in the Arena, but Zolli gets at more than the ability to survive. The second quality captures the specific ways that resilience matter in the context of the movement Katniss leads. Adapting to changing circumstances allows the resilient person or people to retain some foundational thing. The American Revolution probably should not have succeeded given the British Army's advantages. However, by clinging to the mutual pledge of honor in search of a politics that affirmed fundamental equality, the American rebels continually bounced back from challenges that could and should have ended their fight for freedom. Katniss similarly keeps the overall purpose of her fight against President Snow in mind. Her initial act as a leader was to protect her sister at the seeming cost of her own life.

The specific choice Katniss makes helps to explain just what resilience is. Zolli concludes his discussion be summarizing the shape resilience takes in its commitment to some foundational purpose. He notes that the ability to bounce back "cannot simply be imposed from above— instead it must be nurtured in the social structures and relationships that govern people's everyday lives."[29] While an individual may be the example of resilience, ultimately that individual's character reflects a broader social value set. The ability to adapt in order to protect a way of life does not occur when the people involved only want to mind their own concerns. Zolli emphasizes the social nature of resilience. To endure the hardships she encounters throughout The Hunger Games series, Katniss ultimately recognizes that her actions form part of a larger political narrative. As such, the fight for her own life is, in part, a fight for a life that everyone in Panem can say is worth living.

The survival and success of America despite its calcified political dynamics speaks to the power of resilient leaders. Moreover, America's emphasis on freedom and equality serves as a goal that continues to encourage acts of bravery and sacrifice despite the examples we see almost daily of those who would deny the moral foundation of America's successful rebellion. For example, in his speech to his fellow Virginians at a 1775 convention, Patrick Henry supposedly uttered the words that

7. The Rebellion

linger to this day as a rallying cry of the American Revolution: "Give me liberty or give me death." The purpose of the American experiment was to embody this strict either/or. Freedom outweighed a life lived in the shadow of the despotism the Declaration of Independence would speak of a year later.

More than a decade after uttering his famous statement, Patrick Henry would cycle around to this principle in speaking again to his fellow Virginian lawmakers. In 1788, however, his goal was markedly different. He did not need to drum up support for a seemingly impossible fight against the British. Speaking before the Virginia Convention in 1788, Patrick Henry needed to convince his fellow lawmakers to codify the new American government's principles by ratifying the Constitution.

Henry's argument reaches back to the core principle that proved resilient. He tells his colleagues: "Guard with jealous attention the public liberty. Suspect everyone who approaches that jewel. Unfortunately nothing will preserve it, but downright force: Whenever you give up that force you are inevitably ruined."[30] The success of the Revolution must continue by protecting the core value it was based on and ultimately achieved in victory: public liberty. Individual freedoms exist within this concept, but Henry's point of emphasis is telling with respect to the unwavering commitment he and others had to the moral basis for the Declaration of Independence and subsequent war with Britain. Freedom is collective in nature and this principle is worth protecting through force. People should recall the right and the duty that the Declaration makes plain. There exists an obligation of the governed to reject a political leader who does not preserve human freedom. If required, force is a legitimate way to protect freedom because true freedom can generate unified political voice that can overcome even the gravest of threats.

This is the unwavering commitment Katniss brings to the rebels throughout The Hunger Games series. She never completely loses site of the moral imperative that drives her actions, which is why she can overcome even the loss of her closest friend. Gale may reach the point where his attitude toward others is no different than President Snow's but Katniss pushes ahead toward her goal of a life where kids are not killed in the Arena and she, like everyone else, will be free to live the life she wants to live.

8. President Coin

The war between the rebels and President Snow is finally over. Amidst heavy losses on both sides, a final battle in the Capitol finally brings to an end the game that began when Prim's name was selected at the reaping. Having surveyed the destruction this final conflict caused, the President sits down to plan the country's next steps.

The war has taught some important lessons about the districts. In order to prevent future conflicts, the decision is made to keep the fences up around the districts in order to limit movement. The districts will continue to focus on producing particular staples. The airwaves were shown to be risky tools throughout the war, so access to programming will be limited and what can be viewed will be carefully scripted. Finally, the decision is made to hold the Hunger Games in the coming year as a reminder of why the war was fought and to remind everyone of who emerged victorious.

Based on these two paragraphs, is it clear who won the war? A quick read would seem to suggest that in this scenario President Snow prevailed in the war with the rebels. However, a closer read reveals that nothing here precludes these events from describing a world where the rebels won the war and President Coin finally has the chance to give Panem a new leader.

Though she obviously does not survive the end of *Mockingjay*, a world that she governs could well turn out to be similar to life under President Snow. This introductory thought experiment serves to establish just how closely President Coin's leadership mirrors that of President Snow. Her shared title offers a clue to the complicated (and complicating) role she plays for the rebels. On the one hand, she instills a level of discipline in District Thirteen that allows the rebellion to simmer for years. When Katniss shows up, President Coin's discipline not only provides a safe haven from which the rebellion can unfold, it also surrounds the rebel leaders with a well-trained military force to fight the war.

8. President Coin

Despite the benefits she brings to the rebel cause, there is an unmistakable quality about President Coin that makes her almost impossible to root for. Lindsey Issow Averill provides an accurate summary of why this is the case: "Although President Coin leads the resistance, she uses the same problematic strategies that define President Snow's politics. She jails and tortures innocent people (Katniss's prep team), she drops bombs on her own people (and Prim and other rebel medics), and she's prepared to sacrifice more innocent children."[1] When we stop and think about the decisions President Coin makes, we see a familiar and problematic use of violence. We see a willingness to use life as a means to an end that is narrowly conceived. When a leader is willing to cause the deaths of those who are fighting on her behalf, we should consider her leadership along the same critical lines with which we brought into focus the deeply troubling dynamics that the rebels are fighting against. Katniss makes the problem clear at the beginning of *Mockingjay*: "In some ways, District 13 is even more controlling than the Capitol."[2]

Part of the reason President Coin gets away with her disregard for those whom she governs lies in the Spartan nature of life in District Thirteen. Luxury is almost impossible because of the district's isolation. Building a sustainable society underground and under constant threat of military action demands some of the sacrifices that President Coin asks of everyone. To her credit, she does not seem to play favorites with anyone. The rules in place to ration out every aspect of life in District Thirteen do not seem bendable. In fact, the concessions Katniss wrings from President Coin in the early stages of *Mockingjay* seem to be the only exceptions to the way things are done in District Thirteen.

When contrasted with life in Capitol, it seems easy to sympathize with President Coin. She does a decent job with the hand she has been dealt. To survive in the conditions she must manage would seem to be based on a virtue that is decidedly absent in the Capitol. For President Coin, food must be dolled out on the basis of needed calories. In the Capitol, President Snow's parties have drinks that will induce vomiting so that people can each as much as they want with no concern for nutrition. Despite the very different pictures we see in the capitols of each side to this war, Christina Van Dyk argues that we should actually see the Capitol and District Thirteen as defined by consonant political realities: "At first blush, the hidden discipline and excessive luxury of the

The Politics of *The Hunger Games*

Capitol look nothing like the incredibly regimented life of District 13. But both have the same outcome: a lack of genuine autonomy that leaves the citizens with only those outlets for self-expression that are approved and tightly controlled by their governments."[3] Regardless of the specifics, we find life lived in circumstances defined by a heavy political hand. Van Dyk's specific insight that neither the Capitol nor District Thirteen allow the autonomy that lies at the heart of a healthy politics demands a focused examination of President Coin.

At the core of her politics, we find an imbalance that smothers the kinds of principles that inspire political action. President Coin, like President Snow, does not rely on encouraging the best among those who live in District Thirteen. Rather, her main focus seems to be proactively eliminating anything that might disrupt her carefully crafted plans. The consequence is a kind of political flat lining. Even the refugees from other districts who take shelter in District Thirteen seem to converge on a somewhat listless way of going about life. There is an upside to this state of affairs in that District Thirteen's residents do remain calm in the face of the Capitol's threat. When the Capitol bombs the district, the residents efficiently activate an evacuation more deeply into the ground without casualties. Once in the emergency shelter, however, life quickly regresses to the monotonous scheduling Katniss so desperately tries to avoid.

This discipline comes at a cost, a fact made plain when we get to see a flash of the sorts of things that make life bearable. At Finnick's and Annie's wedding, we see Katniss reveal a skill that few probably guessed she had prior to the wedding. Katniss, along with just about everyone else from District Twelve, can dance. Katniss explains this oddity with obvious pride: "We may have been the smallest, poorest district in Panem, but we know how to dance."[4] The value of this skill in light of that poverty is clear: "Dancing transforms us."[5] Finding a way to celebrate amidst difficult circumstances is a cultural legacy with biblical roots. District Twelve's embrace of dancing as a way to enjoy life echoes strongly the balance of good and bad outlined in the famous third chapter of Ecclesiastes. Katniss could easily be quoting the famous introductory lines: "For everything there is a season, and a time for every matter under heaven."[6] Life is not all positive; tears balance out the times that make us smile.

8. President Coin

In celebration of Finnick and Annie, everyone who lives in District Thirteen has the chance to set aside the strain of living beneath the ground. We can hear the words in Ecclesiastes beating beneath the District Twelve residents' feet as they show others how to do one of life's great pleasures: "there is a time to weep, and a time to laugh; a time to mourn, and a time to dance."[7] The cold realities of life underground do not disappear, but dancing allows everyone to remember that joy that joy can be found amidst despair. Importantly, this reminder comes from outside District Thirteen. This is not a message President Coin gives (and, most likely, it is not a message she could give if she tried). Katniss and her fellow residents from District Twelve make clear in their celebration the ways that President Coin cancels out the positive counterweights to the somber realities outlined in Ecclesiastes and lived out in District Thirteen every single day.

The downside of this lack of energy is that as the rebellion's legal leader, President Coin simply cannot inspire a movement that will chant for liberty or death. Katniss is the spark, but Katniss's decision to accept the role as the rebels' Mockingjay does not come about because President Coin appeals to the things Katniss values. On the contrary, Katniss only makes the decision by openly challenging President Coin with a list of demands to play a role that she could ultimately do on her own. Amazingly, Katniss gets everything she wants with very little significant compromise. President Coin attaches conditions, but none erase the outright challenge to her established authority as the rebel leader in name.

The shock we perceive amidst those in the room (and even Katniss hints as her nerves) results in part from the brash nature of Katniss's demands. The requests themselves turn out to be acceptable; we can assume this because President Coin agrees to them. The very act of speaking a way that disagrees with President Coin marks this exchange as significant. Simply put, people do not challenge President Coin. She is in charge and the unstated expectation is that her word is final even before it is spoken

What we find here is a hint of a political tactic that links President Coin and President Snow. A blanket unwillingness to question a political leader reveals an underlying fear of punishment. This fear, though unspoken, says a lot about life in District Thirteen. Aristotle offers a helpful summary of how to think about this lingering fear: "*Fear* is an occasion which leads to sedition among two classes of person-wrongdoers, who are afraid of punishment; and persons expecting to suffer wrong, who are anxious to anticipate what they expect."[8] The distinction Aristotle offers helps to identify when fear is in the air even if no one states that s/he is afraid. The anticipation of punishment defines a society framed by fear. Aristotle helps us to focus not on those who expect punishment for wrongdoing; is generally the norm in any society where there is some level of order. The telling point lies in the anxiety people experience when they do nothing wrong. The exchange between Katniss and Coin is tense in part an earnest and legitimate request anticipates in everyone's eyes that Katniss will be punished for insubordination. In other words, anxiety reflects the concern that justifiable actions will be punished as thought they are wrong. Fear marks the mindset that punishment can come from both right and wrong actions, which in turn captures the mindset we see in those who interact with President Coin.

Fear serves President Snow well, a fact we saw in the discussion of how Machiavelli's famous dictum "it is better to be feared than loved" conveys the essence of President Snow's political mindset. Given the similarities between President Snow and President Coin, a return to Machiavelli's *The Prince* will prove helpful. Specifically, Machiavelli speaks to the assumptions about the governed that lead to a politics of fear: "in constituting and legislating for a commonwealth it must needs be taken for granted that all men are wicked and that they will always give vent to the malignity that Is in their minds when opportunity offers."[9] In short, Machiavelli advises rulers to assume the people under their influence are intrinsically tuned to bad actions. This, in turn connects to the discussion of Hobbes' contributions to political philosophy. When faced with wicked people, rulers should emphasize security to minimize the risk that our supposedly negative dispositions pose to the political elite. By these standards, President Coin outshines President Snow. There is no dissent in District Thirteen, which suggests that her efforts to head off the potential for internal conflict is successful in its extremism.

Despite the outward success in controlling District Thirteen, President Coin encounters the same problem that President Snow cannot avoid: the impact someone who does not fit within their political frame-

8. President Coin

work can have. Katniss quickly upends the careful discipline in District Thirteen and this is exactly what Machiavelli says will prove inevitable. He writes: "The evil dispositions often do not show themselves for a time is due to a hidden cause which those fail to perceive who have had no experience of the opposite; but in time—which is said to be the father of all truth—it reveals itself."[10] One explanation for the unavoidable appearance of truth can be found in the logical outcome of the assumption that everyone is wicked. If this is the case, and if this is the guiding principle for governing the residents of District Thirteen, then President Coin paints herself into a corner. By her own political argument she is also a constant risk, intrinsically inclined to self-interest, and thus a threat to a stable political order.

Katniss is the one who recognizes this clearly. In time, others gradually follow Katniss's lead in their willingness to throw off President Coin's authority. One of the most telling examples of the shift in allegiance away from President Coin to Katniss occurs after the rebels have successfully taken the Capitol. President Snow has been sentenced to death and awaits execution while Katniss recovers from her injuries. Gradually she emerges from her place of recovery to go see President Snow. When she reaches the door the room where President Snow is locked up, guards prevent her from entering. After the first guard tells her that she cannot go in the room, the second guard adds: "You can't go in, Soldier Everdeen. President's orders."[11] President Coin does not want anyone to disrupt her plan of action for bringing about justice for President Snow. As a result, even the person who was instrumental in bringing about the rebels' victory cannot go in the room. The mistrust is obvious. Despite the success Katniss brings about, she remains just another solider whom President Coin will not allow to act outside of an established protocol (which is ultimately self-serving).

We wait with Katniss, though given the basis of the order, there is no reason to expect she will be able to enter the room. However, a voice emerges to override President Coin's order. Paylor, who knows Katniss from the heroic display at the District Eight hospital, tells the guards: "Let her go in."[12] Paylor demands that Katniss be allowed to do what President Coin said was not allowed. Paylor elaborates to the guards: "On my authority…. She has a right to anything behind that door."[13] There is no legal and/or military authority for this command as President Coin has the final say on such matters. Further, though she is a respected solider, Paylor is not a member of the rebels' executive leadership. The explanation, then, does not seem like the kind of thing the guards would yield to given that they know who Katniss is and enforce the prohibition against entering the room with President Snow. However, as Katniss remarks in her narration after Paylor speaks up, "These are [Paylor's] soldiers, not Coin's."[14] The discipline President Coin demands does not outweigh the virtues that rule on the battlefield. Loyalty does not come with the title of President. Loyalty remains something that leaders earn and Paylor commands this respect from the guards.

Moreover, Katniss has earned respect from Paylor, which explains the truly interesting bit of Paylor's explanation to the guards. Specifically, Paylor acknowledges Katniss's contribution the one who led the rebels to victory. She has earned the right to do what she wants, even if what she wants violates a direct order from President Coin. The official rules thus give way to an unspoken but ultimately more important way of deciding who is in charge. Paylor allows Katniss to enter because of her leadership both in the early stages when she speaks to a hospital in need of hope and at the conclusion of a very difficult military campaign.

Once inside, Katniss recognizes something is out of place in President Snow's supposed cell. The fact that he awaits his fate in relative comfort strikes her as misplaced given his crimes. As she processes her first impressions, however, the reason behind his cozy cell becomes apparent. Katniss narrates: "I'd supposed he would be secured in the deepest dungeon that the Capitol had to offer, not cradled in the lap of luxury. Yet Coin left him here. To set a precedent, I guess. So that if in the future she ever fell from grace, it would be understood that presidents—even the most despicable—get special treatment."[15] President Coin reveals in her choices about President Snow's imprisonment an underlying inequality. She does not count herself as bound by the same restrictions she imposes on everyone else. Though she maintains an outward appearance to the contrary, hidden behind a locked door Katniss realizes that President Coin very much anticipates political power of the kind President Snow exercise. To cement the comparison, President Coin makes sure that President Snow rests comfortably just in case she should ever find the tables turned. If she ever falls from power, she wants the next ruler to know that she gave due preferential treatment to her colleague.

8. President Coin

President Snow's first remarks to Katniss offer his condolences for Prim's death. Katniss reacts in a way that assumes President Snow is still playing his political game. He is still trying to harm her and through psychological warfare. His supposed sympathy for her loss is, in Katniss's eyes, obscene in its inauthenticity (though by the end of the interaction at the conclusion of *Mockingjay* President Snow reprimands Katniss for doubting his honesty; he states again that he they had an agreement not to lie on another.

Seeing Katniss's response to his serious expression of sympathy, President Snow wastes little time in confirming the hunch Katniss has when she enters the room. He reiterates that he sees her death as unnecessary. He tells her: "So wasteful, so unnecessary."[16] He then explains that at the point the parachutes exploded, killing Prim and so many others, he was prepared to surrender. His word choice catches Katniss's attention; she cannot figure out what President Snow means when he narrates that "they"[17] caused the explosion.

The next portion of President Snow's remarks serve in essence to expose President Coin for who she really is. As Katniss struggles to put the pieces together regarding what happened, President Snow explains what does not quite make sense: "Forget the obvious fact that if I'd had a working hovercraft at my disposal, I'd have been using it to make an escape. But that aside, what purpose could it have served? We both know I'm not above killing children, but I'm not wasteful. I take life for very specific reasons. And there was no reason for me to destroy a pen full of Capitol children."[18] Beneath the surface of terrible violence—bombing children who are working medics—we see President Coin's cold self-interest, though, unexpectedly, the source of this revelation is President Snow. He would have saved himself happily and left the consequences of the war for others to handle. Further, he had nothing to gain by killing those children. We see, then, the honesty President Snow announces when he first talks with Katniss at the beginning of *Catching Fire*. He has absolutely no problem killing children because it is part of his political tool kit. The fact that he does not shy away from the most damning accusation he faces while awaiting execution highlights that the is telling the truth in this exchange.

Katniss resists the obvious. "He's lying"[19] she tells herself. This way of understanding the death of her sister is more palatable than the actual

The Politics of *The Hunger Games*

truth, which she cannot avoid forever. President Coin ordered the bombing that killed so many children. In its outcome, President Coin's decision is no different than the Hunger Games. The motivation is the same as well. President Coin saw in the bombing the chance to advance her own political ambition. The difference that Katniss must comes to terms with is that President Snow accepts responsibility for his actions while President Coin attempts to blame someone else for all those deaths. The difference is subtle, but important (and it does not excuse the outcome; obviously bombing children is wrong). President Coin's willingness to kill children will be an even worse scenario for the political reality in Panem after the way. The same tactics will be on the table; she just will not be honest about her willingness to use them.

The point here is not to argue that President Snow is a moral paragon. The key takeaway in the context of the current discussion is that President Snow reveals President Coin's true character. When President Snow walks Katniss through the bombing that killed Prim, he exposes a truth that will ultimately drive her actions once she is set to kill President Snow. In short, if it is possible, President Coin is actually a worse political leader than President Snow in that she uses fear as a means to serve her ends and then tries to hide this fact.

The face-to-face between Katniss and President Snow brings together many different political threads from The Hunger Games series. One of the key takeaways, however, is a bit unexpected. The acknowledgement of wrongdoing is indirect but clear. President Snow confesses to Katniss the terrible things he happily did for his own purposes without any way of benefiting from doing so. President Coin is the only one who can alter what will inevitably happen, so the honesty toward Katniss is legitimate. More importantly, this honesty casts an important light on what Katniss can expect from life in a Panem ruled by President Coin. In essence President Snow presents himself as an example of what is to come in order to make sure she knows that President Coin is no different at her core. If anyone gets the strategies that President Coin is using and the decisions she has made to consolidate her power, it is President Snow. We do not have to like him, but we should take his final message seriously. A politics of fear has clear consequences, something Katniss knows well based on her experiences. The person who would use fear against the people s/he governs should be treated with the utmost suspicion.

8. President Coin

Ascending the political ranks to the point of ruling over an entire country invariably brings power into someone's hands. There is simply no way to avoid the fact that the person in charge will have more influence than just about everyone else. There is, in other words, an inevitable inequality when it comes to political influence (though, importantly, this inequality should not impact the foundational equality that all people have a right to). The strange thing about President Coin is that she could achieve a lot of her goals without resorting to the tactics she does. President Snow himself explains to Katniss that the rebels had won the fight before President Coin bombed a bunch of children.

The problem lies in the way power can lead to a mindset that will not allow some inequality to coexist with rights that ensure a foundational equality of all people. Aristotle helps us understand the issue: "The quality of being happy is not the same order as the quality of being even. The quality of being even may exist in a whole without existing in either of its parts: the quality of being happy cannot."[20] When the notions of happiness and equality are conflated, there is an almost inevitable need to choose one over the other. If a person in a position of influence must tend toward one or the other, we can expect s/he will opt for a path that protects her/his happiness first. We see this clearly with President Coin. Her interests not only supersede the basic rights of everyone else, they also align her with a way of thinking that actively encourages inequality.

For Aristotle, the tilt toward inequality locates a society's political shortcomings in the decisions of those who cannot ensure happiness for everyone. He writes: "It is impossible for the whole of a state to be happy unless most of its parts, or all, or at any rate some, are happy."[21] Assuming that one's own happiness takes precedent over the happiness of others will lead to decisions that protect the happiness of a few at the expense of the many. This, in turn, ensures that there will always be unhappiness in a population. So long as unhappiness exists, divisions of power, wealth, and other social markers will become toxic within a culture. They need not be. If the happiness of those with less can be seen as the same in kind (and not necessarily quantity), then political leaders can make decisions that will bring about their own happiness along with the happiness of others. In being deceitful and treating her power as independent of the others under her guise, President Coin sets the postwar Panem world toward inevitable conflict.

Ironically, it takes someone at the extreme end of inequality to make Katniss realize this. President Snow helps Katniss (and us) realize the danger of President Coin's political mindset. This is an important consideration in thinking about the reasons that Katniss ultimately decides to assassinate President Coin. Once the pageantry of the event has been orchestrated, much like the reaping, Katniss steps in the public view in order to experience the demand she asked for in agreeing to be the Mockingjay. She gets to kill President Snow. At the moment when the script duly asks her to fulfill her task, she realizes that the script's author has an ulterior motive. As her bow strains, an arrow pointed at President Snow, Katniss finally realizes what President Snow has been saying about President Coin. She accepts his honesty and perhaps the most unexpected (and politically significant) moment in the entire series she improvises. "The point of my arrow shifts upward. I release the string. And President Coin collapses over the side of the balcony and plunges to the ground. Dead."[22] Like President Snow, President Coin cannot outrun the consequences of her decisions. She dies the death a lot of us probably think she deserves. At the same time, the fact that Katniss kills President Coin should have serious ramifications. However, she is home after a couple of days of captivity. Why? She killed President Coin in cold blood in front of an entire nation. What can we make of this unexpected twist?

Two things come together in Katniss's assassination of President Coin. The first is that President Coin's mistakes catch up to her. She bets on fear and Katniss shows one final time that fear cannot inspire people. Further, when given a choice of following fear or embracing hope, people will choose the latter because at the heart of politics they expect and desire someone who can speak to values that are lasting and can secure a good life for everyone.

If we continue to rewind the events at the end of *Mockingjay*, this message from President Coin verifies the conclusion Katniss comes to regarding President Coin's motivations when she sends Peeta to replace Soldier Leeg 2 after she dies on the Capitol streets. The crack rebel team needs to be at full strength, so President Coin sends Peeta—who up to the point has shown a willingness to kill Katniss because of his torture at the hands of President Snow—to fill out the roster. There seems to be a consensus among the prior team members that Peeta is a dangerous

8. President Coin

replacement, but, Peeta makes clear any such concerns have been overruled. He announces on his arrival that Boggs's calls to protest are useless. "'It won't matter,' Peeta tells the rest of us. 'The president assigned me herself. She decided the propos needed some heating up.'"[23] Katniss knows immediately what President Coin's goal is. She narrates: "if Coin sent Peeta here, she's decided something else as well. That I'm of more use to her dead than alive."[24] This is a stunningly destructive act. Under the guise of giving the rebels' best military team needed manpower, President Coin sets in motion her plan to kill off Katniss. The decision echoes a political strategy that we have seen elsewhere, namely in Herod and President Coin. Each of these rulers perceives that killing off a threat can bring about a political benefit. This expected outcome overrides the obvious risks of the plan should it not work (and it never does) and it pretends that other, more lasting ways of rallying people are not possible. In a way this last assumption is true. It simply does not acknowledge that their own leadership the reason such inspiration is not possible.

On some level, President Coin understands what people want, even if she cannot provide it herself. This explains her rationale for getting Katniss to be the Mockingjay. The motivation for this symbol is to inspire the rebels, but the assumptions behind the inspiration President Coin envisions ultimately serve to expose her anticipated hope as fraudulent. After an explosion on the streets of the Capitol as the rebels advance, everyone assumes that Katniss and her team are dead. President Snow even airs a statement pointing out this perceived outcome. Ever the shadow to President Snow, President Coin then gets Beattee to air a message regarding Katniss's death. President Coin herself provides the climactic statement: "Dead or alive, Katniss Everdeen will remain the face of this rebellion. If ever you waver in your resolve, think of the Mockingjay, and in her you will find the strength you need to rid Panem of its oppressors."[25] For President Coin, Katniss's memory should live on as a martyr for the cause of freedom (importantly, Boggs is the one who first uses this term to explain a motivation for the rebels' propos; martyrs who plan their death in hopes of being a martyr tend to be received as inauthentic). Ironically, there is a lot of truth in these words. Katniss is the symbol of liberation from oppression; the thing President Coin misses is that this message ultimately lumps her in with those oppressors.

When we look back at this message after what President Snow reveals about President Coin, we can see what she is really after in making this statement so quickly. She needs Katniss to encourage the strength that her own leadership is not able to generate. President Coin must recognize that this equation ultimately proves that Katniss is more important to the rebellion, so in fact a dead Katniss is really the preferred outcome for inspiring hope. A martyr, in other words, provides a symbol without the living presence of someone who can rally a nation. The thing with martyrs is that they need to be the ones who decide to sacrifice themselves. When a tyrant kills a person in hopes of manufacturing such a sacrifice, s/he is only deceiving her/himself.

In the end, self-deception characterizes President Coin. She accomplishes a lot to gather resources and wait for the right time to unleash the rebels' military counter to President Snow's tyranny. At this point, we can still affirm her as a good leader. However, effective and efficient are not the same things as morally sound. The events that unfold after the rebellion start make clear that such praise is misplaced. President Coin is, in the end, no different than President Snow. She resorts to the same violence and the same fear in hopes of achieving the same things. She even recognizes and tacitly admits that Katniss provides the rebels with the inspiration they really need. Her response to this shows her political failure in with respect to the things that really matter. She cannot ignite the passion that drives a politics in search of an honorable life, so she hides behind her own failures in hopes that she can kill off those who might expose her weakness. As a result, the rebels' final victory comes when President Coin crumples beneath the weight of Katniss's arrow.

9. The Capitol's Residents

Part of what makes The Hunger Games series so appealing is the way Collins invites readers into a challenging world from Katniss's perspective. Her age, her life in District Twelve, and her relationships are just a few of the things that make the books so fascinating to read. Our ability to sympathize with her fight against President Snow stems in large part from the intimate look we get at how his actions affect not only her outward actions, but also her inward thoughts.

As the basis for understanding the political climate in Panem, Katniss's perspective opens into many different points of interest. The preceding chapters in this book show the depth of the political insights Katniss's viewpoint offers. At the same time there have been moments where the ability to step outside that perspective in the movies versions of The Hunger Games series provides important considerations. Politics is not just a matter that concerns District Twelve, Katniss, or the handful of rebels we get to know well. The ability to offer different perspectives that are unavailable in the books because they are written from Katniss's perspective is one of the significant ways the films have enhanced the discussion of political themes throughout The Hunger Games series.

Given the value of multiple perspectives, particularly in thinking about politics, this chapter will attempt to understand in a bit more detail an unspoken perspective in Panem: that of the citizens in the Capitol. Alongside Katniss, it is easy to see the Capitol's citizens as complicit with the fear and violence President Snow exhibits. However, simply lumping the Capitol's everyday citizens in with a detached tyrant is a bit simplistic. As Chad William Timm points out clearly, we should stop and consider what those who live in the Capitol think about a variety of things: "Our knowledge of the Capitol is limited to reports from Katniss, an outsider, so we don't know about all the forms of cultural capital that Capitol residents value."[1] This matters because of the impact our own cultural experiences have on our identities. Further, Sam Sommers explains in *Situations Matter: Understanding How Context Transforms Your World*, where we come from cannot be separated from who we are: "The culture in which you grow up teaches you how to think about yourself through both explicit instruction and more subtle reminders."[2] The impact our surroundings have may not always be visible, but each of us carries in our way of understanding the world a collection of cultural values that matters. There are ways of thinking about the world that lie behind the heavily made up faces of those whom Katniss routinely scorns.

With respect to the specific realm of politics, it is worth recalling some of the key signposts that have guiding the discussions in the previous chapters. As a social matter, politics ultimately involves everyone. Thus, the citizens who live in the Capitol also go about life within the troubling realities we have criticized in examining President Snow's political mindset. There is a very real threat of violence out in the Districts. It is easy to assume that this threat does not exist in the same way in the Capitol, but the assumption rests on the fact that we simply do not have access to the perspectives of those who can speak to the matter.

Though rigorous, Jeffrey Stout's book on moral diversity, *Ethics After Babel: The Languages of Morals and Their Discontents*, provides a helpful framework for traversing what on the surface appears to be difficult ethical ground. It is easy to reject the notion that the Capitol's citizens are morally culpable for watching and enjoying the Hunger Games. However, Stout cautions that moral questions are questions because they do not always have a clear answer. Challenging issues almost always reveal that there are multiple and legitimate perspectives. According to Stout: "there are many moral languages in use around us, each with its own assumptions about reality and complicit in a distinct way of life, and granted that our condition is often one of discord and misunderstanding."[3] The important point to lift out of Stout's claim here is the importance of our assumptions in articulating moral ideas (and ideals). Further, Stout highlights what we see frequently in thinking about Katniss's own understanding of the world. Personal experience goes a long way toward explaining why we think the way we do.

When Katniss enters the Arena for the first time, she does so as a tribute within an established tradition. Given the number of times the

9. The Capitol's Residents

Games have occurred, we find that multiple generations of citizens will grown up and lived adult lives in the shadow of a political world where having kids fight to the death is normal. This is not to say that those who think that the Hunger Games have always been there so there is no problem have a moral escape hatch. Rather, the point is to identify the basis for the assumptions that will explain why someone thinks this way. The same rigid mindset presumably characterizes those living in the Capitol. If they have only known the Games as entertainment, they will have a difficult time envisioning a different perspective on the matter. Absent intervention, it becomes difficult to articulate a scenario that would lead to a different way of thinking about the world. Their assumptions, in other words, have not encountered a political alternative to the world they know. Further, the absence of any such alternative stems directly from President Snow's totalizing grip on power. We can assume his focus on restricting political thought and action covers the Capitol's residents as well as the districts. Given this reality, it makes sense (even if there remains a moral question) that the Capitol citizens are stuck in their ways.

This kind of problem emerges forcefully when we think about Effie. She is very much a part of the Capitol world; she embraces fully the culture surrounding the Hunger Games. As a result, she interacts with Katniss from a perspective that sees the Hunger Games as bringing about good things. When she is riding on the train with Katniss during the Victory Tour, Effie (once again) calls attention to the material luxuries available. She then tells Katniss to enjoy it because she has "earned it."[4] Katniss responds harshly: "Yes, by killing people."[5] This clash of perspective highlights just how far apart these two worlds are. The same thing is diametrically opposed in each person's understanding of what the Victory Tour means.

At the same time, we see that Effie is not a one-dimensional character. She does struggle with her place at the intersection of these two worlds. She clearly has an emotional attachment to the "team"[6] from District Twelve that emerges throughout the *Catching Fire* movie. Just before Peeta and Katniss will go back into the Arena, she brings Haymitch a gold bracelet and Peeta a gold locket to match Katniss's gold pin and her gold hair. Her gold token is absurd, but it offers a way for her to include herself in a group that would probably be justified in turning their backs on her. Even when she is in the Spartan world of District Thirteen in the *Mockingjay* film, we see Effie take strides toward understanding a world different than her own. The facial expressions she shows as Haymitch discusses the Mockingjay costume Cinna designed and the strategy for the propos indicate that she is, on the whole, a positive presence in the room (and she manages to twist a gray rag into something resembling the kind of extreme hats she prefers).[7]

The broad point to make, then, is to caution against rejecting someone else's perspective out of hand. Someone else's moral language may well turn out to be bankrupt, but we should arrive at this conclusion after considering what they might think about a given issue. Assuming that someone's moral perspective lacks legitimacy is a mindset that reflects the same kind of problematic things President Snow does. Recent events in Ferguson, Missouri, provide a prominent example of this point. After Darren Wilson, a police officer, shot Michael Brown, an unarmed teenager, protests and riots erupted. There were immediately suspicions as to motives for the shooting and the possibility of justice for the victim. Perhaps the crucial element of the event is the fact that Officer Wilson is white and the victim is black. As such, the question of whether force was justified from a legal perspective passed through a moral and cultural question of race.

A grand jury was convened. The grand jury declined to indict Officer Wilson, which led to further demonstrations on the streets of Ferguson. One particular statement to highlight in the context of the current discussion is the decision by five members of the St. Louis Rams, a professional football team, to make a very public statement about Michael Brown's death. As they were introduced before a game against the Oakland Raiders, five players came onto the field and assumed a "hands up and don't shoot" posture. The image recalled the way some witnesses describe Michael Brown acting as he was shot. The message the Rams players wanted to send was clear: they felt the grand jury's decision not to indict Officer Wilson was based on race and a political structure that would not give Michael Brown justice.

The St. Louis Police Officers Association (SLPOA) responded forcefully to what the Rams players did. From the outset, the SLPOA statement reveals assumptions that dismiss out of hand the moral framework out of which the Rams players acted. The statement reads: "The St. Louis

9. The Capitol's Residents

Police Officers Association is profoundly disappointed with the members of the St. Louis Rams football team who chose to ignore the mountains of evidence released from the St. Louis County Grand Jury this week and engage in a display that police officers around the nation found tasteless, offensive and inflammatory."[8] In the SLPOA's opinion, the decision to assume the "hands up and don't shoot" position ignores the legal conclusion the grand jury reached. The players, of course, knew what the decision was and made their statement anyway. They were not engaging in a legal conversation; they were making a moral and cultural statement that was based on fact. An unarmed black teenager had been shot dead.

The telling moments in the SLPOA statement emerge as it lays out its grievance. The statement continues: "it is unthinkable that hometown athletes would so publicly perpetuate a narrative that has been disproven over-and-over again."[9] The narrative in this case is the one that exonerates the police officer involved in the shooting without questioning whether the grand jury's decision had any suspect elements.[10] In short, the supposedly objective standard by which protests should be measured includes only one moral perspective.

How this moral high ground is claimed reveals the core point in this example. The SLPOA Business Manager, Jeff Roorda, specifically cited addresses the political foundation for the Rams players' gesture. The SLPOA statement includes Roorda's insights on free speech: "I know that there are those that will say that these players are simply exercising their First Amendment rights. Well I've got news for people who think that way, cops have first amendment rights too, and we plan to exercise ours."[11] Two crucial assumptions surface in Roorda's remarks. First, he acknowledges an established legal and moral right the players hold to say what they want about the events that happened. The players have a right to say what they want. However, Roorda acknowledges their First Amendment rights to suggest that they are not a legitimate basis for articulating their understanding of what happened to Michael Brown. The second point is more subtle and ultimately more damaging. Roorda cites the officers' rights to free speech (though the specific manifestation of those rights in the statement as made is unclear) as a zero-sum counter to the Rams players. In other words, Roorda is claiming that the police officers' rights to free speech carry more weight than the Rams' players' same rights. The unstated logic is the assumption that given two different perspectives on what happened, only one side should be accepted as legitimate in the moral conversation surrounding the death of an unarmed teenager at the hands of one of Roorda's "brothers."[12]

The bias is obvious, yet Roorda and the entire SLPOA statement show no awareness of the blatant double standard its statement rests upon. One problem the Rams players' want to call attention to is the way police officers often get an unchecked benefit of the doubt when unarmed people are shot. In many instances the racial identities of the parties involved reflect a long-standing racial dynamic that privileges white perspectives in America. Because a different perspective—one that gives the victim and his cultural memory an equal moral voice—challenges the SPLOA narrative, Roorda will quickly and completely dismiss what the Rams players did as conflicting directly with his own set of values. Crucially, he does so on the basis of a moral claim, the right to free speech, that he denies the same right to others in order to justify his conclusion.

This is precisely the approach that Stout cautions against in articulating a basis for productive political discourse. Stout states: "there are distinct moral languages and [we must] consider implications for our conception of comparative ethics, moral philosophy, constructive moral thought, and moral change."[13] Again, in moral matters we should expect varied perspectives that are based on specific experiential matters that cannot be discarded just because they challenge an existing mindset. In other words, we considered how others understand a series of events, we must be careful not to let the difference of another perspective be dismissed just because it does not line up with our own perspective. For Katniss and the rest of the rebels, this means that they should consider how the citizens who live in the Capitol understand life under the rule of President Snow.

There is a clear question that surfaces when we stop and think about how politics might be understood in the eyes of those Capitol residents. Specifically, an important question exists about whether they ultimately support the Hunger Games and, therefore, carry moral responsibility for what happens in the Arena. Do the Capitol's citizens have an obligation to stop watching the Hunger Games in order to help bring them to a halt? The extent to which a population can—or should—share guilt

9. The Capitol's Residents

for the impact their political leader has warrants consideration and this chapter will attempt to shed some light on the matter.

The challenge of different moral voices within a political context comes in the form of finding consensus. If different perspectives claim exclusive understandings of an issue, then moral uncertainly results. Further, as we have just seen the more powerful voice in terms of social and political standing will tend to break these impasses by claiming to be right. The implication, of course, is that the other side is necessarily wrong. There exists, then, an important question regarding the ability to balancing competing moral claims.

Niebuhr recognizes the challenge when the goal is to affirm different ways of thinking about an issue. If we take some objective and virtuous standard as the goal of thinking about our common moral voice, then we immediately find ourselves in a tense situation because within a population there will be different opinions. According to Niebuhr, this risks frustrating our honest attempts to solve difficult moral questions. He writes: "The development of social justice does depend to some degree upon the extension of rationality. But the limits of reason make it inevitable that pure moral action, particularly in the intricate, complex and collective relationships, should be an impossible goal."[14] Though we may want to think through matters objectively (i.e. with our reason), often these attempts will bump up against conditions that undermine our reason. Anger, for example, can frustrate attempts to compromise with a perspective that is responsible for suffering. The important thing in Niebuhr's comments is the implicit acknowledgement that sometimes reason cannot be the only factor in defining what is "right." Anger and other emotions can and should be legitimate considerations. Conflict-free relationships are impossible because sometimes resolving conflict can ask someone to deny her/his legitimate experiences and resulting perspectives. To return briefly to the discussion above from Ferguson, the result of the grand jury, which is a reasonable conclusion based on the law, cannot simply be taken as "truth" because doing so would deny the voices of those who feel Michael Brown did not get justice.

We see a quick willingness to deny other perspectives throughout The Hunger Games series. The surprising thing comes with the realization that the rebels are just as culpable of considering that Capitol residents should not be condemned as a matter of course. Gale, who knows a bit about suffering himself, shows this characteristic when he is hunting above District Thirteen with Katniss. He asks her why she is so concerned about her prep team, which she knows at this point has been imprisoned and tortured. Based on her experience, the prep team has not simply, as Gale puts it, "spent the last year prettying [her] up for slaughter."[15] The challenge is clear and absolute. They played a role in the Hunger Games, so they deserve whatever suffering they are now enduring.

Katniss responds by acknowledging that the question of guilt is not this simple. She tells sputters out a response: "It's more complicated than that. I know them. They're not evil or cruel. They're not even smart. Hurting them, it's like hurting children. They don't see.... I mean they don't know...."[16] Katniss asks Gale to recognize a couple of important points both in this moment and in the broader context of this chapter. The first is that he condemns them in the abstract. He assumes things about their character without ever having interacted with them. Because she knows these people personally, Katniss can see past their complicit roles in the Hunger Games. Further, she argues for a higher standard of proof when it comes to assigning responsibility. They simply do not understand that the Hunger Games is part of a larger political game, so to treat them as willing participants in that broader game is unfair. In fact, judging them in this way ignores the motivations for their actions: trying to stay alive.

The basis for her attitude is twofold. First, Katniss knows the very real suffering of the Arena and thus she rejects out of hand an argument that casts the prep team in a similar role as the tributes. They are pawns, not proactive actors in President Snow's political world. Second, she tells Gale that: "they don't view [The Hunger Games] the way we do.... They're raised on it and—."[17] Though she has trouble processing her argument, Katniss acknowledges internally that she is "defending"[18] the prep team. Importantly, this is not a full-throated statement that they are blameless. Rather, it is an honest attempt from Katniss, based on her own experiences, to understand the specifically human aspects of the Hunger Games from a perspective other than her own.

When we pit one individual's experiences against another's in an attempt to determine who is right, we encounter biases that can easily be taken as objective. In this scene, Katniss's understanding of the Capi-

9. The Capitol's Residents

tol's residents does not account for a different perspective. We have to account for other perspectives, particularly when there is a commonality as there is here. The motivation for Katniss's critique is what President Snow has done to her and she disperses her justifiable anger and other emotions in response to President Snow across everyone else in the Capitol. As Niebuhr cautions, this necessarily means that we cannot treat Katniss's conclusions as immediately applicable because her moral thought process is not entirely thorough.

The understandable biases in Katniss's reaction translate into a broader social dynamic that complicates how she (and therefore we) views those Capitol citizens. Niebuhr explains: "Men will never be wholly reasonable, and the proportion of reason to impulse becomes increasingly negative when we proceed from the life of individuals to that of social groups, among whom a common mind and purpose is always more or less inchoate and transitory, and who depend therefore on a common impulse to bind them together."[19] Societies form around shared values. Though these values are often positive, they can also be negative and/or tinged with a troubling bias. Police officers overwhelmingly constitute a positive force in our lives, but this characterization can also cause a collectively negative response to the idea that individual police officers may have run afoul of what we consider acceptable.

In other words, we often have a hard time separating the individual from the group of which that individual is a part. The thing that binds us together—a social understanding of a group of people—can prevent us from thinking about individuals within that collective in terms other than those that apply broadly. When we hear what Katniss has to say about her prep team, we can see that she glosses over what they might think individually to assume that they think in the same way and that their way of thinking supports President Snow just because they live in the Capitol. What we do not read about is Katniss *asking* anyone on her prep team what s/he thinks about President Snow. If she were really interested in a thorough moral analysis of what those in the Capitol believe, this would seem like a reasonable question to ask. We can understand why she does not pause to ask this kind of thing, but we should not mistake that kind of understanding as some kind of proof that the prep team members lack a moral compass.

The probable reason why Katniss does not explore how Capitol citizens think about President Snow is that she cannot untie herself from the experiences that define her as a citizen of District Twelve. She has grown up not only with the slanted history President Snow pedals, but also the response of her immediate friends, family and fellow residents to that falsified history. As a result, her mindset will, like most, default to social values she knows best. According to Niebuhr, the social grounding is almost inevitable: "Men may achieve a rational unity of impulse around the organizing centre of the possessive instinct or the will-to-power, and yet have a faint sense of obligation to achieve social objectives, which transcend, or are in conflict with, their will to power."[20] When push comes to shove, most of us are going to stick with what we know when trying to resolve a difficult matter. What we know is almost always filtered clearly (and with bias) through the particular circumstances in which we grew up. To engage critically with any moral perspective, then, we must be able to bracket our own assumptions and consider the assumptions of others as based on a set of experiences that for those people are just as important as our own. Only then can we move to critique why a set of beliefs contains problematic ways of thinking about moral questions.

Though they ultimately fail to see Katniss for who she is—an individual who has suffered greatly at the hands of President Snow and as a citizen of District Twelve—the prep team shows a willingness to try. After their first round of work with her, Flavius exclaims: "Excellent! You look almost like a human now!"[21] This should not give them a pass for thinking about a fellow citizen as less than human, but it should head off any claims that they are as despotic in their political mindset as President Snow is. In short, we see in the prep team a flicker of a moral struggle that cannot get past its own default understanding of the political reality in which they live their lives. This, Niebuhr explains, is an apt summary for most people: "The individual character of conscience does not preclude the determination of most moral judgments by the opinions of the group. Most individuals lack the intellectual penetration to form independent judgments and therefore to accept the moral opinions of their society."[22] Essentially, most of us will fail to appreciate fully the moral and political perspectives of those who are different from us, even though this is the crucial skill required to bridge legitimate differences in understanding. Because we often struggle to

9. The Capitol's Residents

out ourselves *fully* in another person's shoes, we will drift back to the social ways of thinking that we grew up with. The result is just what we expect in the way Katniss thinks about the prep team as citizens of the Capitol. In the end she can only see them first and foremost as Capitol residents; she cannot quite get to the point of thinking about the prep team as individuals who happen to live in the Capitol.

Even when someone can set aside her/his own way of thinking to affirm the value of a truly different perspective, a further hurdle exists that prevents the kind of political and moral discourse that allows mutually exclusive opinions to coexist (as an aside, this is very much the status quo in American political discourse at the moment; individual voices on either side of the aisle cannot break through partisanship in pursuit of a commonly beneficial politics). Once again Niebuhr explains the dynamic: "Even when they do form their own judgments there is no certainty that their sense of obligation toward moral values, defined by their own mind, will be powerful enough to overcome the fear of social disapproval."[23] What we need, then, is someone who can not only set aside her/his own way of thinking, but also someone who will do so publicly even though doing so may be dangerous in the context of her/his surroundings.

Hopefully some readers will have thought of the name that needs to be introduced here: Cinna. In the Capitol's culture where the Games are accepted both morally and politically, Cinna is the one voice that straddles both perspectives Niebuhr identifies. Given the fear President Snow instills across Panem, we can understand to some degree why no one speaks up. It is difficult to be the voice of reason when being heard will result in cruel punishment.[24] Cinna understands what is at stake and he makes a coded but overtly public statement that challenges President Snow. During the movie version of *Catching Fire*, we see the moment clearly when Cinna's life is going to end. President watches as the camera pans to Cinna taking a bow when Caesar Flickerman acknowledges him as the designer of Katniss's Mockingjay dress. President Snow recognizes what is going on and less than 24 hours later Cinna will be beaten to death as Katniss waits in her tube to enter the Arena.

We get a sense that Cinna is different when he first meets Katniss. Notably, he looks her directly in the eye, an act that signals he takes the circumstances in which they meet seriously. If this is not enough of a surprise, he then skips past any niceties to acknowledge an implicit point. He remarks: "How despicable we must seem to you."[25] The movie version of *The Hunger Games* highlights this difference by turning Cinna's directness into an apology for what happened.[26] In both cases, the statement takes Katniss by surprise, but she ultimately misreads its purpose. Cinna then moves on to explain her costume for the parade. His matter-of-fact nature stands out to Katniss: "It crosses my mind that Cinna's calm and normal demeanor masks a complete madman."[27] Her perception of Cinna as a madman, even though he gives a clue that she should think otherwise, fails to recognize that he is different in a way that will become important. He remains on an even keel amidst a terrible job responsibility. With time we realize that Cinna's calm ultimately reveals his commitment to what Katniss represents in the political struggle against President Snow.

The outline of this narrative speaks to Cinna's political courage, but this virtuous mindset is only part of the story. Cinna is not just brave; he is brave because he authors a political message powerful enough to outlast President Snow. It takes until *Mockingjay* when she gets her official uniform as the rebel symbol for Katniss to realize that Cinna was playing a long game with his statement. He essentially sacrifices his life halfway through the rebellion in order to create for Katniss the ability to bring the rebellion to a full out and eventually successful conflict (his attention to detail in this respect is mirrored in the detail he brings to the Mockingjay suit, down to the easily accessible place for a suicide pill so that the Mockingjay can be a martyr at her own hand if captured). Moreover, he undertakes this program in full recognition of what his participation will cost him.

The curious thing about Cinna's role in The Hunger Games series is that he seems to be acting alone. There is no suggestion that he routinely engaged the hidden rebels in the Capitol even though his sketchbook of the Mockingjay suit obviously show he was in contact with Plutarch and others. The vision of what the Mockingjay is and can be flows from his own creative political mind. In this respect he exhibits the reason no tyrant can even dismiss completely the possibility of rebellion. Cinna has what Niebuhr recognizes as an intrinsic capacity for political action based on moral goodness: "But it is important to point out that men do possess, among other moral resources, a sense of obli-

9. The Capitol's Residents

gation toward the good, as their mind conceives it."[28] Cinna's creativity points to a world other than the one where he designs costumes for kids who are about to die in the Arena. This vision should not be taken for granted. We see throughout The Hunger Games series that most people struggle to identify and act upon a morally sound political agenda. Cinna, however, manages not only to conceive of the good as a citizen of the Capitol, but also act on that vision in a way that bridges the gap between his own cultural surroundings as those of someone from District Twelve.

This subtle influence is important in the context of building a rebellion step by step. A final point from Niebuhr's analysis captures why someone like Cinna is so valuable in a cultural context where almost everyone lacks the moral capacity to reject an unjust political power structure. Niebuhr writes: "Conscience is a moral resource in human life, but it is not as powerful as those moralists assume, who would save mankind by cultivating the sense of duty. It is more potent when it supports one impulse against another than when it sets itself against the total force of an individual's desires."[29] Effie is hardly a moral paragon, but we see her develop from a one-dimensional Capitol citizen to someone who struggles with competing political realities. In other words, she cannot reject the Capitol outright and on her own, but she can absorb the example of those around her. Katniss has this effect; we see this when Effie struggles to announce Katniss's name as the female tribute at the reaping for the 75th Hunger Games. Effie also exhibits the impact of being around Cinna when she hints at her sadness when Katniss is about to enter the Arena.

We do not see Effie other than when she is around characters like Katniss, Cinna, and Haymitch who do possess the moral strength to reject President Snow's political reality. We do see her struggle to reconcile the two worlds that she knows. Even if these instances are only part of how she spends her time, we can see the effect these moments have. Of the Capitol residents whom we read most about, she shows that moral and political transformation can occur even in those who clearly benefit from the presence of the Hunger Games in their lives.

It is natural, though not necessarily in a good way, to uphold political dynamics that are self-serving. When the playing field is tilted in favor of personal or social interests, motivation for change will almost

The Politics of *The Hunger Games*

always need to come from outside those who occupy the position of benefit. Just about any political matter in our culture today meets these criteria. Entrenched interests will almost always override arguments—be they political, moral, or both—to bring about change that would clearly benefit those outside the group that benefits from a contemporary political climate. In the case of the leader like President Snow, the point is obvious. However, a close look at perhaps the most long-standing beneficiary of the Hunger Games among the Capitol's residents will introduce yet another layer in thinking about the political mindset of those living in the Capitol. Caesar Flickerman is a complicated character in this respect. On the one hand, he glamorizes the Games in a way that no one else can. He manipulates emotional responses in his audience by ignoring the reality of what awaits the kids he interviews the night before the Games being. On the other hand, there seems to be a touch of humanity to his bonds with some of the tributes. His exchanges with Peeta in both *The Hunger Games* and *Catching Fire* suggest that he actually relates to Peeta outside of his role as MC of an annual infanticide.

More than anyone, Caesar captures the way a mindset of it's always been this way can allow an unjust thing like the Hunger Games to continue. He shows the inability of clever people to recognize and/or hold accountable the political leaders that rely on such events to maintain power. In *Eco-Republic: What the Ancients Can Teach Us about Ethics, Virtue, and Sustainable Living*, Melissa Lane identifies a specific way of relating to others that sheds light on the confusion a character like Caesar creates. She writes: "Attachment to the status quo also makes it difficult to establish a standard of assessment for imaginative and social change. Just because we have always drawn the boundaries of harm in one way, those boundaries appear natural and necessary to us, and benefit from our existing bias in favour of them."[30] The issue is not necessarily an unwillingness to think about alternatives to a political order. The problem, which turns out to be far more damaging, is that people who have been a part of the Games cannot think of a world without them. They are used to the Hunger Games.

The entire process, from the reaping to the victory tour, subsumes the kind of creative vision that we see in Cinna's work. Caesar should know better than anyone the manufactured appeal of the Games, as well as the political implications of every step. Though he should, he never

9. The Capitol's Residents

shows an ability to think how he might use his role to challenge what the Games represent. Because we cannot know if he is capable of admitting the moral reality of his job, we cannot get to the point of considering whether Caesar would be willing to stand up to President Snow if the moment were right. Like Katniss (though Caesar is far more entangled in the role he plays), then, he cannot get fully outside of the world he knows.

While it may be tempting to give the moral and political crown to Katniss and the rebels, in the end there is a lot in common between the rebels and the people who perform roles that serve President Snow's power. In thinking about morality in The Hunger Games series, George A. Dunn zeroes in on a shared moral weakness across stakeholders in this narrative. Dunn summarizes a quality that binds just about everyone together: "We'd like to believe that we always act from the most high-minded intentions, but in fact our motives are probably seldom, if ever, entirely pure."[31] Dunn's argument cautions against tidy moral judgments about the political roles different people play. Even the rebels have their own shortcomings. The inverse would also seem to be true. Even those who appear morally flawed have redeeming qualities. The Peacekeepers, for example, hardly seem like sympathetic characters. However, we eventually find out that their position of relative power does not provide a life of luxury. They struggle with many of the same things that define life in the districts. In fact, the Peacekeepers in District Twelve seem to live a life closer to Katniss than to the powers that be back in the Capitol. As Thread reveals when Haymitch talks him down from punishing Katniss, even the head Peacekeeper works within the fearful world President Snow presides over. The application of power certainly lies in the hands of the Peacekeepers, but as individuals they seem to be very much in the same boat as Katniss and her fellow rebels.

One key question remains in light of the analysis this chapter presents. Even if the residents of Panem and the Peacekeepers do not ultimately embrace President Snow's way of governing, are they not morally responsible for failing to stand up to what they know is wrong? This is an important question when it comes to circumstances where a relative handful of people undertake clearly immoral things like the Hunger Games. Even if we can get ourselves to the point where we can understand why Caesar Flickerman might not be able to acknowledge his role in the Hunger Games, should we be willing to grant him a reprieve from moral responsibility for the killing of children? Even if he does not actively participate in the violence themselves, should we deem him morally responsible for what happens in the Arena?

These questions get at some of the deepest moral challenges in a politics that takes seriously the different perspectives of a diverse population. When we see the systemic abuse of a group of people while another group does nothing to demand change. When people go about life as though nothing is wrong, there is a strong inclination to hold those people morally accountable for their political inaction. In the end, the point of this chapter is to revisit the question of how much we can know about the citizens of Panem who live in the Capitol regarding their opinions of the Games and President Snow.

Ultimately, the answer may lie in the words of those who have shown political courage that few of us can muster. Frankl, who has more reasons than most to condemn an entire population, offers a powerful way of thinking about this issue. He states: "As for the concept of collective guilt, I personally think that it is totally unjustified to hold one person responsible for the behavior of another person or a collective of people."[32] The argument that people should do something if they live under the shadow of a tyrant even if they do not suffer the full extent of the tyrant's political abuses makes sense. What Frankl challenges us to do, however, is to maintain our moral focus in holding the true authors of political abuse accountable. Caesar Flickerman is hardly a moral paragon, but he is not of the same moral kind as President Snow. This challenge, in other words, is to remember who bears responsibility for truly immoral circumstances and to distinguish this person of those people from others who may actually have more in common with us than we think.

10. The Media

September 26, 1960, probably does not seem like a pivotal point in our political history. Senator Kennedy engaged Vice President Nixon in a televised debate and the transcript reveals a mix of occasionally bland statements, hyperbole, and hints of the kind of ideological arguments that would come to define our current political discourse.

In his opening statement, Kennedy traverses some interesting ground. He is clear in his vision of what America can be, but his supporting evidence could easily be labeled lacking. For example, he states: "This is a great country, but I think it could be a greater country; and this is a powerful country, but I think it could be a more powerful country. I'm not satisfied to have fifty percent of our steel-mill capacity unused."[1] The introductory idea that America is great but could be greater stands on well-worn political ground. Something would be amiss if a presidential candidate did not make a statement of this sort. The curious thing lies in the example Kennedy uses to illustrate how America falls short of its potential. In the midst of the Cold War, he points to unused steel mill capacity as the place where America can do better.

Alongside this strange rhetorical development we find hyperbole that strains credibility. Kennedy also claims in his opening remarks an understanding of historical context that relies on a hyperbolic analogy: "In the election of 1960, and with the world around us, the question is whether the world will exist half-slave or half-free, whether it will move in the direction of freedom, in the direction of the road that we are taking, or whether it will move in the direction of slavery."[2] There certainly existed in 1960 a deep ideological divide between American and Soviet political philosophies. Further, much was at stake in the geopolitical struggle between these two oppositional ways of thinking about the world. All that being said, the comparison with slavery drifts into a political strategy that generally fails to stick. Slavery was abusive and deeply immoral in its systemic violence and denial of basic human rights. Simply put, slavery and communism are not really the same kind of thing. This did not prevent Kennedy from making an obvious move to pander to the mindset of millions of Americans who would have been happy to accept the analogy as intellectually sound.

Nixon does not exactly outshine Kennedy in his own opening remarks. He, too, opens with a ringing statement about American potential. In fact, he agrees with President Kennedy: "I subscribe completely to the spirit that Senator Kennedy has expressed tonight, the spirit that the United States should move ahead."[3] He disagrees about the pace of progress, however: "I think we disagree on the implication of his remarks tonight and on the statements that he has made on many occasions during his campaign to the effect that the United States has been standing still."[4] The point of disagreement is understandable. Is America maintaining its leadership on the global stage? Or is it failing to live up to its potential? These were serious questions in a time when the Soviet Union posed a legitimate threat to American leadership and ideals across the globe.

At this point, then, Nixon could have be incisive in articulating how America can get moving again. Whereas President Kennedy pointed to the steel mills, President Nixon might articulate a more visionary way to recover momentum in the ideological struggle against communist ideology. Instead, President Nixon defaults to a similarly bland economic point: "Now last year, of course, was 1958. That happened to be a recession year. But when we look at the growth of G.N.P. this year, a year of recovery, we find that it's six and nine-tenths per cent and one of the highest in the world today. More about that later."[5] The emphasis on economics within the context of geopolitical leadership does make sense; communism fails to generate the level of economic growth that President Nixon describes. As such, the point he makes is not irrelevant to his broader the claim. That being said, diving into economic metrics does not provide the kind of inspiration one might expect given the way President Nixon framed his statement.

When we set the transcript aside and instead focus on the appearance of each man, a different story comes into focus. The YouTube clip of the debate mentioned above provides significant insight if paused at the 0:08 mark than the entire transcript reveals.[6] On the right hand of

10. The Media

the screen, President Nixon sits awkwardly. His right foot is slight forward while his left foot is pulled back in a way that echoes but does not quite mimic a 19th century nobleman's posture. His hands do not look comfortable and his shoulders hunch forward slightly. He looks over at President Kennedy with a passionate-less stare. In short, President Nixon looks out of place.

President Kennedy, on the other hand, looks confidently at the camera. His hands are folded in a calm pose that expresses confidence with the context of the debate. His right leg is crossed over his left in a way that conveys a sense of being relaxed. Even his suit establishes in contrast with President Nixon who seems more at home on television. President Kennedy's dark jacket hangs loosely at his side because he followed common protocol and unbuttoned the jacket. President Nixon's lighter colored suit bunches up because he did not unbutton it.

As a matter of content, the winner of this debate is very much open to discussion. As a matter of appearance, however, it is roundly accepted that President Kennedy wins handily, a conclusion that applies to each of the televised debates from this election cycle. September 26, 1960, matters a great deal because it cements the role of the media in political processes. During the 1960 campaign, President Kennedy established a new way to political victory: controlling the media message.

This brief comparison highlights the tenor of the debate between Presidents Kennedy and Nixon. Though both men point to an American ideal at the outset and sound this note elsewhere in the debate, if one reads through the entire debate transcript a fairly wonky story unfolds. The point, then, is not to highlight either side as a transcendent political voice, but rather to introduce how a seemingly bland policy debate actually laid the foundation for an important political reality in America. Further, the intersection of media and politics has the sometimes beneficial but often problematic tendency of obscuring objective facts. As a result, the media becomes the basis for avoiding responsibility and shifting blame.

From the outset of The Hunger Games series, we find that the media will be a negative kind of political presence. Katniss reveals the impact the airwaves have on how the realities of life are characterized. With respect to the starvation, she describes how events unfold: "you hear the wails from a house, and the Peacekeepers are called in to retrieve the body. Starvation is never the cause of death officially. It's always the flu, or exposure, or pneumonia."[7] Though the reports of what supposedly happened "fools no one,"[8] the refusal to be transparent in an official sense speaks to the intentional use of the media to distribute false information. The fact that this strategy never wavers despite the ability of people to recognize what is at stake in false reports only shows the extent to which those in control of the media put on political blinders and pretend that their version of reality will be taken as true.

The media lurks throughout The Hunger Games series. Almost everything that occurs across the three books gets broadcast. Katniss spends a good deal of her time looking for ways not to appear on some screen. Despite its constant presence, however, the media also tends to linger in the background of the action. Still, when the books are read looking for the media, it quickly becomes apparent just how important the media is in affecting how events unfold in Panem.

A specific outcome of this constant presence deserves attention. When cameras are present, a couple of important things happen. First, there is an immediacy to the dynamics that we have seen throughout this book so far. Violence and fear are not only the basis for President Snow's politics, they are also an inescapable background to daily life because they appear explicitly and implicitly at seemingly every turn. The violence can reach anyone almost anywhere. This ubiquity brings the second point into focus: the things everyone watches are hears present a reality that is continually manipulated. No matter the intent of those broadcasting, the message will require editing. When the intent is specifically malicious, the ability to manipulate what hits the airwaves proves to be a very toxic mix.

On August 2, 1990, the world saw something unprecedented: the start of a war on live television. Green and grainy images of bombs falling on Baghdad at night kept eyes glued to the television. War had come to the American living room. Some commentators will focus on the way that broadcasting the First Gulf War made war immediate to an American audience, but there exists a certain irony in this claim. Yes, broadcasts of those images from Baghdad introduced tens of millions of people to the chaos of combat, but the broadcast had a strangely detached quality. People saw cruise missiles smash into buildings from thousands of feet in the air. Explosions were recognizable, but only from a distant

10. The Media

perspective. In short, the familiarity of war on television showed very little, if any, of the humans who were firing those missiles and dying in those explosions.

The paradox in broadcasting war nationwide is something that is inescapable in both the viewing of the Hunger Games and, eventually, the coverage of the war between the rebels and the Capitol. We read about the constant presence of cameras and propaganda, which ultimately gloss over the human costs around which broadcast messages are built. The core problem emerges when the accessibility of events on television becomes synonymous with the gruesome, exhausting experiences of those who play the unwitting role of television stars. When viewers mistake a broadcast of war with war itself, they implicitly sanction those who manipulate the images through their ignorance of the fuller picture from which the broadcast content comes.

In a telling article entitled "The War Photo No One Would Publish," *The Atlantic* writer Torie Rose DeGhett explores the decision by multiple media outlets in America not to publish a challenging photo of an Iraqi soldier who died inside a burning truck. Taken at the tail end of the First Gulf War, the photo reveals a side of war that is so often scrubbed from the media. This is, DeGhett argues, the very reason the photo never appeared in major news outlets. She writes: "In the case of the charred Iraqi soldier, the hypnotizing and awful photograph ran against the popular myth of the Gulf War as a 'video-game war'—a conflict made humane through precision bombing and night-vision equipment. By deciding not to publish it, *Time* magazine and the Associated Press denied the public the opportunity to confront this unknown enemy and consider his excruciating final moments."[9] Several salient points surface here this summary explanation. Framed as a "video-game war," the conflict that so many experienced from their homes too often left out the impact war has on people. The photo in question (which can be viewed online with DeGhett's article) forces readers to experience a deeply physical example of suffering and the human will to live. Though DeGhett rightfully calls attention to the fact that the photo's subject is Iraqi, the broader point here has to do with the need to confront the impact violence has on people. Death haunts as it lays bare what war does to those fighting.

This is not to say, of course, that we should ignore DeGhett's more focused critique of the decision not to publish the photo in American news outlets. As she notes, the photo was not deemed inappropriate for the news. Several outlets abroad published the photo: "The image was not entirely lost. The *Observer* in the United Kingdom and *Libération* in France both published it after the American media refused."[10] There was, then, a specific decision from a specific perspective to maintain a crafted narrative regarding the war. In DeGhett's words, the American media wanted to highlight: "The hardware-focused coverage of the war removed the empathy that Jarecke says is crucial in photography, particularly photography that's meant to document death and violence."[11] War should not be thought of as a detached, top-down ideological battle. These things play their parts, but at its core war involves people fighting and killing. This struggle surfaces in a photo that unsettles a mechanistic narrative, so the photo never reached the mainstream media.

Ultimately, DeGhett's article calls attention to the ways truth can be negotiated through the media. Perspective matters a great deal and as we see in The Hunger Games series, the opportunity to bend truth to meet one's own interests makes the media one of the definitive battlegrounds where political sway can be won or lost. Purdy recognizes what this negotiation exposes when it comes to specifically political messages. He writes: "Rather than expressions of conviction, public statements are moves made according to the shifting rules of an elaborate game."[12] As we have seen on multiple occasions, the entire *Hunger Games* series is one long, dangerous, and carefully scripted political chess match. Importantly, the moral core of politics that Purdy wants to recover runs counter to the purpose of political messages. The media becomes a way to generate sound bites rather than statements of conviction. Truth becomes something other than its definition says it should be. Political messaging in the media is about manipulation.

Though both the rebels and President Snow play this game, it is clear that President Snow embraces more fully the superficial nature of what he puts on the air. As a result, he presides over a politics that is literally a spectator sport. He thus mirrors Purdy's deeper analysis regarding politics and the media: "The most prevalent attitude toward politics after indifference treats it as a hybrid of spectator sport and *People* magazine's celebrity culture."[13] A politics run through the media becomes a distraction for its core aim of protecting individual freedoms and providing a moral foundation for culture. In the stead of these aims we find

10. The Media

a world defined by what sells. Those who are buying (i.e. the population) become interested in superficial things and expect sound bites rather than substantive leadership.

When the facts on the airwaves lack substance, ignorance comes to pass as knowledge. This kind of politics quickly reduces what should be a vigorous and critical search for compromise to arguments where adherence to a position, regardless of whether the position is intellectually sound, becomes the assumed basis for political leadership. In 2011, a troubling poll was released. The poll showed that viewers of Fox News were actually less informed about world events than people who did not watch any news. Specifically, reporter Michael A. Memoli points out: "respondents were first asked whether, to the best of their knowledge, opposition groups in Egypt had been successful in bringing down the Mubarak regime."[14] The results are startling. "Among NPR listeners, 68 percent correctly said they had been; only 49 percent of Fox News viewers answered correctly. In fact, the survey found, Fox viewers were 18 percentage points less likely to answer correctly than those who watched no news at all."[15] The numbers here make clear that information presented on Fox News does not seem to undergo critical review before reaching the airwaves. When not watching a source of information provides a better understanding of world events than a broadcast that ostensibly should provide its viewers facts, criticism of that news source is more than warranted.

The point here is not to claim that Fox News viewers are the only ones who lack substantive news. To balance the discussion, it is worth pointing out that those who watch predominantly left-leaning political television likewise exhibited clear bias in how they understood events. Memoli notes: "And it seems Jon Stewart may be more reliable than cable news anchors. On Occupy Wall Street, the survey found viewers of "The Daily Show" were 12 percentage points more likely to say protesters were predominantly Democratic. MSNBC viewers were the most likely to say the protesters were mainly Republicans."[16] Satire plays an important role in the way societies think about important issues, but when satire stands as the most reliable source of information, more traditional media have generally failed to provide reliable information. The common denominator between those watching Fox News and those who prefer MSNBC remains a willingness to accept tidy sound bites as the basis for a culture's political discourse.

While on the victory tour in *Catching Fire*, Peeta and Katniss experience the full force of President Snow's media-driven politics. In the Capitol, there are feted with an elaborate party at the presidential mansion to bring their publicity tour to a crescendo. The movie version of *Catching Fire* does well to convey the lavishness and ridiculousness of this party. The camera follows Peeta, Katniss, and Effie as they walk toward President Snow's brightly lit and fantastically decorated mansion. An enormous, cheering crowd surrounds the trio as they make their way indoors. Effie, beaming at the attention, tells Peeta and Katniss with obvious pride: "Everyone who's anyone is hear tonight."[17] Social standing comes with being at a party designed to celebrate two people who managed to survive infanticide in service of the host's political purposes. Peeta and Katniss are clearly and rightfully uncomfortable in that they recognize the absurdity of the event. The events that led to their celebrity are tragic, yet they are treated as cultural icons.

The party at the Snow mansion is unsettling as a political event, but a more telling exchange on the victory tour between Katniss and Effie makes plain the problem with a politics that plays out through the media. Filtered through the Capitol's media objectives, the Games are, for Effie, a moment of achievement. She feels proud that her tributes one the event and she is obviously interested in the attention she will receive for leading the team that prepped Peeta and Katniss. This social currency blinds her to the truth Katniss cannot help but state in response to Effie's remark that Katniss has earned something. Winning the games is not and should not be about celebrity and its rewards; it is about cold-blooded killing when no other options exist. This is done in service of a fear-based politics that sows fear through the artifice of celebrity it bestows on those who manage to survive. Effie, then, represents the impact the media has on political life in Panem while Katniss exposes the empty nature of this same political framework. The world of the Games, broadcast throughout Panem, hide the truth of what is actually happening within the carefully honed and largely artificial world of the celebrity.

If we take a step back from the particular effect of manufacturing social value based on the Games, we see a deeply troubling pattern. The media can appeal easily to a population if the message is right. The problem comes when those who accept that message at face value then fail to see how those manipulating the message are achieving troubling

10. The Media

things through propaganda. Specifically, the façade of meaning that can be created via the media becomes an effective way of spreading bad information.

Vladimir Putin may deserve the prize for best abuse of the media to support his political goals and not just because he is willing to be photographed shirtless while riding a horse. In a recent *Time* overview of Putin, we read about a danger that mirrors the way President Snow abuses facts throughout The Hunger Games series. Madeline Albright, the former Secretary of State and accomplished political scientist, explains what is so troubling about Putin: "Through his illegal actions in Ukraine, Putin has reminded us that leaders of great countries are most dangerous when they make up their own facts. Putin's world is colored by toxic fictions."[18] Albright highlights the specific consequences a media-based politics can have: the creation of "facts" that justify immoral and illegal actions. Through his propaganda, Putin justifies the invasion of a sovereign state to his own people and gets away with it (polls in Russia throughout the year have shown Putin with approval ratings of nearly 70 percent despite biting economic sanctions[19]).

Fiction is an apt description for Putin's manipulation of facts within the Russian media. Despite his justifications for invading Ukraine—alongside the more troubling denial of responsibility for allowing a commercial airliner to be shot down—Putin cannot escape the obvious outside the context of the media message he controls. Erik Pineda offers a good outline of the specific ways Putin changes reality in constructing a narrative about Russia's invasion of Ukraine. According to Pineda, Putin's propaganda insists on four things that are demonstrably false: "Russia, in fact, is coming to Ukraine's rescue; Russia originally and rightfully owns Crimea; No Russian troops inside Ukraine; Down of Malaysia Airlines MH17 is Ukraine/NATO fault."[20] A general narrative takes shape in these four points. Russia becomes a protagonist in pursuit of Ukraine's rescue without defining the thing that Ukraine needs to be rescued from while simultaneously blaming Western interests for this unstated crisis. In short, these manipulated facts allow Putin to claim to Russians that they are pursuing some moral good while in reality Putin's political machine undertakes a power grab on the basis of violence and fear.

Behind this manufactured narrative, we find a further disturbing

The Politics of *The Hunger Games*

pattern in how Putin uses propaganda to obscure the truth of the events he is driving. The fictions not only describe current events, they also create a past that is similarly false. The unsubstantiated claim that Russia is only reclaiming what it owns similarly assumes a manufactured set of facts. In turn, these supposed facts become the justification for a politics that wants to extend its own power at the cost of innocent lives. Timm highlights the extent to which President Snow relies on controlling the population as opposed to encouraging its freedom: "Discovering and exposing those methods of control isn't an easy task. The Capitol works hard to keep them invisible in order that its power be taken for granted. The trick is to get people to control themselves, to fall into certain habits that perpetuate the existing social order."[21] In the broadcasts of the Games, we find a frequent "trick" used to obscure what is actually going on in the Arena. The history of Panem lays responsibility for the Games at the feet of the districts, which implicitly argues that the tributes deserve their fate. Importantly, the broadcasts and public statements to this effect never explicitly make this claim. Rather, it is left unsaid, which makes identifying and rejecting it all the more difficult. This is a further consequence of the spectator sport of politics. When claims are not made explicitly, they are much harder to critique.

Exposure to this slanted history begins at an early age for the children in Panem's districts. Timm highlights the use of propaganda in schools as an important piece of justifying the Games. He explains: "One way to do this is through education—or perhaps we should say *mis*education. What children learn in Panem, at home and in school, prepares them to take their place in the social order. In school they learn that the Hunger Games and the Capitol's superiority are just the way things are, while being taught skills that guarantee they will have the same dangerous and low-paying jobs as their parents."[22] There exists a manufactured social order that allows for violence to be used in order to maintain the political status quo. Putin would be proud. By rewriting history to serve contemporary political ends, and then broadcasts that history at every opportunity, President Snow nurtures a fiction that ultimately prevents the districts from resisting the violence and fear that exists within the Capitol's way of governing Panem.

Within this approach to molding history in a convenient way Timm sees the lessons District Twelve's kids learn as specifically problematic.

10. The Media

Katniss grows up hearing an enhanced version of a convenient history: "Schooling in District 12 reinforces inequality in an even more deliberate and insidious way: by teaching children from the Seam to accept the Capitol's power."[23] Blind acceptance of existing power is what this kind of education wants to accomplish. The specifics of this power should be troubling to the kids who learn these lessons because they are the ones who may suffer the most for what this fiction allows. Timm makes the connection here explicit: "One way Katniss's school does this is by using school time to teach students about the Hunger Games, so they will accept the Games as an ordinary fact of life…. By teaching about the Games and making them part of the school's curriculum, the school is explicitly reaching students that the Games are a necessary and normal part of life."[24] The blasé acceptance of violence, fear, and possible death in the Arena as part of life undermines so much of what politics should be, particularly for children. In Putin's case, the fictions he manufactures and manicures are meant to placate an adult population. In Panem, these same kinds of false lessons obscure the country's violent identity from children.

This long-term strategy is effective. The politic dynamic in Panem occurs over the meaning of symbols like the Arena, events like the reaping, and the fear a heavy-handed security state creates. Jill Olthouse's essay "I Will Be Your Mockingjay": The Power and Paradox of Metaphor in the Hunger Games Trilogy" articulates clearly why it matters how people understand the basic facts of the relationship between the Capitol and the districts. She writes: "the fight against the Capitol is conducted with more than just guns and explosives. Alongside the physical fight is an ideological battle of words, images, and associations."[25] Physical conflict becomes just another part of the story, but when we meet Katniss and first read about the Games, the conflict centers on the way the media presents the Games. Citizens become passive recipients of the narrative that begins in schools and, as such, they are not tuned to be critical of what they are about to see. The population, in other words, remains ignorant, a goal that drives much of the fiction that President Snow upholds. When ideological battles unfold, a misinformed opponent is the best kind.

History offers numerous examples of how leaders who have no problem resorting to violence curate a propaganda campaign with the intent of obscuring reality. A look at Hitler's *Mein Kampf* reveals the tactical purpose propaganda serves. He offers a simple playbook for establishing the kind of toxic fiction we have been examining throughout this chapter. Hitler's basic premise reflects much of the slanted history we read about in The Hunger Games series: "The receptivity of the great masses is very limited, their intelligence is small, but their power of forgetting is enormous. In consequence of these facts, all effective propaganda must be limited to a very few points and must harp on these in slogans until the last member of the public understands what you want him to understand by your slogan."[26] When a large group consumes the same message, the ability to critique that message subsides. Ignorance can be forced through numbers. The caveat is that effective use of propaganda must be consistent in presenting the same key points over and over. So long as they hear the same message, people will gradually accept the takeaway those writing the propaganda want to serve as the key takeaway.

A crucial feature of this simplicity is to demure from factual discussions. Hitler cautions against creating space for critical thinking: "It is a mistake to make propaganda many-sided, like scientific instruction, for instance."[27] Rather, effective propaganda limits the facts to those things that uphold the particular narrative one wants to spread across a culture. Hitler continues: "The function of propaganda is, for example, not to weigh and ponder the rights of different people, but exclusively to emphasize the one right which it has set out to argue for. Its task is not to make an objective study of the truth, in so far as it favors the enemy, and then set it before the masses with academic fairness; its task is to serve our own right, always and unflinchingly."[28] Propaganda works when those conveying the message stick to the flawed story. Putin continues to lie to Russians, but because he is consistent in the lies he attracts significant support. President Snow can act with impunity because the history that justifies the Games takes shape early in life; by the time anyone might know better, s/he has internalized a false history. The summary benefit for those who would use propaganda remains the ability to act wholly out of self-interest with little threat of consequence.

In The Hunger Games series, the media enables propaganda because it calls into question Panem's values. By recasting fact as fiction and inventing a self-serving history, President Snow obscures the things politics should be about and replaces them with questions he answers in

10. The Media

the form of the Capitol's broadcasts in a variety of contexts. This strategy highlights the problems of reducing politics to a matter of the media. In his monograph *God and Caesar in America: An Essay on Religion and Politics* Senator Gary Hart focuses on the consequences of using the media as a primary setting for political discourse. He identifies the use of fictions that exclude all but the ruling power as disconcerting: "coded political communications require rather cynical use of special language, including 'dog whistle' messages. As the phrase suggests, these are communications sent on a frequency that only the select can hear. If your ears are not keen enough to be tuned to the secret frequency, you will not be able to get the message."[29] When people like President Snow dictate the message, there exists a serious risk if someone is unable to hear the secret code. As we see often, those who are not on the inside continually experience violence and are exposed to manipulative fears.

The broader issue here revolves around the way that things like political value become defined in narrow terms. Hart explains: "this approach, presuming it is not totally cynical, is fraught with monumental peril."[30] The peril lies in the way a single, normative understanding of corporate things like cultural values get talked about within a media-driven propaganda. Hart casts light on the dynamic that exists within the message we continually see in Panem's media: "Like defining the terms of a debate, he who gets to choose the values dominates the political discussion."[31] These kind of exclusive values have a long history of denying rights to people and enforcing the ban through the use of violence. Any time we see a serious political matter framed in a way that allows for only one opinion, we should be suspicious. When the message is enforced through violence, we should reject the message altogether because its purpose is to extend the power of a political elite at the cost of everyone else's liberty and security.

Throughout the lengthy discussion above, the focus has been on the ways that the Capitol's use of the media is problematic. Importantly, the rebels also rely on the media to advance their own cause. In the process of playing the same game, they ultimately risk smothering the energy that drives their cause. A particular example will help to clarify how playing the media game creates risks for the rebels. Once Katniss has agreed to become the Mockingjay, a public relations campaign unfolds. Specifically, the leaders of the rebellion have a plan to distribute propos across Panem's airwaves to accomplish a dual purpose. First, they want to provide an encouraging message to the districts who are fighting against the Capitol. Second, the rebel leaders want to provide a different narrative to those living in the Capitol in hopes of attacking the credibility of President Snow.

In playing the same game as the Capitol, the rebels would seem to have a good plan. If they can reframe the argument, they can call into question President Snow's leadership. The plan's foundation requires that Katniss follow a script that the rebel leaders deem likely to achieve the two goals noted above. The problem, of course, is that scripting Katniss's behavior so closely comes across as unnatural. The results of the force propos are obvious to everyone. The strategy has a flaw; it regresses into an inauthentic portrayal of what matters. It casts Katniss as a robotic figure specifically designed to counter the propaganda that comes out of the Capitol.

The solution emerges once Katniss goes off script. When she is free to act normally, she becomes an inspirational figure who is very effective in sending a message. The contrast with the Katniss we see in the rehearsals reveals an important shortcoming of political messaging through the media. Editing the message creates the possibility that the truly important content gets left out. When this happens, it becomes very easy to manipulate the entire media-based strategy of defining the political narrative in favorable and fictional terms. We see her impact clearly in the *Mockingjay* movie when she presents herself as a leader in her own terms while fighting in District Eight.

When the rebels and the Capitol coexist on the same stage, these problems become apparent very quickly. While Peeta is held captive at the beginning of *Mockingjay*, he becomes a mouthpiece for Capitol propaganda against the rebels' military campaign. He is forced to speak against what the rebels fight for and pleas for them to lay down their arms. In the battle for control of minds across Panem, the strategy makes sense; they use the popular guy who is comfortable on camera to encourage the rebels to give up.

Unfortunately for President Snow, the strategy backfires in a variety of ways. The first example of this occurs when Peeta effectively warns the rebels that a bombing raid on District Thirteen is imminent. In his own coded language he gives District Thirteen just enough time to acti-

10. The Media

vate an emergency plan that saves innumerable lives. His ease in front of the camera is supposed to get the rebels to stop fighting. Instead he flips the script and provides the rebels with an advantage.

The Hunger Games are part of an elaborate use of media to further a political end. The broadcast is well oiled and effective in presenting political violence as a justifiable and enjoyable thing to watch. The strategy reveals the depravity of President Snow's way of ruling Panem and the seeming willingness of those who watch to be passive in their exposure to unconscionable programming. Still, for the most part the media remains a crucial aspect of both sides' struggle, particularly in *Mockingjay*.

Despite the prevalence of the media as a political reality in the way we read about in *Mockingjay*, the definitive example of why the media cannot provide a legitimate political message occurs in *Catching Fire*. At the televised interviews the night before the 75th Hunger Games, the tributes—all of whom would be more or less known as media stars in Panem—stand on stage per the script of how the night should go.

What happens at the climactic moment, however, completely undermines the media-driven strategy President Snow relies on. After all of the tributes have been interviewed they stand up for the anthem that marks the end of the program. The music starts, but it does something other than bring the evening to a rousing, Capitol-affirming conclusion. As the anthem plays, the tributes take one another's hand and stand in a unified line. As Katniss narrates, the effect is powerful: "By the time the anthem plays its final strains, all twenty-four of us stand in one unbroken line in what must be the first public show of unity among the districts since the Dark Days. You can see the realization of this as the screens begin to pop into blackness. It's too late, though. In the confusion they didn't cut us off in time. Everyone has seen."[32] The broadcast that was supposed to trumpet the Capitol's yearly celebration of power enables the first public viewing of resistance. The tributes do not act as pieces in the game. They announce clearly that a Quarter Quell designed to reiterate the Capitol's power has become an announcement that people have had enough of that power. The media, ever the source of quick political turns, makes sure that all those required viewers see the show of unity against the Capitol.

11. Public Violence

At the outset, I will emphasize that the following chapter is dense. Methodologically it adds an important layer to the argument that emerges throughout this book. For readers who do not want to work through a denser academic discussion, this chapter can be skipped. Jumping to the conclusion will not impact the arc of the discussion that has unfolded thus far. Though important in thinking about the role violence plays as a public reality, the discussion here is not crucial to understanding the broader argument in this book.

In *The Scapegoat*, René Girard analyzes the specific phenomenon of *collective* violence. The corporate nature of Girard's project is significant in the context of this project and, as such, Girard's discussion of violence warrants extended treatment. When violence is pervasive, there is a complex dynamic at play that goes beyond a tyrant's decisions. Those decisions may still be in the causal point in a violent dynamic, but, as Girard makes clear, sustained violence against a particular kind of person requires a social dimension. The deep cultural role that violence plays in The Hunger Games series is evident from all angles. How the Games are celebrated in the Capitol and tolerated in the Districts invites Girard as a critical point of departure.

While the presence of violence may be easy to recognize, the *type* of violence President Snow prefers is an important thing to consider. The Hunger Games are overtly violent; there is no shortage of graphic passages throughout the books and movies to verify the claim. What matters at the outset of a Girardian analysis is to articulate the target of the violence. For Girard, recognizing the commonalities of cultural violence helps underscore the role violence plays in those societies. Girard explains that the person driving the violence is telling: "unity is easy to find … there are violent crimes which choose as object those people whom it is most criminal to attack, either in the absolute sense or in reference to the individual committing the act: a king, a father, the symbol

11. Public Violence

of supreme authority."[1] Two salient considerations surface in the thread that stitches public violence together. First, there exists a clear leader who enables the violence. Due to the person's stature within a particular culture, he (and it is almost always a he) implicitly sanctions the violence as normative through the political power he wields.

The second point to consider here is the consistency in the targets these political authorities select. Whatever legal, moral, or cultural standard might otherwise protect the victim is set aside on the authority of the person who authorizes violence. Obvious criminal acts become permissible, which further underwrites the goal the violence pursues. That is, the political role this kind of violence plays allows the victim to be recast as demanding violence. As a result, the victim becomes the one who perpetuates the public violence, which, in turn, further sanctions the use of violence. The result is, usually, that a social undercurrent embraces violence in a way that holds the victim accountable for her/his suffering.

There is a strongly inverted relationship between the victim's role within the society and the use of violence against the victim. We have a cultural legacy of leaders who underwrite violence against the defenseless: "in biblical and modern societies [victims are] the weakest and most defenseless, especially young children."[2] As we saw in the Introduction, this is precisely the approach the binds Herod and President Snow together. In killing children, each man exerts a political authority in which "it is the strictest taboos that are transgressed."[3] From our perspective, this point seems clear enough; infanticide is one of our strongest taboos. The capacity in which this taboo is set aside, however, illustrates the way that public violence serves the power structure that perpetuates the breaking of taboos. As shocking as we may find Herod's and President's Snow's actions, their respective campaigns mask an important nuance in the dynamics this kind of violence enables. Killing children is essentially an "attack [on] the very foundation of cultural order, the family and the hierarchical difference without which there would be no social order."[4] Consequently, these men employ violence in a way that weakens the cultural order over which they rule. This is a risky game to play. Creating a hidden disorder through the use of violence against kids might become initiate a political response from those who recognize the victims' plight that seeks to overthrow those who permit public violence.

In reality, however, these political superstructures tend to withstand the risks they create. The reason for the success of this strategy lies in how those who align themselves with the ruling political power react to the role of public violence. Attacking the foundational social order is political risk that ultimately seeks to rewrite a more unified social order. Girard explains: "If the wrongdoers, even the diabolical ones, are to succeed in destroying the community's distinctions, they must either attack the community directly ... or else they must begin the destruction of difference within their own sphere."[5] President Snow assumes great risk in his leadership regarding the Hunger Games's violent campaign. The goal is to maintain and strengthen his power. He could wipe out the adults who oppose him in each district, but he opts for the Hunger Games's more subversive and psychological campaign because this approach is built on unpredictability. Through violence, he is able to undermine the social bonds that are most threatening because he succeeds in pulling all of Panem into the spectacle that is the Hunger Games. Even those who are the clear victims buy in to the spectacle because it is so pervasive as a cultural presence. In effect, President Snow tries to erase the differences between the Capitol and the districts though the annual slaughter of children. The taboo against killing children fades from the minds of those whom the Hunger Games affects because, per Girard's analysis, the entire equation is based on the portrayal of the victims as the ones who are ultimately responsible for the games.

How violence is structured in public conversation reveals a lot about those involved in the conversation. Particularly important voices to consider include those who represent cultural authority: the kings, the fathers, the elite, etc. Together, they are bound by an inability to tell the truth about the role violence plays in their powerful positions. Girard describes the mindset that erases violence from the public conversation: "So helpless were they that telling the truth did not mean facing the situation but rather giving in to its destructive consequences and relinquishing all semblance of normal life."[6] Violence in service of a few powerful figures does not constitute a normal politics; it requires a different kind of leadership. This alternative finds acceptable of whatever consequences come about when violence has run its course. This mindset runs against the grain of the purpose for politics: structuring life within the polis. Convincing some people to buy into this skewed under-

11. Public Violence

standing of political influence is part of the challenge. The second and more invasive task is to quell the victims' anger at the violence they experience. The entire population, must, in Girard's words, "share in this type of blindness."[7]

President Snow is myopic in his commitment to upholding this lie. The pervasive publicity that surrounds the game has a single purpose: to recast the Games as normative for Panem. If the Games are embraced in the Capitol and accepted in the Districts, President Snow will keep all sides united in blindness. The history of Panem laces all aspects of the Games. Two manifestations of this history as presented in service of justifying public violence are worth considering.

The Games present a specific challenge in continually redefining the Games as something other than they are. Every year there is a victor. A child who has killed other children must re-enter society. S/he is a presence that always threatens to expose the public lie that President Snow must sustain. It is not surprising, then, that victors are celebrated as heroes and invited to be part of the Capitol. This crossing over from the Districts to the Capitol is an important symbolic journey for President Snow's purposes. For the citizens of the Capitol, the victim's identity as victim assumes the appearance of normal life from the perspective of those who are not cast into the arena. Victimhood vanishes as the winner-turned-celebrity sanctions the lie her/his victory could have exposed. The violence against the districts' children is acceptable to the victor because s/he now has far more than s/he ever could. Betraying the false message would require giving up a life of material comfort that would otherwise be impossible and, moreover, would invite further violence on the victor and her/his family, friends, and fellow members from her/his home district.

The victim, then, has very little choice in resisting the role of violence, but s/he assumes an outsized role in maintaining the lie. This dynamic is what Girard means when he uses the term Scapegoat.[8] The victim who wears this label (not by choice) reveals how: "The perpetual conjunction in myths of a very guilty victim with a conclusion that is both violent and liberating can only be explained by the extreme force of the scapegoat mechanism."[9] Girard continues: "the order that is either absent or compromised by the scapegoat once more establishes itself or is established by the intervention of someone who disturbed it in the first place."[10] The violence that unfolds in the arena is, potentially, a revelation that would undermine the complicated edifice President Snow maintains and expands through the Games. His success defines his tyranny both in its willingness to uphold his power through all means necessary and explains why he is able to maintain power in the midst of such a devastating use of public violence.

Girard summarizes the dark magic cast in perpetuating the scapegoat mechanism. Leaders like President Snow are in their insidiousness adept at their political use of violence. Girard writes: "The transgressor restores and even establishes the order he has somehow transgressed in anticipation. The greatest of all delinquents is transformed into a pillar of society."[11] The nearly universal toleration and/or embrace of President Snow in this regard points to an important component of the lie's success. If citizens were honest, they would recognize that "Terrified as they are by their own victim, they see themselves as completely passive, purely reactive, totally controlled by this scapegoat at the very moment when they rush to his attack. They think that all initiative comes from him."[12] However, as people bound by the lie the Hunger Games perpetuates, the citizens of the Capitol cannot look beyond the assumption that they are passive. If we recall the way the historical justification for the Hunger Games is explained, the basis for the passivity can be identified. The Capitol did nothing wrong; it was not the aggressor that started the war. By extension, it must remain passive as the Hunger Games continue. Importantly, this mindset never mentions the actual violence that occurs. If people can watch kids killing other kids in the arena and see it for its simple truth—violence in service of the Capitol—then it is hard to imagine that the Hunger Games would be so popular. However, the citizens do not make this connection because their understanding is based on the broader lie that sanctions the violence that occurs in the Arena.

In the wake of violence in service of an existing power structure, one must ask how the popular misunderstanding of violence can continually avoid detection for what it is. Girard summarizes the issue well: "Such things can happen, *especially in our time,* but they cannot happen, even today, without the availability of an eminently manipulatable mass to be used by the manipulators for their evil purposes."[13] In short, the masses who miss the truth of what happens at the hands of their culture share a common quality: they can be molded to participate in the false

11. Public Violence

narrative without recognizing their complicity. They "allow themselves to be trapped in the persecutors' representation of persecution."[14] In his description Girard highlights a willing laziness among the populace when it comes to engaging critically with their own politics. Reverting to simplistic answers creates space for those who stand to benefit from perpetuating the lie of violence to bend the masses away from truth. President Snow's psychological edge is a crucial component in this respect. Even if those who accept the perpetrator's version of events are able to recognize what is really going on, any questions they ask surface within a culture framed by the lie.

In other words, there exists a narrative surrounding the existing political rulers that exhibits clear falsehoods. The problem is that the ruling elites go to great lengths to harden the narrative as truth. Those familiar with *Braveheart* will hear the echo of King Robert the Bruce's opening monologue: "History is written by those who have hanged heroes."[15] The truth Girard exposes in discussing this point is that to recover the truth from the lie we must begin to unravel the long narrative used to justify violence by focusing on the person who reveals and erases the perpetrators' responsibility: the victim. The efforts taken to hang the heroes thus become apparent. As the old saying goes, without a body, it is hard to convict a murderer. To extend the lie that supports violence, the victim cannot be seen as a victim.

Katniss does her part in reversing the tide, but on this particular point Finnick is most instructive. Finnick reveals the privileged role that victors experience is anything but terrible: "If a victor is considered desirable, the president gives them as a reward or allows people to buy them for an exorbitant amount of money. If you refuse, he kills someone you love. So you do it."[16] Victory, in other words, only intensifies the threats faced in the Arena. The significant difference is that President Snow is willing to extent the violence and fear to others in order to control those who win the Hunger Games.

If this were not enough to give pause to those watching, Finnick then exposes President Snow's range of targets. His tyranny is not reserved only for those in the districts; he also acts with similar ruthlessness within the Capitol's highest political circles. Finnick explains that President Snow has left a string of dead rivals under mysterious circumstances. Poison is his preferred method of assassination. Notably, the treatment is not reserved only for rivals. Finnick shares that President Snow also killed off "his allies who had the potential to become threats."[17] Finnick's insights present a clear portrait to all of Panem. The political tools President Snow brings to bear on the districts are likewise in use throughout the Capitol. In the end, those living in the districts are thus no difference than those living in the Capitol. Anyone who might stand in the way of President Snow's power will be quickly killed off.

While Finnick plays his part in exposing the lie that underwrites the Games, Katniss is the causal force in exposing President's Snow's reliance on the scapegoat mechanism. For all the elaborate avoidance of truth, the lie remains in plain sight. Those who perpetuate the lie are, importantly, so confident in the masses' inability or unwillingness to recognize what is really happening that they can actively call attention to their political violence. As Girard points out: "they hide none of the objective traces of their persecution."[18] This brazenness focuses the collective mindset on the victim's supposed agency as the necessitating factor for violence. Katniss turns out to be the anti-victim in that she retrains the public's gaze on the obviousness of the violence. As the climactic storm clouds gather near the end of the 75th Hunger Games, Katniss, fully televised, literally short-circuits the entire façade. The openness of the Games regarding the role violence plays in Panem's politics begins the ultimate rewriting of the lie as a truth. The Games are a manufactured way of justifying an existing political reality. Once this truth is broadcast live, President Snow's collapse is inevitable.

Girard uses a telling metaphor to discuss the impact the outsider has in exposing the lie that justifies violence. Victims are necessarily cast as other than the group that puts forth and sustains the lie. He writes: "The signs that indicate a victim's selection result not from the difference within the system but from the difference outside the system, the potential for the system to differ from its own difference, in other words not to be different at all, to cease to exist as a system."[19] Though complex, Girard's analysis reveals the *reason* those who rely on the scapegoat mechanism do so: they are intrinsically fragile as political leaders. They may obscure this fragility through a leadership that gets the populace to buy into the lie of violence, but doing so does not remove the underlying instability that characterizes those who resort to such measures.

11. Public Violence

Girard uses the body as an analogy. A serious health condition is unnerving because it is often visible. The perception of difference from a healthy body is, at first glance, the thing that unsettles. However, Girard's point is that serious health conditions actually expose a different and more troubling cause for concern. They are reminders that the entire body is fragile. The outward appearance of strength that a healthy body exhibits can disappear in an instant. The result is, crucially, to articulate how "Difference that exists outside the system is terrifying because it reveals the truth of the system, its relatively, its fragility, its mortality."[20] The political body is no different in this capacity. The very thing that can be defined as a problem within the context of the political body is ultimately a reminder that every body is problematic. Every ruler's grip on power is tenuous, a point cast into particularly sharp focus when the ruler who consolidates power through violence denies that power can evaporate. The purpose of the lie of violence thus becomes apparent for what it is: a denial of the body's mortality. In extreme cases like President Snow (and, importantly, President Coin), violence makes sense as the basis for the denial; there is no better way to convince members of a political body of existing power structures than to expose *others* as mortal. The message is built on the always incorrect assumption that the perpetrator's own mortality is not similarly fragile.

Katniss is an outsider in two ways, which helps explain why she is the exception that escapes President Snow's infanticide. Rather than reassert the victimhood of the districts, Katniss successfully exposes President Snow's fragility because she is outside the system in multiple respects. As a resident of District Twelve, she is already on the fringes of the broad narrative build on and through the Hunger Games. Tributes from District Twelve usually do not win because they do not grow up with experiences that will be relevant in the Arena. She is, then, different in her outward weakness because she comes from District Twelve.

Ironically and importantly, this weakness is merely perceived in how Katniss represents District Twelve. Her abilities with a weapon and her survival skills establish her as an outsider from District Twelve in that she does not follow the typical progression of the helpless tribute. She literally goes beyond the fence that is supposed to contain her. In the woods, she and Gale learn how what is needed to be a victim who can turn the entire violent narrative around. Further, in the woods she and Gale can think about their lives and discuss the implications of what is happening without being constrained by the limits that President Snow imposes on each district. Her outsiderness in this respect creates a tribute from District Twelve that belies the expectations of the system. This, in turn, allows her to be the tribute *within* the Games that can expose the entire system for what it is.

Conclusion

From the moment Katniss volunteers to go into the Arena in Prim's place, a political shift occurs. The District Twelve residents salute her in an almost forgotten way of showing unity. Though everyone faces an uphill struggles against President Snow, this initial awareness of what the Hunger Games symbolize surfaces again and again until the rebels' momentum cannot be stopped. As the rebellion spreads out across the districts in *Catching Fire*, Katniss reflects on what might be happening as she prepares for the Victory Tour: "Gale is right. If people have the courage, this could be an opportunity. He's also right that, since I have set it in motion, I could do so much."[1] The problem is that Katniss has to get past the fear that holds her back: "I may have been a catalyst for rebellion, but a leader should be someone with conviction, and I'm barely a convert myself."[2] She lit a spark, but she does not think she can fan the flames that are building.

What Katniss does not recognize as the uprisings spread is that she has revealed her conviction at the initial reaping. She showed all of Panem that she was ultimately immune to President Snow's worst weapon: fear. She protected her sister regardless of her own safety. When she is about to be paraded through the Capitol's streets in the tributes' parade, Katniss and Cinna have a brief exchange that anticipates what will follow from her participation in the Hunger Games. Cinna explains that the District Twelve costumes will appear to be on fire, but she and Peeta will be fine. Thus, Cinna tells them, "Don't be afraid."[3] Katniss responds almost as Cinna finishes speaking: "I'm not afraid."[4] She is focused even as she is about to trotted out as a sacrificial piece in President Snow's political games. Though she has no idea how the particulars will work out, her quick remark to Cinna reveals the underlying courage that in the moment and throughout The Hunger Games series allows her to be an effective political leader. She can withstand the worst President Snow can do.

Conclusion

The political arc that Katniss follows three general steps. The first, as noted above, is simply the recognition that Panem's political core is rotten. Though this may seem obvious, there exists a pervasive fear that undermines independent political thought. To admit the problem is to take the first step toward a solution. We see a specific result of this recognition. Katniss does not yield to fear. Rather, she stands firm and thus strengthens her resolve.

The crucial final step is to act. Bonhoeffer's call to action against Hitler included the following famous quote: "If I see a madman driving a car into a group of innocent bystanders, then I can't as a Christian, simply wait for the catastrophe and then comfort the wounded and bury the dead. I must try to wrestle the steering wheel out of the hands of the driver."[5] Once we recognize the source of injustice, we must act to remove the source of that injustice from our political processes. We must be proactive in our political engagement. In this respect, Katniss exemplifies political courage. She consistently fights against an unjust ruler despite the likelihood that she will not survive the struggle.

In Chapter 1, we looked at Gale's initial suggestion for how to undermine President Snow. If we just stop watching, then his entire plan will fall apart. This is partly true, but as we see in Bonhoeffer's call to action, tuning out must be a clear step forward. It cannot be an excuse to say that enough has been done, or, in Gale's case, the first step toward a political mindset that ultimately mirrors the injustices he fights against.

As this exploration of political themes in *The Hunger Games* wraps up, it is worth considering whether the rebels are successful as political actors in their victory and, if not, to consider the implications. In one respect they clearly succeed; they dispose of both President Snow and President Coin. The latter's death, however, signals a point of concern with respect to the question of whether the rebels ultimately erase the underlying moral bankruptcy that they set out to eliminate.

As discussed earlier, President Coin's death is problematic. While it does ensure that her own brand of political abuse will not prevail, the circumstances of her death achieve a moral good at the cost of assassination. Having evaluated this point already, the focus here will be on the significant conversation that occurs just before her death. As she moderates a conversation with important rebel figures, President Coin informs a small gathering that a decision has been reached not to kill

Conclusion

all Capitol citizens. Instead, she tells the group an alternative: "in lieu of eliminating the entire Capitol population, we have a final, symbolic Hunger Games, using the children directly related to those who held the most power."[6] The justification for this is to mirror the effects the Hunger Games had on the districts. Given the lengthy period of suffering in the shadow of the Arena, it makes sense, President Coin argues, to return the favor. Violence was used to remind the rebels of the Capitol's strength. To balance out the scales, the victorious rebels should do the same to those whom they have just defeated.

President Coin offers this supposed way out of killing everyone in the Capitol with two clear assumptions that must be noted. First, she casts the idea as somehow merciful, even though vengeance is the obvious motivation in the symbolic event a final Hunger Games would constitute. Second, though she asks those in attendance to vote on the matter, the decision is not really democratic. President Coin explains: "A majority of four will approve the plan" to hold or not to hold a final Hunger Games and "No one may abstain from the vote."[7] The goal, of course, is to absolve herself of responsibility, a fact she makes clear in stating that the result of the vote will be announced so that "it will be known it was done with your approval."[8] Katniss votes yes to honor Prim's memory, though the legacy runs counter to everything Prim stood for. Haymitch casts the deciding vote and says yes to align himself with Katniss. President Coin is satisfied with the vote, so much so that she tells Katniss she will let President Snow know what has been decided just before he is executed.

As they take the first steps toward rebuilding Panem, then, the rebels retain a troubling dynamic that they just fought to overcome. They move forward by casting blame on a victim in a way that justifies violence toward that victim. Holding a Hunger Games with Capitol children as the tributes would simple reverse the power dynamic that led to rebellion rather than adopting a political framework that preserves the basic rights of every citizen. Beattee recognizes this when he votes against the plan: "It would set a bad precedent. We have to stop viewing one another as enemies. At this point, unity is essential for our survival."[9] Beattee is right, but his common sense argument cannot override the deep-seated desired for revenge. It turns out Machiavelli was on point. Old wounds cannot easily be forgotten.

Conclusion

When Martin Luther King, Jr., accepted his Nobel Peace Prize in 1964, he outlined the steps needed to carry a culture defined by injustice toward a place where the core values of a truly free society would be possible. He claims: "Nonviolence is the answer to the crucial political and moral questions of our time—the need for mankind to overcome oppression and violence without resorting to violence and oppression."[10] King identifies the core dynamic that the rebels cannot shake in their victory: violence. Their decision to hold a Hunger Games retains the cycle that must be broken. Even after this decision, when Katniss seems to reverse course by assassinating President Coin, the change is brought about by another act of violence. So long as someone is oppressed freedom will be tainted by a violence that denies someone his or her rights.

King lays bare a reality that defines much of our political culture and history. We embrace noble ideals, but too often those ideals conflict with the practical application of political power. Quite simply, we do not recognize a basic truth King calls attention to in his acceptance speech: "Civilization and violence are antithetical concepts."[11] In order to break these opposites apart, King points toward the recovery of our moral ideals: "If this is to be achieved, man must evolve for all human conflict a method which rejects revenge, aggression and retaliation. The foundation of such a method is love."[12] The only way forward, King argues, is to recover a deeply moral commitment to one another and build a political identity on this foundation. Beattee is right. Revenge must give way to something that brings people together.

For all of the terrible things that happen as *Mockingjay* races toward its conclusion, there exists a brief moment when the reality of what King is talking about surfaces. As the rebels flee the lizards, Peeta reaches the point where he asks Katniss just to leave him to his death. Katniss reflects on what this would mean: "I really will have killed him. And Snow will win. Hot, bitter hatred courses through me. Snow has won too much already."[13] Peeta cannot continue is his current condition, yet Katniss cannot leave him. Like pointing the arrow at Finnick at the end of *Mockingjay*, she finds that she must make a decision that will ripple through the entire political narrative she is a part of. Peeta's life symbolizes what is good in Panem; in this moment his desire to reject the logic of the Hunger Games comes clearly into focus. If Katniss leaves Peeta, she will be handing President Snow an absolute symbolic victory.

Conclusion

Ever the fighter, Katniss refuses to give in. She tries the one thing has not tried in the context of her battle with President Snow. She acts out of love. "It's a long shot, it's suicide maybe, but I do the only thing I can think of. I lean in and kiss Peeta full on the mouth. His whole body starts shuddering, but I keep my lips pressed to his until I have to come up for air. My hands slide up his wrists to clasp his. 'Don't let him take you from me.'"[14] Katniss commits herself fully to her feelings amidst terrible circumstances and, in so doing, she finally reverses President Snow's attempt to use Peeta as a weapon against her. The kiss opens into the possibility that there is more than revenge. As a result, she asks Peeta for the simplest and most difficult thing he can do in this moment: "Stay with me."[15] Peeta's answer shows that there is still good amidst a war contested through the violent, self-serving politics of both President Snow and President Coin. He tells Katniss: "Always."[16]

In many ways it is a shame that Katniss's risk in this moment does not stay with her for the conclusion of the war. This act offers a chance to embark upon a political journey that could, once and for all, place commitment to others at the center of Panem's politics. Lane outlines how simple acts can create new frameworks for a society: "Once our values and habits are recreated, new frameworks for judging harm and value, cost and benefit, will produce new evaluations of what is lost and what is gained."[17] For Katniss and the other rebels, the challenge continues to be the willingness to reevaluate what is lost and gained. The emphasis on gaining through revenge impacts very important decisions. Even Katniss cannot fully let go of violence and revenge. Collectively, the rebels fail to find a "social imagination"[18] that can stop the cycle of violence in which they are trapped.

Lane offers some difficult words regarding the collective inability to let go of the negative politics we have seen throughout The Hunger Games series and, indeed, within our own political culture. She explains what amounts to a collective political failure: "the lesson we failed to learn from each one of these crises is that the excessive greed of a few was merely the exaggeration of a system made broadly in their image: a system which was set up to allow people to push the limits for the purpose of material accumulation without any requirement to consider the bigger picture."[19] When a handful of powerful people make decisions based on self-interest, and then pursue the perceived benefits of those

Conclusion

decisions without regard to the collective population, the outcomes are predictable. Importantly, these results rarely bode well for anyone in the end. Even those who benefit in the short term do so by burying intrinsic social weaknesses. When those wounds come into focus, we often find the destructive tit-for-tat cycle of political abuse that we see at the end of *Mockingjay*.

In recognizing the parallels between the political themes throughout The Hunger Games series and the state of our own political reality, it is easy to be discouraged. Further, we can see uncomfortable parallels between our own culture's fascination with spectator sports and violent entertainment. We are not about to send kids into an arena to fight to the death, but we do support a multi-billion dollar professional football league that brings violent sport into our homes for almost half a year's worth of weekends. We spend billions of dollars on a combination of grotesquely violent horror films and video games. We have become addicted to reality television. We can say the violence in The Hunger Games series is fiction, but if we look around, we can locate our culture on a spectrum that embraces violence in the name of entertainment.

During a recent TED Talk, Steven Pinker offers some surprising claims about public violence in our world today. For one, he argues that violence is receding as a social reality: "Although we don't have statistics for warfare throughout the Middle Ages to modern times, we know just from conventional history—the evidence was under our nose all along that there has been a reduction in socially sanctioned forms of violence."[20] When we considered this kind of in macro terms, we can easily jump to the great wars of the 20th century and the terror-driven violence of the 21st century. Pinker's point, however, is that in a localized capacity our culture has distanced itself from violence. For example, he notes: "For example, any social history will reveal that mutilation and torture were routine forms of criminal punishment. The kind of infraction today that would give you a fine, in those days would result in your tongue being cut out, your ears being cut off, you being blinded, a hand being chopped off and so on."[21] Violence used to be a default for many things including small legal infractions to voicing one's own political opinion. The world Pinker describes from the past reflects the state of politics in Panem. In our own world, we recognize that such violence destabilizes our collective good.

Conclusion

Though he outlines several explanations for our collective distance from violence, one point in particular is worth dwelling on: we increasingly value life. According to Pinker: "there is a widespread sentiment that life is cheap. In earlier times, when suffering and early death were common in one's own life, one has fewer compunctions about inflicting them on others. And as technology and economic efficiency make life longer and more pleasant, one puts a higher value on life in general."[22] Though our politics may not serve us in a variety of ways, on the whole life is better for more people in that we live longer and more securely than in the past. Despite the clear political biases that infringe upon the freedoms of a number of demographics, in general Americans experience autonomy and opportunity (though it is important to note that in no way is the "game" here played on a level playing field). If we can generally make a living and know our families will be safe, we are less inclined to turn toward violence as a means of achieving political ends. If we think back to the protests in Ferguson, the tension over a legal decision laced with our country's politics did not erupt into outright violence because those protesting did not erupt in their anger. They led in their choice to exercise their rights to speak freely.

There is, in other words, hope that despite our political failures we still exhibit the core values that America was built upon. In his 2nd Inaugural Address, President Lincoln points to the mindset that, ironically, looked to war as a way of resolving a fight over a deeply immoral political reality. Lincoln stated: "While the inaugural address was being delivered from this place, devoted altogether to *saving* the Union without war, insurgent agents were in the city seeking to *destroy* it without war—seeking to dissolve the Union and divide effects by negotiation. Both parties deprecated war, but one of them would *make* war rather than let the nation survive, and the other would *accept* war rather than let it perish, and the war came."[23] Conflict united two halves of a nation built on shared principles. Notably, Lincoln binds the two sides together as complicit in the war. The point is clear. The war came about because all sides embraced it.

Lincoln (obviously) lays moral blame on one side of the conflict, but this does not prevent him from looking past the specific wrongs to a broader goal. Unity as a nation can override even the deepest wounds. The conclusion of the 2nd Inaugural Address points to this reconcilia-

Conclusion

tion as possible: "With malice toward none, with charity for all, with firmness in the right as God gives us to see the right, let us strive on to finish the work we are in, to bind up the nation's wounds, to care for him who shall have borne the battle and for his widow and his orphan, to do all which may achieve and cherish a just and lasting peace among ourselves and with all nations."[24] Anger must give way to the basic rights that everyone enjoys as individuals. Out of this reclaimed common ground, politics can be rebuilt to treat the wounded and achieve a stable, lasting peace that affirms everyone as equal parts of the country's political tapestry.

Chapter Notes

Introduction

1. "Herod I," *Jewish Encyclopedia*, available at: http://jewishencyclopedia.com/articles/7598-herod-I (accessed 28 August 2014).

2. Professor H. Graetz, *History of the Jews* (Philadelphia: Jewish Publication Society of America, 1896), 76.

3. Matthew 2:1–4. All quotes from the Bible come from the *HarperCollins Study Bible New Revised Standard Version*, Society of Biblical Literature, eds. Harold W. Attridge and Wayne A. Meeks (New York: Harper One, 2006).

4. One could argue that the prophecy cited as the basis for identifying Jesus as a threat can be read as political. The fact that the new king will emerge out of a lowly political place (Matthew 2:6) suggests an inversion of existing political order. Further, the language of "ruler" has obvious political implications. However, a quick meeting between Herod and the Jewish leaders in Jerusalem would presumably have clarified that Bethlehem's new prominence and the role of the new ruler were theological in nature. Both characteristics elaborate on the image of the "shepherd" as a religious rather than a political concept.

5. Matthew 2:7–8.
6. Matthew 2:12.
7. Matthew 2:16.
8. As a North American society, Panem can be considered part of our own history. Thus, even though a connection to Judeo-Christianity is never stated explicitly in *The Hunger Games* (and this is not surprising given that religion in general is absent from the plot and narrative of the series), historical continuity allows for this suggestion.

9. Suzanne Collins, *Mockingjay* (New York: Scholastic Press, 2010), 306.
10. Ibid., 311.
11. See Aristotle, *The Ethics of Aristotle: The Nicomachean Ethics*, Penguin Classics, trans. J.A.K. Thomson (New York: Penguin Books, 1976), I.i. This is a very quick summary remark about how Aristotle conceptualizes individual virtue. His ideas are, of course, far more complex than I cover here. A deeper exploration of how Aristotle arrives at his conclusion and, moreover, how that conclusion fits within the larger context of an individual's social context is an intellectual journey that I very much encourage but will not cover within the scope of this book.
12. Aristotle, *Ethics*, I.vii.
13. Luke 6:31. This is not to make an explicit religious or theological argument. Rather, I refer to the Bible because it is the most common *moral* text in our culture.
14. Luke 6:37–38.
15. Aristotle, *Ethics*, I.iii.
16. Ibid.

Chapter 1

1. Suzanne Collins, *The Hunger Games* (New York: Scholastic Press, 2008), 15.
2. Ibid., 6.
3. Ibid., 16.
4. *The Hunger Games*, directed by Gary Ross (Los Angeles: Lionsgate, 2012), DVD.
5. Ibid.
6. Ibid.
7. Eberhard Bethge, *Dietrich Bonhoeffer: A Biography*, ed. Victoria J. Barnett (Minneapolis: Fortress Press, 2000), 736.
8. Ibid.

9. Eric Greitens, *The Heart and the Fist: The Education of a Humanitarian, the Making of a Navy SEAL*, Reprint Edition (New York: Mariner Books, 2012), 11.

10. Ibid., 36.

11. The timing of Greitens' service in the military affords a counterpoint to much of the extreme political discourse of late–20th and early 21st century American politics. He served in a time when America's political identity struggled to make sense of the world's post–9/11 political topography. The entire book is a worthwhile read for his insights, but the specific insights he offers during his time in Kenya speak to the impact localized political decisions can have.

12. Jedediah Purdy, *For Common Things: Irony, Trust, and Commitment in America Today* (New York: Vintage, 2000), 83.

13. United Nations, "The Universal Declaration of Human Rights," available at: http://www.un.org/en/documents/udhr/ (accessed 20 October 2014).

14. Purdy, xiii.

15. "The Universal Declaration of Human Rights."

16. Ibid.

17. Ibid.

18. Purdy, xv.

19. Reinhold Niebuhr, *Moral Man and Immoral Society* (New York: Charles Scribners's Sons, 1960), 34.

20. *The Hunger Games: Catching Fire*, directed by Francis Lawrence (Los Angeles: Lionsgate, 2013), DVD.

21. Ibid.

22. Ibid.

23. *The Hunger Games*, DVD.

24. Suzanne Collins, *Catching Fire* (London: Scholastic, 2009), 283.

25. *The Hunger Games*, 142.

26. *Catching Fire*, 274.

27. Jill Olthouse, "'I Will Be Your Mockingjay': The Power and Paradox of Metaphor in The Hunger Games Trilogy," *The Hunger Games and Philosophy: A Critique of Pure Treason*, eds. George A. Dunn and Nicolas Michaud (Hoboken, NJ: John Wiley & Sons, 2012) 53.

28. Andrew Zolli and Ann Marie Healy, *Resilience: Why Things Bounce Back*, Reprint Edition (New York: Simon & Schuster, 2013), 19.

Chapter 2

1. *Gladiator*, directed by Ridley Scott (Los Angeles: Paramount, 2000), DVD.

2. Ibid.

3. Horace, *Sermones*, Verity Platt, *Facing the Gods: Epiphany and Representation in Graeco-Roman Art, Literature* (Cambridge, UK: Cambridge University Press, 2011), 355.

4. *The Hunger Games*, 144.

5. Ibid., 144–145.

6. Plutarch, *Lives: Demosthenes and Cicero. Alexander and Caesar*, trans. Bernadotte Perrin, Loeb Classical Library (Volume VII) (Cambridge, MA: Harvard University Press, 1919), 5.4.

7. Ibid.

8. Ibid.

9. Cicero, *Letters*, ed. Evelyn S. Shuckburgh, Perseus Digital Library, Tufts University, available at: www.perseus.tufts.edu (accessed 31 October 2014).

10. Olthouse, 45.

11. Tacitus, *A Dialogue on Oratory*, eds. Alfred John Church and William Jackson Brodribb, Perseus Digital Library, Tufts University, available at: www.perseus.tufts.edu (accessed 31 October 2014).

12. "Interview with Suzanne Collins," Scholastic Book Clubs, available at: https://clubs-kids.scholastic.co.uk/clubs_content/18829 (accessed 31 October 2014).

13. Andrew Shaffer, "The Joy of Watching Others Suffer: Schadenfreude and the Hunger Games," *The Hunger Games and Philosophy: A Critique of Pure Treason*, eds. George A. Dunn and Nicolas Michaud (Hoboken, NJ: John Wiley & Sons, 2012), 79.

14. Charles Murray, "Deeper into the Brain," *National Review* (2000).

15. Edward Baptist, *The Half Has Never Been Told: Slavery and the Making of American Capitalism* (New York: Basic Books, 2014).

Notes—Chapter 3

16. "Our Withdrawn Review Blood Cotton," *The Economist*, Online Extra (4 September 2014), available at: http://www.economist.com/news/books/21615864-how-slaves-built-american-capitalism-blood-cotton (accessed 30 October 2014).
17. Online extra (4 September 2014).
18. Ibid.
19. Ibid.
20. Quoted in Jeffrey Sachs, *The End of Poverty: Economic Possibilities for Our Time*, Reprint Edition (New York: Penguin Books, 2006), 311..
21. Ibid.
22. Victor W.A. Mbarika and Irene Mbarika, "Africa Calling: Burgeoning Wireless Networks Connect Africans to the World and to Each Other," *IEEE Spectrum* (1 May 2006), available at: http://spectrum.ieee.org/telecom/wireless/africa-calling (accessed 30 October 2014).
23. Sachs, 311.
24. Charles Murray, "Interview on Race and IQ," *Think Tank with Ben Wattenberg*, PBS (1994), television show.
25. *Mockingjay*, 223
26. Ibid.
27. Seneca, *On the Shortness of Life*, trans. C.D.N. Costa, Penguin Great Ideas (New York: Penguin Books, 2005), XIII.6.8.
28. Ibid.
29. Aurelius, Marcus Aurelius, *The Meditations*, trans. George Long, The Internet Classics Archive, available at: http://classics.mit.edu/Antoninus/meditations.mb.txt (accessed 1 November 2014).
30. Ibid.
31. Purdy, 48.
32. Ibid., 71.

Chapter 3

1. President George W. Bush, "Securing the Homeland, Strengthening the Nation," available at: http://www.dhs.gov/securing-homeland-strengthening-nation (accessed 30 October 2014).
2. Ibid.
3. Ibid.
4. Ibid.
5. Jean-Jacque Rousseau, *The Social Contract*, available at: http://www.constitution.org/jjr/socon_01.htm (accessed 24 October 2014).
6. Ibid.
7. Jacob G. Hornberger, "Ten Ways a Libertarian Society Would Be Different," The Future of Freedom Foundation, available at: http://fff.org/2013/02/01/ten-ways-a-libertarian-society-would-be-different/ (accessed 1 November 2014).
8. Tiffany Gabbay, "Elizabeth Warren on Class Warfare: 'There is nobody in this country who got rich on his own,'" *The Blaze* (21 September 2011), available at: http://www.theblaze.com/stories/elizabeth-warren-on-class-warfare-there-is-nobody-in-this-country-who-got-rich-on-his-own (accessed 2 September 2014).
9. Ibid.
10. Ibid.
11. Frank Newport, "Congress Approval Sits at 14% Two Months Before Elections." *Gallup*, available at: http://www.gallup.com/poll/175676/congress-approval-sits-two-months-elections.aspx (accessed 1 November 2014).
12. "Voter Turnout," The Center for Voting and Democracy, available at: http://www.fairvote.org/research-and-analysis/voter-turnout/ (accessed 1 November 2014).
13. T. Becket Adams, "Prediction: Major Voter Turnout for Midterm Elections." *Washington Examiner* (August 25, 2014), available at: http://www.washingtonexaminer.com/prediction-major-voter-turnout-for-midterm-elections/article/2552429 (accessed 1 November 2014).
14. Rousseau, *The Social Contract*.
15. Ibid.
16. Ibid.
17. Ibid.
18. Thomas Hobbes, *The Leviathan*, 1660, available at: http://oregonstate.edu/instruct/phl302/texts/hobbes/leviathan-contents.html (accessed 2 November 2014).
19. Ibid.
20. *Catching Fire*, 21.
21. Hobbes, *Leviathan*.
22. Ibid.
23. Ibid.

24. Benjamin Franklin, "Pennsylvania Assembly: Reply to the Governor," The Papers of Benjamin Franklin, available at: http://franklinpapers.org/franklin/framedVolumes.jsp?vol=6&page=238a (accessed 7 November 2014).
25. Purdy, 46.
26. Luke 12:48.
27. Purdy, 46.
28. Luke 11:17.
29. Purdy, 25.

Chapter 4

1. *Catching Fire*, DVD.
2. Ibid.
3. Ibid.
4. *The Hunger Games*, DVD.
5. Ibid.
6. *Catching Fire*, DVD.
7. Niccolò Machiavelli, *The Prince*, The Constitution Society, available at: http://www.constitution.org/mac/prince00.htm (accessed 7 November 2014).
8. *The Hunger Games: Mockingjay—Part I*, directed by Francis Lawrence (Los Angeles: Lionsgate, 2014), film.
9. Machiavelli, *The Prince*.
10. *The Hunger Games*, DVD.
11. Ibid.
12. Ibid.
13. Machiavelli, *The Prince*.
14. *Catching Fire*, DVD.
15. Confucius, *Analects: With Selections from Traditional Commentaries*, trans. Edward Slingerland (Indianapolis: Hackett Publishing Company, 2003), 2.19.
16. Machiavelli, *The Prince*.
17. Ibid.
18. Adolf Hitler, *Mein Kampf*, The Internet Archive, available at: https://archive.org/details/meinkampf035176mbp (accessed 20 November 2014).
19. Niccolò Machiavelli, *The Discourses*, trans. Leslie J. Walker, S.J., ed. Bernard Clark, Penguin Classics (New York: Penguin Books, 2003).
20. Ibid., Book 4.
21. Ibid.
22. Niebuhr, 33.
23. Michel Foucault, *The History of Sexuality, Vol. 1: An Introduction*, trans. Robert Hurley, Reissue Edition (New York, Vintage, 1990), 1.86.
24. Niebuhr, 34.
25. Machiavelli, *The Discourses*, Book 4.
26. Ibid.

Chapter 5

1. *The Hunger Games*, DVD.
2. *The Hunger Games*, 23.
3. Ibid., 19.
4. John 28:29–31.
5. John 28:38.
6. See Matthew 27:15–23.
7. Matthew 27:24.
8. See Exodus 3:11 and Jeremiah 1:6 respectively.
9. Zolli, 6.
10. Viktor E. Frankl, *Man's Search for Meaning* (New York: Washington Square Press, 1984), 172.
11. See Genesis 38:16ff.
12. Genesis 50:20.
13. Frankl, 173.
14. *Mockingjay*, film.
15. Confucius, *Analects*, 2.1.
16. Purdy, 201.
17. Ibid., 40.
18. Plato, *The Republic*, trans. Desmond Lee, Penguin Classics, Second Edition (New York: Penguin Books, 2003).
19. Purdy, 40.
20. Greitens, 58.
21. *Mockingjay*, 215.
22. Ibid.
23. Ibid., 217.
24. Ibid.
25. Martin Luther King, Jr., "Acceptance Speech," The Nobel Peace Prize, 1964, available at: http://www.nobelprize.org/nobel_prizes/peace/laureates/1964/king-acceptance.html (accessed 26 November 2014).
26. Ibid.
27. Ibid.
28. Greitens, 189.
29. *The Bourne Ultimatum*, directed by Paul Greengrass (Los Angeles: NBC Universal, 2007), DVD.

Chapter 6

1. *The Hunger Games*, 19.
2. Ibid., 24.
3. Ibid., 25.
4. William Shakespeare and Paul Werstine, *King John*, ed. Barbara A. Mowat, Folger Shakespeare Library (New York: Simon & Schuster, 2006), 1.4.116–117.
5. *Catching Fire*, 224.
6. Ibid., 226.
7. Machiavelli, *The Prince*.
8. Aristotle, *Ethics*, VI.ii.
9. Ibid., VI.ii.
10. Ibid.
11. Ibid.
12. *Catching Fire*, 293.
13. *Catching Fire*, DVD.
14. Aristotle, *Ethics*, VI.v.
15. See Sahil Kapur, "Mitch McConnell Filibusters His Own Bill to Lift Debt Ceiling," TPM (6 December 2012), available at: http://talkingpointsmemo.com/dc/mcconnell-filibusters-his-own-bill-to-lift-debt-ceiling (accessed 1 December 2014).
16. Aristotle, *Ethics*, VI.v.
17. Ibid., VI.i.
18. Ibid., VI.v.
19. Ibid., VI.viii.
20. Malcolm Gladwell, *The Tipping Point: How Little Things Can Make a Big Difference*. (London: Abacus, 2006), 36.
21. Ibid., 54.
22. Albert-László Barabási, *Linked: How Everything Is Connected to Everything Else and What It Means for Business, Science, and Everyday Life* (New York: Plume Books, 2003), 53.
23. Zolli, 258.
24. Ibid.
25. *Catching Fire*, 228.
26. Machiavelli, *The Prince*.

Chapter 7

1. Thomas Jefferson, The Declaration of Independence, available at: http://www.archives.gov/exhibits/charters/declaration_transcript.html (accessed 24 October 2014).
2. Ibid.
3. Ibid.
4. Ibid.
5. Benjamin Franklin, "At the Signing of the Declaration of Independence" available at: http://www.ushistory.org/franklin/quotable/quote71.htm *(accessed 24 October 2014).*
6. Thomas Jefferson, "First Inaugural Address," 1801, The Heritage Foundation, available at: http://www.heritage.org/initiatives/first-principles/primary-sources/jeffersons-first-inaugural-address (accessed 24 October 2014).
7. *Catching Fire*, 432.
8. Ibid., 433.
9. Ibid., 437.
10. Lincoln Krause "Playing for the Breaks: Insurgent Mistakes," *Parameters* (2009), available at: http://strategicstudiesinstitute.army.mil/pubs/parameters/Articles/09autumn/krause.pdf (accessed 15 November 2014), 49.
11. Ibid., 50.
12. Ibid.
13. Ibid.
14. Ibid., 51.
15. Ibid.
16. Ibid., 54–55.
17. Ibid., 55.
18. Ibid., 56.
19. *Mockingjay*, 204.
20. Ibid.
21. Ibid.
22. Ibid., 205.
23. Ibid.
24. Ibid.
25. Ibid.
26. Aristotle, *The Politics of Aristotle*, trans. and ed. Ernest Barker (Oxford: Oxford University Press, 1958) III.ii $2.
27. Greitens, 301.
28. Zolli, 6.
29. Ibid., 211.
30. Patrick Henry, "Speech of Patrick Henry Before the Virginia Ratifying Convention," *The Essential Federalist and Anti-Federalist Papers*, ed. David Wootten (Indianapolis: Hackett Publishing Company, 2003) 26.

Chapter 8

1. Lindsay Issow Averill, "Sometimes the World Is Hungry for People Who Care: Katniss and the Feminist Care Ethic," *The Hunger Games and Philosophy: A Critique of Pure Treason*, eds. George A. Dunn and Nicolas Michaud (Hoboken, NJ: John Wiley & Sons, 2012), 179.
2. *Mockingjay*, 36.
3. Christina Van Dyk, "Discipline and the Docile Body: Regulating Hungers in the Capitol," *The Hunger Games and Philosophy: A Critique of Pure Treason*. Eds. George A. Dunn and Nicolas Michaud. Hoboken, NJ: John Wiley & Sons, 2012), 262.
4. *Mockingjay*, 226.
5. Ibid., 227.
6. Ecclesiastes 3:1.
7. Ecclesiastes 3:4.
8. Aristotle, *Politics*, V.iii §4.
9. Machiavelli, *The Prince*.
10. Ibid.
11. *Mockingjay*, 354.
12. Ibid.
13. Ibid.
14. Ibid.
15. Ibid., 355–356.
16. Ibid., 356.
17. Ibid.
18. Ibid.
19. Ibid.
20. Aristotle, *Politics*, II.viii §27.
21. Ibid.
22. *Mockingjay*, 372.
23. Ibid., 261.
24. Ibid.
25. Ibid., 294.

Chapter 9

1. Chad William Timm, "Class Is in Session: Power and Privilege in Panem," *The Hunger Games and Philosophy: A Critique of Pure Treason*, eds. George A. Dunn and Nicolas Michaud (Hoboken, NJ: John Wiley & Sons, 2012), 280.
2. Sam Sommers, *Situations Matter: Understanding How Context Transforms Your World* (New York: Riverhead Books, 2011), 131.
3. Jeffrey Stout, *Ethics After Babel: The Languages of Morals and Their Discontents* (Princeton: Princeton University Press, 2001), 2.
4. *Catching Fire*, DVD.
5. Ibid.
6. Ibid.
7. *Mockingjay*, film.
8. Ryan Van Bibber, "St. Louis Police Officers Association Criticizes Rams Players for 'Hands Up Don't Shoot' Gesture," SB Nation (30 November 2014), available at: http://www.sbnation.com/nfl/2014/11/30/7312145/rams-players-hands-up-dont-shoot-police *(accessed 30 November 2014)*.
9. Ibid.
10. While it is not the purpose of this discussion to delve into the legal circumstances of the grand jury's decision, it is worth noting that, legally speaking, there are serious questions involving how the grand jury was convened and run. For a helpful summary of some of these points, see Judd Legum, "How One Woman Could Hit the Reset Button in the Case Against Darren Wilson," Think Progress (2 December 2014), available at: http://thinkprogress.org/justice/2014/12/02/3598082/one-woman-could-appoint-a-special-prosecutor-and-bring-justice-to-ferguson/ (accessed 2 December 2014).
11. Van Bibber.
12. Ibid.
13. Stout, 4.
14. Niebuhr, 34–35.
15. *Mockingjay*, 53.
16. Ibid.
17. Ibid.
18. Ibid., 54.
19. Niebuhr, 35.
20. Ibid.
21. *The Hunger Games*, 62.
22. Niebuhr, 36.
23. Ibid.
24. Though I won't delve into further detail here about biblical echoes—there is enough such exploration elsewhere in this book—I would like to emphasize the strong parallel here between the arrival of the savior figure (Katniss/Jesus) with someone who comes just before to start clearing the

way (Cinna/John). Someone else has to do a lot of heavy lifting to prime a society for a political message based on true moral commitment. John the Baptist loses his head for his work preparing the way for Jesus just as Cinna pays with his life for creating the outline of the Mockingjay.

25. *The Hunger Games*, 65.
26. *The Hunger Games*, DVD.
27. *The Hunger Games*, 67.
28. Niebuhr, 37.
29. Ibid., 39.
30. Melissa Lane, *Eco-Republic: What the Ancients Can Teach Us About Ethics, Virtue, and Sustainable Living*, Reprint Edition (Princeton: Princeton University Press, 2013), 13.
31. George A. Dunn, "The Odds Have Not Been Very Dependable of Late": Morality and Luck in The Hunger Games Trilogy," *The Hunger Games and Philosophy: A Critique of Pure Treason*, eds. George A. Dunn and Nicolas Michaud (Hoboken, NJ: John Wiley & Sons, 2012), 71.
32. Frankl, 174.

Chapter 10

1. Commission on Presidential Debates, "September 26, 1960, Debate Transcript," available at: http://www.debates.org/index.php?page=september-26–1960-debate-transcript (accessed 13 November 2014).
2. Ibid.
3. Ibid.
4. Ibid.
5. Ibid.
6. Though the transcript offers everything one needs to get a handle on the relatively blasé debate, watching a video of the debate will help convey the point at hand with additional nuance. The debate can be found at: https://www.youtube.com/watch?v=gbrcRKqLSRw (accessed 28 November 2014).
7. *The Hunger Games*, 28.
8. Ibid.
9. Torie Rose DeGhett, "The War Photo No One Would Publish," *The Atlantic* (8 August 2014). Available at: http://www.theatlantic.com/features/archive/2014/08/the-war-photo-no-one-would-publish/375762/ (accessed 28 November 2014).
10. Ibid.
11. Ibid.
12. Purdy, 42.
13. Ibid., 43.
14. Michael A. Memoli, "Fox News Viewers Less Informed About Current Events, Poll Shows," *Los Angeles Times* (21 November 2011), available at: http://articles.latimes.com/2011/nov/21/news/la-pn-fox-news-poll-20111121 (accessed 1 December 2014).
15. Ibid.
16. Ibid.
17. *Catching Fire*, DVD.
18. Madeline Albright, "Vladimir Putin: The Leader Who's Testing the West." *Time* (23 April 2014), available at: http://time.com/70855/vladimir-putin-2014-time-100/ (accessed 1 December 2014).
19. "Russians' Approval of Putin Hits Near All-Time High, Poll Shows," RT (28 October 2014), available at: http://rt.com/politics/196212-piutin-approval-grows-poll/ (accessed 1 December 2014).
20. Erik Pineda, "4 Lies Fed by Putin to Russians to Justify Invasion of Ukraine, Europe and Nuclear Showdown with America. *International Business Times* (29 November 2014), available at: http://au.ibtimes.com/articles/574377/20141129/putin-russia-ukraine-europe-invasion-world-war.htm#.VHyMUoe2K5Q (accessed 2 December 2014).
21. Timm, 278.
22. Ibid.
23. Ibid.
24. Ibid.
25. Olthouse, 42.
26. Hitler, *Mein Kampf*.
27. Ibid.
28. Ibid.
29. Gary Hart, *God and Caesar in America: An Essay on Religion and Politics* (Golden, CO: Fulcrum Publishing, 2005), 21.
30. Ibid.
31. Ibid.
32. *Catching Fire*, 290–291.

Chapter 11

1. René Girard, *The Scapegoat*, trans. Yvonne Freccero (Baltimore: Johns Hopkins University Press, 1986), 15.
2. Ibid.
3. Ibid.
4. Ibid.
5. Ibid.
6. Ibid., 2–3.
7. Ibid., 3.
8. Ibid., 42.
9. Ibid.
10. Ibid.
11. Ibid.
12. Ibid., 43.
13. Ibid., 40. Emphasis added.
14. Girard, 40.
15. *Braveheart*, directed by Mel Gibson (Los Angeles: Paramount, 1995), DVD.
16. *Mockingjay*, 178.
17. Ibid., 171.
18. Girard, 26.
19. Ibid., 21.
20. Ibid., 20.

Conclusion

1. *Catching Fire*, 140.
2. Ibid.
3. *The Hunger Games*, DVD.
4. Ibid.
5. Quoted in Russel Moldovan, *Martin Luther King, Jr.: An Oral History of His Religious Witness and Life* (San Francisco: International Scholars Publications, 1999), 26.
6. *Mockingjay*, 369.
7. Ibid.
8. Ibid.
9. Ibid., 370.
10. Martin Luther King, Jr., "Acceptance Speech," The Nobel Peace Prize, 1964, available at: http://www.nobelprize.org/nobel_prizes/peace/laureates/1964/king-acceptance.html (accessed 1 December 2014).
11. Ibid.
12. Ibid.
13. *Mockingjay*, 313.
14. Ibid., 314.
15. Ibid.
16. Ibid.
17. Lane, 12.
18. Ibid.
19. Ibid., 30.
20. Steven Pinker, "The Surprising Decline in Violence," TED2007, transcript available at: https://www.ted.com/talks/steven_pinker_on_the_myth_of_violence/transcript?language=en (accessed 8 December 2014).
21. Ibid.
22. Ibid.
23. Abraham Lincoln, "Second Inaugural Address," Bartelby, available at: http://www.bartleby.com/124/pres32.html (accessed 3 December 2014).
24. Ibid.

Bibliography

Adams, T. Becket. "Prediction: Major Voter Turnout for Midterm Elections." *The Washington Examiner* (25 August 2014). Available at: http://www.washingtonexaminer.com/prediction-major-voter-turnout-for-midterm-elections/article/2552429.

Albright, Madeline. "Vladimir Putin: The Leader Who's Testing the West." *Time* (23 April 2014). Available at: http://time.com/70855/vladimir-putin-2014-time-100/.

Aristotle. *The Ethics of Aristotle: The Nicomachean Ethics*. Penguin Classics. Trans. J.A.K. Thomson. New York: Penguin Books, 1976.

_____. *The Politics of Aristotle*. Trans. and Ed. Ernest Barker. Oxford: Oxford University Press, 1958.

Aurelius, Marcus. *The Meditations*. Trans. George Long. The Internet Classics Archive. Available at: http://classics.mit.edu/Antoninus/meditations.mb.txt.

Averill, Lindsay Issow. "Sometimes the World Is Hungry for People Who Care: Katniss and the Feminist Care Ethic." *The Hunger Games and Philosophy: A Critique of Pure Treason*. Eds. George A. Dunn and Nicolas Michaud. Hoboken, NJ: John Wiley & Sons, 2012. 162–176.

Baptist, Edward. *The Half Has Never Been Told: Slavery and the Making of American Capitalism*. New York: Basic Books, 2014.

Barabási, Albert-László. *Linked: How Everything Is Connected to Everything Else and What It Means for Business, Science, and Everyday Life*. New York: Plume Books, 2003.

Bethge, Eberhard. *Dietrich Bonhoeffer: A Biography*. Ed. Victoria J. Barnett. Minneapolis: Fortress Press, 2000.

The Bourne Ultimatum. Directed by Paul Greengrass. Los Angeles: NBC Universal, 2007. DVD.

Braveheart. Directed by Mel Gibson. Los Angeles: Paramount, 1995. DVD.

Bush, President George W. "Securing the Homeland, Strengthening the Nation." Available at: http://www.dhs.gov/securing-homeland-strengthening-nation.

Cicero, M. Tullius. *Letters*. Ed. Evelyn S. Shuckburgh. Perseus Digital Library, Tufts University. Available at: www.perseus.tufts.edu.

Collins, Suzanne. *Catching Fire*. London: Scholastic, 2009.

_____. *The Hunger Games*. New York: Scholastic Press, 2008.

_____. *Mockingjay*. New York: Scholastic Press, 2010.

Commission on Presidential Debates. "September 26, 1960, Debate Transcript." Available at: http://www.debates.org/index.php?page=september-26–1960-debate-transcript.

Confucius. *Analects: With Selections from Traditional Commentaries*. Trans. Edward Slingerland. Indianapolis: Hackett Publishing Company, 2003.

DeGhett, Torie Rose. "The War Photo No One Would Publish." *The Atlantic* (8 August 2014). Available at: http://www.theatlantic.com/features/archive/2014/08/the-war-photo-no-one-would-publish/375762/.

Dunn, George A. "The Odds Have Not Been Very Dependable of Late": Moral-

Bibliography

ity and Luck in The Hunger Games Trilogy." *The Hunger Games and Philosophy: A Critique of Pure Treason.* Eds. George A. Dunn and Nicolas Michaud. Hoboken, NJ: John Wiley & Sons, 2012. 56–74.

Foucault, Michel. *The History of Sexuality, Vol. 1: An Introduction.* Trans. Robert Hurley. Reissue Edition. New York, Vintage, 1990.

Frankl, Viktor E. *Man's Search for Meaning.* New York: Washington Square Press, 1984.

Franklin, Benjamin. "At the Signing of the Declaration of Independence." Available at: http://www.ushistory.org/franklin/quotable/quote71.htm.

———. "Pennsylvania Assembly: Reply to the Governor." The Papers of Benjamin Franklin. Available at: http://franklinpapers.org/franklin/framedVolumes.jsp?vol=6&page=238a.

Gabbay, Tiffany. "Elizabeth Warren on Class Warfare: 'There is nobody in this country who got rich on his own.'" *The Blaze* (21 September 2011). Available at: http://www.theblaze.com/stories/elizabeth-warren-on-class-warfare-there-is-nobody-in-this-country-who-got-rich-on-his-own.

Girard, René. *The Scapegoat.* Trans. Yvonne Freccero. Baltimore: Johns Hopkins University Press, 1986.

Gladiator. Directed by Ridley Scott. Los Angeles: Paramount, 2000. DVD.

Gladwell, Malcolm. *The Tipping Point: How Little Things Can Make a Big Difference.* London: Abacus, 2006.

Graetz, H. *History of the Jews.* Philadelphia: Jewish Publication Society of America, 1896.

Greitens, Eric. *The Heart and the Fist: The Education of a Humanitarian, the Making of a Navy SEAL.* Reprint Edition. New York: Mariner Books, 2012.

HarperCollins Study Bible New Revised Standard Version. Society of Biblical Literature. Eds. Harold W. Attridge and Wayne A. Meeks. New York: Harper One, 2006.

Hart, Gary. *God and Caesar in America: An Essay on Religion and Politics.* Golden, CO: Fulcrum Publishing, 2005.

"Herod I." *Jewish Encyclopedia.* 1906. Available at: http://jewishencyclopedia.com/articles/7598-herod-I.

Henry, Patrick. "Speech of Patrick Henry Before the Virginia Ratifying Convention." *The Essential Federalist and Anti-Federalist Papers.* Ed. David Wootten. Indianapolis: Hackett Publishing Company, 2003.

Hitler, Adolf. *Mein Kampf.* The Internet Archive. Available at: https://archive.org/details/meinkampf035176mbp.

Hobbes, Thomas. *The Leviathan.* 1660. Available at: http://oregonstate.edu/instruct/phl302/texts/hobbes/leviathan-contents.html.

Horace. *Sermones.* Verity Platt, *Facing the Gods: Epiphany and Representation in Graeco-Roman Art, Literature.* Cambridge, UK: Cambridge University Press, 2011.

Hornberger, Jacob G. "Ten Ways a Libertarian Society Would Be Different." The Future of Freedom Foundation. Available at: http://fff.org/2013/02/01/ten-ways-a-libertarian-society-would-be-different/.

The Hunger Games. Directed by Gary Ross. Los Angeles: Lionsgate, 2012. DVD.

The Hunger Games: Catching Fire. Directed by Francis Lawrence. Los Angeles: Lionsgate, 2013. DVD.

The Hunger Games: Mockingjay—Part I. Directed by Francis Lawrence. Los Angeles: Lionsgate, 2014. Film.

"Interview with Suzanne Collins." Scholastic Book Clubs. Available at: https://clubs-kids.scholastic.co.uk/clubs_content/18829.

Jefferson, Thomas. *The Declaration of Independence.* United States Government Archives. Available at: http://

Bibliography

www.archives.gov/exhibits/charters/declaration_transcript.html.

———. "First Inaugural Address." 1801. The Heritage Foundation. Available at: http://www.heritage.org/initiatives/first-principles/primary-sources/jeffersons-first-inaugural-address.

Kapur, Sahil. "Mitch McConnell Filibusters His Own Bill to Lift Debt Ceiling." TPM (6 December 2012). Available at: http://talkingpointsmemo.com/dc/mcconnell-filibusters-his-own-bill-to-lift-debt-ceiling.

"Kennedy-Nixon First Presidential Debate 1960." YouTube. Available at: https://www.youtube.com/watch?v=gbrcRKqLSRw.

King, Martin Luther, Jr. "Acceptance Speech." The Nobel Peace Prize, 1964. Available at: http://www.nobelprize.org/nobel_prizes/peace/laureates/1964/king-acceptance.html.

———. "Letter from Birmingham Jail." 1963. Available at: http://www.uscrossier.org/pullias/wp-content/uploads/2012/06/king.pdf.

Krause, Lincoln. "Playing for the Breaks: Insurgent Mistakes." *Parameters* (2009). Available at: http://strategicstudiesinstitute.army.mil/pubs/parameters/Articles/09autumn/krause.pdf.

Lane, Melissa. *Eco-Republic: What the Ancients Can Teach Us About Ethics, Virtue, and Sustainable Living*. Reprint Edition. Princeton: Princeton University Press, 2013.

Legum, Judd. "How One Woman Could Hit the Reset Button in the Case Against Darren Wilson." Think Progress (2 December 2014). Available at: http://thinkprogress.org/justice/2014/12/02/3598082/one-woman-could-appoint-a-special-prosecutor-and-bring-justice-to-ferguson/.

Lincoln, Abraham. "Second Inaugural Address." Bartelby. Available at: http://www.bartleby.com/124/pres32.html.

Machiavelli, Niccolò. *The Discourses*. Trans. Leslie J. Walker, S.J. Ed. Bernard Click. Penguin Classics. New York: Penguin Books, 2003.

———. *The Prince*. The Constitution Society. Available at: http://www.constitution.org/mac/prince00.htm.

Mbarika, Victor W.A., and Irene Mbarika. "Africa Calling: Burgeoning Wireless Networks Connect Africans to the World and to Each Other." *IEEE Spectrum* (1 May 2006). Available at: http://spectrum.ieee.org/telecom/wireless/africa-calling.

Memoli, Michael A. "'Fox News Viewers Less Informed About Current Events, Poll Shows." *Los Angeles Times* (21 November 2011). Available at: http://articles.latimes.com/2011/nov/21/news/la-pn-fox-news-poll-20111121.

Moldovan, Russel. *Martin Luther King, Jr.: An Oral History of His Religious Witness and Life*. San Francisco: International Scholars Publications, 1999.

Murray, Charles. "Deeper into the Brain." *National Review* (2000).

———. "Interview on Race and IQ." *Think Tank with Ben Wattenberg*. PBS (1994). Television show.

Newport, Frank. "Congress Approval Sits at 14% Two Months Before Elections." Gallup Polls (8 September 2014). Available at: http://www.gallup.com/poll/175676/congress-approval-sits-two-months-elections.aspx.

Niebuhr, Reinhold. *Moral Man and Immoral Society*. New York: Charles Scribners's Sons, 1960.

Olthouse, Jill. "'I Will Be Your Mockingjay': The Power and Paradox of Metaphor in The Hunger Games Trilogy." *The Hunger Games and Philosophy: A Critique of Pure Treason*. Eds. George A. Dunn and Nicolas Michaud. Hoboken, NJ: John Wiley & Sons, 2012. 41–54.

"Our Withdrawn Review Blood Cotton." *The Economist*. Online Extra (4 September 2014). Available at: http://www.economist.com/news/books/

Bibliography

21615864-how-slaves-built-american-capitalism-blood-cotton.

Pineda, Erik. "4 Lies Fed by Putin to Russians to Justify Invasion of Ukraine, Europe and Nuclear Showdown with America. *International Business Times* (29 November 2014). Available at: http://au.ibtimes.com/articles/574377/20141129/putin-russia-ukraine-europe-invasion-world-war.htm#.VHyMUoe2K5Q.

Pinker, Steven. "The Surprising Decline in Violence." TED2007. Available at: https://www.ted.com/talks/steven_pinker_on_the_myth_of_violence/transcript?language=en.

Plato. *The Republic.* Trans. Desmond Lee. Penguin Classics. Second Edition. New York: Penguin Books, 2003.

Plutarch. *Lives: Demosthenes and Cicero. Alexander and Caesar.* Trans. Bernadotte Perrin. Loeb Classical Library (Volume VII). Cambridge, MA: Harvard University Press, 1919.

Purdy, Jedediah. *For Common Things: Irony, Trust, and Commitment in America Today.* New York: Vintage, 2000.

Rousseau, Jean-Jacques. *The Social Contract.* Available at: http://www.constitution.org/jjr/socon_01.htm.

"Russians' Approval of Putin Hits Near All-Time High, Poll Shows." RT (28 October 2014). Available at: http://rt.com/politics/196212-piutin-approval-grows-poll/.

Sachs, Jeffrey. *The End of Poverty: Economic Possibilities for Our Time.* Reprint Edition. New York: Penguin Books, 2006.

Seneca. *On the Shortness of Life.* Trans. C.D.N. Costa. Penguin Great Ideas. New York: Penguin Books, 2005.

Shaffer, Andrew. "The Joy of Watching Others Suffer: Schadenfreude and the Hunger Games." *The Hunger Games and Philosophy: A Critique of Pure Treason.* Eds. George A. Dunn and Nicolas Michaud. Hoboken, NJ: John Wiley & Sons, 2012. 75–89.

Shakespeare, William, and Paul Werstine. *King John.* Ed. Barbara A. Mowat. Folger Shakespeare Library. New York: Simon & Schuster, 2006.

Sommers, Sam. *Situations Matter: Understanding How Context Transforms Your World.* New York: Riverhead Books, 2011.

Stout, Jeffrey. *Ethics After Babel: The Languages of Morals and Their Discontents.* Princeton: Princeton University Press, 2001.

Tacitus, Cornelius. *A Dialogue on Oratory.* Eds. Alfred John Church and William Jackson Brodribb. Perseus Digital Library, Tufts University. Available at: www.perseus.tufts.edu.

Timm, Chad William. "Class Is in Session: Power and Privilege in Panem." *The Hunger Games and Philosophy: A Critique of Pure Treason.* Eds. George A. Dunn and Nicolas Michaud. Hoboken, NJ: John Wiley & Sons, 2012. 277–289.

United Nations. "The Universal Declaration of Human Rights." Available at: http://www.un.org/en/documents/udhr/.

Van Bibber, Ryan. "St. Louis Police Officers Association Criticizes Rams Players for 'Hands Up Don't Shoot' Gesture." SB Nation (30 November 2014). Available at: http://www.sbnation.com/nfl/2014/11/30/7312145/rams-players-hands-up-dont-shoot-police.

Van Dyk, Christina. "Discipline and the Docile Body: Regulating Hungers in the Capitol." *The Hunger Games and Philosophy: A Critique of Pure Treason.* Eds. George A. Dunn and Nicolas Michaud. Hoboken, NJ: John Wiley & Sons, 2012. 250–264.

"Voter Turnout." The Center for Voting and Democracy. Available at: http://www.fairvote.org/research-and-analysis/voter-turnout/.

Zolli, Andrew, and Healy, Ann Marie. *Resilience: Why Things Bounce Back.* Reprint Edition. New York: Simon & Schuster, 2013.

Index

action 13–14, 16, 17, 118, 170
Aristotle 7, 8, 92–97, 100, 101, 112–113, 119–120, 125
Aurelius, Marcus 38–39

Barabási, Albert-László 98
Bonhoeffer, Dietrich 13–15, 18, 170
Braveheart 165

Caesar, Julius 28–29
Cicero 29
Confucius 63, 78
creativity 77

The Daily Show 151
deception 62–63
Declaration of Independence 102–103, 106, 115
divide and conquer 52

Ecclesiastes 118–119
economics 146, 151, 175

family 5–6, 175
fear 1, 4–5, 6, 15, 16, 24, 28, 48, 56–58, 60–61, 63–65, 71, 74–75, 80, 90–91, 100, 111, 120, 126, 148, 169–170
Ferguson, MO 132–134, 135, 175
First Amendment 133, 134
Foucault, Michel 67
Fox News 151
Frankl, Viktor 75–77, 144
Franklin, Benjamin 50, 103–104

Girard, René 160–161, 162–164, 165–167
Gladiator 26
Gladwell, Malcolm 98
Gospel of John 72, 73
Gospel of Luke 7, 20
Gospel of Matthew 1, 23, 72
Greitens, Eric 16–17, 50, 80–81, 84, 113–114

Henry, Patrick 114–115
Hitler, Adolf 13–14, 65–66, 156
Hobbes, Thomas 48–50, 53
hope 55–56, 71, 76–77, 81
human rights 11–12, 13, 14, 18–19, 20, 34, 43, 102

inequality 125
Iraq War 148–149
irony 32

Jefferson, Thomas 104
Jesus 2, 71–72

Kenndy, John F. 145–147
King, Martin Luther, Jr. 82–83, 172
Krause, Lincoln 106–108

Leadership 13–14, 122, 161, 166
Libertarianism 43–44
Lincoln, Abraham 175–176
Love 173

Machiavelli, Niccolò 57–58, 60–61, 66–67, 68–69, 90–91, 101, 120–121, 171
martyrdom 127–128
morality 6, 23–24, 26, 37–40, 47, 50–51, 63, 70–71, 78, 83, 85–86, 91–94, 97, 100, 103, 130–131, 132, 133, 134–135, 136–137, 140–141, 143–144, 150, 172, 175
Moses 74, 79, 80
MSNBC 151

Niebuhr, Reinhold 13–14, 20, 67, 68, 135, 137, 138, 139, 140–141
Nixon, Richard 145–147
non-violence 82–83

Pilate, Pontius 72–73
Pinker, Steven 174
Plato 79, 82
privacy 18

Index

psychology 4–5, 6, 48, 53, 63–64, 123, 162, 165
punishment 119, 120
Purdy, Jedediah 18–19, 20, 39–40, 51–52, 78–79, 80, 150
Putin, Vladimir 153–155, 156

Roman Coliseum 26–28, 30
Rousseau, Jean-Jacques 42–43, 45, 46–48, 50–51

Sachs, Jeffrey 34–35
Seneca 37–38

Shakespeare, William 88–89
social class 11–12, 29–30, 32–33, 35–36
stoicism 38
Stout, Jeffrey 130, 134
survival 4

Tacitus 31

virtue 140

Warren, Elizabeth 44–45, 52

Zolli, Andrew 25, 74–75, 98–99, 113–114

www.ingramcontent.com/pod-product-compliance
Ingram Content Group UK Ltd.
Pitfield, Milton Keynes, MK11 3LW, UK
UKHW041919140426
5217IPUK00013B/225